The Diary of an Ennuyée

Mrs. (Anna) Jameson

Imprint

This book is part of TREDITION CLASSICS

Author: Mrs. (Anna) Jameson
Cover design: Buchgut, Berlin – Germany

Publisher: tredition GmbH, Hamburg - Germany
ISBN: 978-3-8424-8579-2

www.tredition.com
www.tredition.de

Marx Joyce
Abbott Hardy Montaigne Machiavelli Chesterton Cooper Emerson Austen
Defoe Melville Haggard Hugo
Christie Eliot Grimm
Stoker Carroll Molière
Wilde Maupassant Byron
Schiller
Garnett Einstein Fitzgerald Engels Smith
Goethe Hawthorne Kafka
Cotton Dostoyevsky Hall
Baum Kipling Doyle Willis
Leslie Dumas Henry Nietzsche
Flaubert Turgenev Balzac
Stockton Vatsyayana Crane
Burroughs Whitman Verne
Curtis Tocqueville Gogol Vinci
Homer Widger Tolstoy Busch
Darwin Thoreau
Potter Freud Zola Twain Plato Scott
Lawrence
Kant Jowett Stevenson Dickens
Andersen Burton Hesse Harte
London Descartes Cervantes
Poe Aristotle Wells Voltaire
Hale James Hastings
Bunner Shakespeare Cooke
Richter Chambers Irving
Doré Swift Dante Chekhov da Shaw Wodehouse Benedict Alcott
Pushkin
Newton

tredition®

tredition was established in 2006 by Sandra Latusseck and Soenke Schulz. Based in Hamburg, Germany, tredition offers publishing solutions to authors and publishing houses, combined with worldwide distribution of printed and digital book content. tredition is uniquely positioned to enable authors and publishing houses to create books on their own terms and without conventional manufacturing risks.

For more information please visit: www.tredition.com

TREDITION CLASSICS

This book is part of the TREDITION CLASSICS series. The creators of this series are united by passion for literature and driven by the intention of making all public domain books available in printed format again - worldwide. Most TREDITION CLASSICS titles have been out of print and off the bookstore shelves for decades. At tredition we believe that a great book never goes out of style and that its value is eternal. Several mostly non-profit literature projects provide content to tredition. To support their good work, tredition donates a portion of the proceeds from each sold copy. As a reader of a TREDITION CLASSICS book, you support our mission to save many of the amazing works of world literature from oblivion. See all available books at www.tredition.com.

Project Gutenberg

The content for this book has been graciously provided by Project Gutenberg. Project Gutenberg is a non-profit organization founded by Michael Hart in 1971 at the University of Illinois. The mission of Project Gutenberg is simple: To encourage the creation and distribution of eBooks. Project Gutenberg is the first and largest collection of public domain eBooks.

Sad, solemn, soure, and full of fancies fraile,

She woxe: yet wist she neither how nor why:

She wist not, silly Mayd, what she did aile,

Yet wist she was not well at ease, perdie;

Yet thought it was not Love, but some Melancholie.

Spenser.

DIARY OF AN ENNUYÉE. [A]

Calais, June 21.—What young lady, travelling for the first time on the Continent, does not write a "Diary?" No sooner have we slept on the shores of France—no sooner are we seated in the gay salon at Dessin's, than we call, like Biddy Fudge, for "French pens and French ink," and forth steps from its case the morocco-bound diary, regularly ruled and paged, with its patent Bramah lock and key, wherein we are to record and preserve all the striking, profound, and original observations—the classical reminiscences—the thread-bare raptures—the poetical effusions—in short, all the never-sufficiently-to-be-exhausted topics of sentiment and enthusiasm, which must necessarily suggest themselves while posting from Paris to Naples.

Verbiage, emptiness, and affectation!

Yes—but what must I do, then, with my volume in green morocco?

Very true, I did not think of that.

We have all read the Diary of an Invalid, the best of all diaries since old Evelyn's.—

Well, then,—Here beginneth the Diary of a Blue Devil.

What inconsistent beings are we!—How strange that in such a moment as this, I can jest in mockery of myself! but I will write on. Some keep a diary, because it is the fashion—a reason why *I* should not; some because it is *blue*, but I am not *blue*, only a *blue devil*; some for their amusement,—*amusement!!* alas! alas! and some that they may remember,—and I that I may forget, O! would it were possible.

When, to-day, for the first time in my life, I saw the shores of England fade away in the distance—did the conviction that I should never behold them more, bring with it one additional pang of regret, or one consoling thought? neither the one nor the other. I leave behind me the scenes, the objects, so long associated with pain; but from pain itself I cannot fly: it has become a part of myself. I know not yet whether I ought to rejoice and be thankful for this opportunity of travelling, while my mind is thus torn and upset; or rather regret [Pg 2] that I must visit scenes of interest, of splendour, of novelty—scenes over which, years ago, I used to ponder with many a sigh, and many a vain longing, now that I am lost to all the pleasure they could once have excited: for what is all the world to me now?—But I will not weakly yield: though time and I have not been long acquainted, do I not know what miracles he, "the all-powerful healer," can perform? Who knows but this dark cloud may pass away? Continual motion, continual activity, continual novelty, the absolute necessity for self-command, may do something for me. I cannot quite forget; but if I can cease to remember for a few minutes, or even, it may be, for a few hours? O how idle to talk of "*indulging* grief:" talk of indulging the rack, the rheumatism! who ever indulged grief that truly felt it? to *endure* is hard enough.

It is o'er! with its pains and its pleasures,
The dream of affection is o'er!
The feelings I lavish'd so fondly
Will never return to me more.

With a faith, O! too blindly believing—
A truth, no unkindness could move;
My prodigal heart hath expended
At once, an existence of love.

And now, like the spendthrift forsaken,
By those whom his bounty had blest,
All empty, and cold, and despairing,
It shrinks in my desolate breast.

But a spirit is burning within me,
Unquench'd, and unquenchable yet;
It shall teach me to bear uncomplaining,
The grief I can never forget.

Rouen, June 25.—I do not pity Joan of Arc: that heroic woman only paid the price which all must pay for celebrity in some shape or other: the sword or the faggot, the scaffold or the field, public hatred or private heart-break; what matter? The noble Bedford could not rise above the age in which he lived: but *that* was the age of gallantry and chivalry, as well as superstition: and could Charles, the lover of Agnes Sorel, with all the knights and nobles of France, look on while their champion, and a woman, was devoted to chains and death, without one effort to save her?

It has often been said that her fate disgraced the military fame of the English; it is a far fouler blot on the chivalry of France.

St. Germains, June 27.—I cannot bear this place, another hour in it will kill me; this sultry evening—this sickening sunshine—this quiet, unbroken, boundless landscape—these motionless woods—the Seine stealing, creeping through the level plains—the dull grandeur of the old chateau—the languid repose of the whole scene—instead of soothing, [Pg 3] torture me. I am left without resource, a prey to myself and to my memory—to reflection, which embitters the source of suffering, and thought, which brings distraction. Horses on to Paris! Vite! Vite!

Paris, 28.—What said the witty Frenchwoman?—*Paris est le lieu du monde où l'on peut le mieux se passer de bonheur;*—in that case it will suit me admirably.

29.—We walked and drove about all day: I was amused. I marvel at my own versatility when I think how soon my quick spirits were excited by this gay, gaudy, noisy, idle place. The different appearance of the streets of London and Paris is the first thing to strike a stranger. In the gayest and most crowded streets of London the people move steadily and rapidly along, with a grave collected air, as if all had some business in view; *here,* as a little girl observed the other day, all the people walk about "like ladies and gentlemen going a visiting:" the women well-dressed and smiling, and with a certain jaunty air, trip along with their peculiar mincing step, and appear as if their sole object was but to show themselves; the men ill-dressed, slovenly, and in general ill-looking, lounge indolently, and stare as if they had no other purpose in life but to look about them. [B]

July 12.—"Quel est à Paris le suprême talent? celui d'amuser: et quel est le suprême bonheur? l'amusement."

Then *le suprême bonheur* may be found every evening from nine to ten, in a walk along the Boulevards, or a ramble through the Champs Elysées, and from ten to twelve in a salon at Tortoni's.

What an extraordinary scene was that I witnessed to-night! how truly *French*! Spite of myself and all my melancholy musings, and all my philosophic allowances for the difference of national character, I was irresistibly compelled to smile at some of the farcical groups we encountered. In the most crowded parts of the Champs Elysées this evening (Sunday), there sat an old lady with a wrinkled yellow face and sharp features, dressed in flounced gown of dirty white muslin, a pink sash and a Leghorn hat and feathers. In one hand she held a small tray for the contribution of amateurs, and in the other an Italian bravura, which she sung or rather screamed out with a thousand indescribable shruggings, contortions, and grimaces, and in a voice to which a cracked tea-kettle, or a "brazen candlestick turned," had seemed the music of the spheres. A little farther on we found two elderly gentlemen playing at see-saw; one an immense corpulent man of fifteen stone at least, the other a thin dwarfish animal with gray mustachios, who held before him what I thought was a child, but on approaching, it proved to be a large stone strapped before him, to render his weight a counterpoise to that of his huge companion. We [Pg 4] passed on, and returning about half an hour afterwards down the same walk, we found the same venerable pair pursuing their edifying amusement with as much enthusiasm as before.

Before the revolution, sacrilege became one of the most frequent crimes. I was told of a man who, having stolen from a church the silver box containing the consecrated wafers, returned the wafers next day in a letter to the Curé of the Parish, *having used one of them to seal his envelop.*

July 27.—A conversation with S** always leaves me sad. Can it then be possible that he is right? No—O no! my understanding rejects the idea with indignation, my whole heart recoils from it; yet if it should be so! what then: have I been till now the dupe and the victim of factitious feelings? virtue, honour, feeling, generosity, you are then but words, signifying nothing? Yet if this vain philosophy lead to happiness, would not S** be happy? it is evident he is *not.*

When he said that the object existed not in this world which could lead him twenty yards out of his way, did this sound like happiness? I remember that while he spoke, instead of feeling either persuaded or convinced by his captivating eloquence, I was perplexed and distressed; I *suffered* a painful compassion, and tears were in my eyes. I, who so often have pitied myself, pitied him at that moment a thousand times more; I thought, I would not buy tranquillity at such a price as he has paid for it. Yet *if* he should be right? that *if*, which every now and then suggests itself, is terrible; it shakes me in the utmost recesses of my heart.

S**, in spite of myself, and in spite of all that with most perverted pains he has made himself (so different from what he once was), can charm and interest, pain and perplex me:—not so D**, another disciple of the same school: he inspires me with the strongest antipathy I ever felt for a human being. Insignificant and disagreeable is his appearance, he looks as if all the bile under heaven had found its way into his complexion, and all the infernal irony of a Mephistopheles into his turned-up nose and insolent curled lip. He is, he *says* he is, an atheist, a materialist, a sensualist: the pains he takes to deprave and degrade his nature, render him so disgusting, that I could not even speak in his presence; I dreaded lest he should enter into conversation with me. I might have spared myself the fear. He piques himself on his utter contempt for, and disregard of, women; and, after all, is not himself worthy these words I bestow on him.

Aug. 25.—Here begins, I hope, a new æra. I have had a long and dangerous illness; the crisis perhaps of what I have been suffering [Pg 5] for months. Contrary to my own wishes, and to the expectations of others, I *live*: and trusting in God that I have been preserved for some wise and good purpose, am therefore thankful: even supposing I should be reserved for new trials, I cannot surely in this world suffer more than I have suffered: it is not possible that the same causes can be again combined to afflict me.

How truly can I say, few and evil have my days been! may I not say as truly, I have not weakly yielded, I have not "gone about to cause my heart to despair," but have striven, and not in vain? I took the remedies they gave me, and was grateful; I resigned myself to *live,* when had I but willed it, I might have died; and when to die and be at rest, seemed to my sick heart the only covetable boon.

Sept. 3.—A terrible anniversary at Paris—still ill and very weak. Edmonde came, *pour me désennuyer.* He has soul enough to bear a good deal of wearing down; but whether the fine qualities he possesses will turn to good or evil, is hard to tell: it is evident his character has not yet settled: it vibrates still as nature inclines him to good, and all the circumstances around him to evil. We talked as usual of women, of gallantry, of the French and English character, of national prejudices, of Shakspeare and Racine (never failing subjects of discussion), and he read aloud Delille's Catacombes de Rome, with great feeling, animation, and dramatic effect.

La mode at Paris is a spell of wondrous power: it is most like what we should call in England a rage, a mania, a torrent sweeping down the bounds between good and evil, sense and nonsense, upon whose surface straws and egg-shells float into notoriety, while the gold and the marble are buried and hidden till its force be spent. The rage for cashmeres and little dogs has lately given way to a rage for Le Solitaire, a romance written, I believe, by a certain Vicomte d'Arlincourt. Le Solitaire rules the imagination, the taste, the dress of half Paris: if you go to the theatre, it is to see the "Solitaire," either as tragedy, opera, or melodrame; the men dress their hair and throw their cloaks about them *à la Solitaire;* bonnets and caps, flounces and ribbons, are all *à la Solitaire;* the print shops are full of scenes from Le Solitaire; it is on every toilette, on every work-table;—ladies carry it about in their reticules to show each other that they are *à la mode;* and the men—what can they do but humble their understandings and be *extasiés,* when beautiful eyes sparkle in its defence and glisten in its praise, and ruby lips pronounce it divine, delicious; "quelle sublimité dans les descriptions, quelle force dans les caractères! quelle âme! feu! chaleur! verve! originalité! passion!" etc.

"Vous n'avez pas lu le Solitaire?" said Madame M. yesterday. "Eh mon dieu! il est donc possible! vous? mais, ma chère, vous êtes perdue de réputation, et pour jamais!" [Pg 6]

To retrieve my lost reputation, I sat down to read Le Solitaire, and as I read my amazement grew, and I did in "gaping wonderment abound," to think that fashion, like the insane root of old, had power to drive a whole city mad with nonsense; for such a tissue of abominable absurdities, bombast and blasphemy, bad taste and bad language, was never surely indited by any madman, in or out of Bedlam: not Maturin himself, that king of fustian,

> "— —ever wrote or borrowed
> Any thing half so horrid!"

and this is the book which has turned the brains of half Paris, which has gone through fifteen editions in a few weeks, which not to admire is "*pitoyable,*" and not to have read "*quelque chose d'inouie.*"

The objects at Paris which have most struck me, have been those least vaunted.

The view of the city from the Pont des Arts, to-night, enchanted me. As every body who goes to Rome views the Coliseum by moonlight, so nobody should leave Paris without seeing the effect from the Pont des Arts, on a fine moonlight night:—

> "Earth hath not any thing to show more fair."

It is singular I should have felt its influence at such a moment: it appears to me that those who, from feeling too strongly, have learnt to consider too deeply, become less sensible to the works of art, and more alive to nature. Are there not times when we turn with indifference from the finest picture or statue—the most improving book—the most amusing poem; and when the very commonest, and every-day beauties of nature, a soft evening, a lovely landscape, the moon riding in her glory through a clouded sky, without forcing or asking attention, sink into our hearts? They do not console,—they sometimes add poignancy to pain; but still they have a power, and do not speak in vain: they become a part of us; and never are we so inclined to claim kindred with nature, as when sorrow has lent us her mournful experience. At the time I felt this (and how many have felt it as deeply, and expressed it better!) I did not *think* it, still less could I have *said it*; but I have pleasure in recording the past impression. "On rend mieux compte de ce qu'on a senti que de ce qu'on sent."

September 8.—Paris is crowded with English; and I do not wonder at it; it is, on the whole, a pleasant place to live in. I like Paris, though I shall quit it without regret as soon as I have strength to travel. Here the social arts are carried to perfection—above all, the art of conversation: every one talks much and talks well. In this [Pg 7] multiplicity of words it must happen of course that a certain quantum of ideas is intermixed: and somehow or other, by dint of listening, talking, and looking about them, people *do* learn, and information to a certain point is general. Those who have knowledge are not shy of imparting it, and those who are ignorant take care not to seem so; but are sometimes agreeable, often amusing, and seldom *bêtes*. Nowhere have I seen unformed sheepish boys, nowhere the surliness, awkwardness, ungraciousness, and uneasy proud bashfulness, I have seen in the best companies in England. Our French friend Lucien has, at fifteen, the air and conversation of a finished gentleman; and our English friend C—— is at eighteen, the veriest log of a lumpish school-boy that ever entered a room. What I have seen of society, I like: the delicious climate too, the rich skies, the clear elastic atmosphere, the *out of doors* life the people lead, are all (in summer at least) delightful. There may be less *comfort* here; but nobody feels the want of it; and there is certainly more amusement—and amusement is here truly "le suprême bonheur." Happiness, according to the French meaning of the word, lies more on the surface of life: it is a sort of happiness which is cheap and ever at hand. This is the place to live in for the merry poor man, or the melancholy rich one: for those who have too much money, and those who have too little; for those who only wish, like the Irishman "to live all the days of their life,"—*prendre en légère monnaie la somme des plaisirs*: but to the thinking, the feeling, the domestic man, who only exists, enjoys, suffers through his affections—

"Who is retired as noontide dew,
Or fountain in a noonday grove—"

to such a one, Paris must be nothing better than a vast frippery shop, an ever-varying galantee show, an eternal vanity fair, a vortex of folly, a pandemonium of vice.

September 18.—Our imperials are packed, our passports signed, and we set off to-morrow for Geneva by Dijon and the Jura. I leave nothing behind me to regret, I see nothing before me to fear, and have no hope but in change; and now all that remains to be said of Paris, and all its wonders and all its vanities, all its glories and all its gaieties, are they not recorded in the ponderous chronicles of most veracious tourists, and what can I add thereto?

Geneva, Saturday Night, 11 o'clock.—Can it be the "blue rushing of the arrowy Rhone" I hear from my window? Shall I hear it to-morrow, when I wake? Have I seen, have I felt the reality of what I have so often imagined? and much, *much* more? How little do I feel the contretemps and privations which affect others—and feel them *only* because they affect others! To me they are nothing: I have in [Pg 8] a few hours stored my mind with images of beauty and grandeur which will last through my whole existence.

Yet I know I am not singular; others have felt the same: others, who, capable of "drinking in the soul of things," have viewed nature less with their eyes than their hearts. Now I feel the value of my own enthusiasm; now am I repaid in part for many pains and sorrows and errors it has cost me. Though the natural expression of that enthusiasm be now repressed and restrained, and my spirits subdued by long illness, what but enthusiasm could elevate my mind to a level with the sublime objects round me, and excite me to pour out my whole heart in admiration as I do now! How deeply they have penetrated into my imagination!—Beautiful nature! If I could but infuse into you a portion of my own existence as you have become a part of mine—If I could but bid you reflect back my soul, as it reflects back all your magnificence, I would make you my only friend, and wish no other; content "to love earth only for its earthly sake."

I am so tired to-night, I can say nothing of the Jura, nor of the superb ascent of the mountain, to me so novel, so astonishing a scene; nor of the cheerful brilliance of the morning sun, illuminating the high cliffs, and throwing the deep woody vallies into the darkest shadow; nor of the far distant plains of France seen between the hills, and melting away into a soft vapoury light; nor of Morey, and its delicious strawberries and honey-comb; nor of that never-to-be-forgotten moment, when turning the corner of the road, as it wound round a cliff near the summit, we beheld the lake and city of Geneva spread at our feet, with its magnificent back-ground of the Italian Alps, peak beyond peak, snow-crowned! and Mont Blanc towering over all! No description had prepared me for this prospect; and the first impression was rapturous surprise; but by degrees the vastness and the huge gigantic features of the scene pressed like a weight upon "my amazed sprite," and the feeling of its immense extent fatigued my imagination till my spirits gave way in tears. Then came remembrances of those I ought to forget, blending with all I saw a deeper power—raising up emotions, long buried though not dead, to fright me with their resurrection. I was so glad to arrive here, and shall be *so* glad to sleep—even the dull sleep which laudanum brings me.

Oct. 1.—When next I submit (having the power to avoid it) to be crammed into a carriage and carried from place to place, whether I would or not, and be set down at the stated *points de vue*, while a detestable laquais points out what I am to admire, I shall deserve to endure again what I endured to-day. As there was no possibility of relief, I resigned myself to my fate, and was even amused by the absurdity of my own situation. We went to see the junction of the Arve [Pg 9] and the Rhone: or rather to see the Arve pollute the rich, blue transparent Rhone, with its turbid waters. The day was heavy, and the clouds rolled in prodigious masses along the dark sides of the mountains, frequently hiding them from our view, and substituting for their graceful outlines and ever-varying contrast of tint and shade, an impenetrable veil of dark gray vapour.

3rd.—We took a boat and rowed on the lake for about two hours. Our boatman, a fine handsome athletic figure, was very talkative and intelligent. He had been in the service of Lord Byron, and was with him in that storm between La Meillerie and St. Gingough, which is described in the third canto of Childe Harold. He pointed out among the beautiful villas, which adorn the banks on either side, that in which the empress Josephine had resided for six months, not long before her death. When he spoke of her, he rested upon his oars to descant upon her virtues, her generosity, her affability, her goodness to the poor, and his countenance became quite animated with enthusiasm. Here, in France, wherever the name of Josephine is mentioned, there seems to exist but one feeling, one opinion of her beneficence and *amabilité* of character. Our boatman had also rowed Marie Louise across the lake, on her way to Paris: he gave us no very captivating picture of her. He described her as "*grande, blonde, bien faite et extrêmement fière*:" and told us how she tormented her ladies in waiting; "*comme elle tracassait ses dames d'honneur*." The day being rainy and gloomy, her attendants begged of her to defer the passage for a short time, till the fogs had cleared away, and discovered all the beauty of the surrounding shores. She replied haughtily and angrily, "Je veux faire ce que je veux—allez toujours."

M. le Baron M— —n, whom we knew at Paris, told me several delightful anecdotes of Josephine: he was attached to her household, and high in her confidence. Napoleon sent him on the very morning of his second nuptials, with a message and billet to the ex-empress. On hearing that the ceremony was performed which had passed her sceptre into the hands of the proud, cold-hearted Austrian, the feelings of the *woman* overcame every other. She burst into tears, and wringing her hands, exclaimed "Ah! au moins, qu'il soit heureux!" Napoleon resigned this estimable and amiable creature to narrow views of selfish policy, and with her his good genius fled: he deserved it, and verily he hath had his reward.

We drove after dinner to Copet; and the Duchesse de Broglie being absent, had an opportunity of seeing the chateau. All things "were there of her"—of her, whose genuine worth excused, whose all-commanding talents threw into shade, those failings which belonged to the weakness of her sex, and her warm feelings and imagination. The servant girl who showed us the apartments, had been fifteen years in [Pg 10] Madame de Staël's service. All the servants had remained long in the family, "elle était si bonne et si charmante maîtresse!" A picture of Madame de Staël when young, gave me the idea of a fine countenance and figure, though the features were irregular. In the bust, the expression is not so prepossessing:—*there* the colour and brilliance of her splendid dark eyes, the finest feature of her face, are of course quite lost. The bust of M. Rocca [C] was standing in the Baron de Staël's dressing-room: I was more struck with it than any thing I saw, not only as a chef-d'œuvre, but from the perfect and regular beauty of the head, and the charm of the expression. It was just such a mouth as we might suppose to have uttered his well-known reply—*"Je l'aimerai tellement qu'elle finira par m'aimer."* Madame de Staël had a son by this marriage, who had just been brought home by his brother, the Baron, from a school in the neighbourhood. He is about seven years old. If we may believe the servant, Madame de Staël did not acknowledge this son till just before her death; and she described the wonder of the boy on being brought home to the chateau, and desired to call *Monsieur le Baron* "Mon frère" and "Auguste." This part of Madame de Staël's conduct seems incomprehensible; but her death is recent, the circumstances little known, and it is difficult to judge her motives. As a *woman*, as a *wife*, she might not have been able to brave "the world's dread laugh"—but as a *mother*?— —

We have also seen Ferney—a place which did not interest me much, for I have no sympathies with Voltaire:—and some other beautiful scenes in the neighbourhood.

The Panorama exhibited in London just before I left it, is wonderfully correct, with one pardonable exception: the artist did not venture to make the waters of the lake of the intense ultramarine tinged with violet as I now see them before me;

> "So darkly, deeply, beautifully blue;"

it would have shocked English eyes as an exaggeration, or rather impossibility.

THE PANORAMA OF LAUSANNE.

Now blest for ever be that heaven-sprung art
Which can transport us in its magic power
From all the turmoil of the busy crowd,
From the gay haunts where pleasure is ador'd,
'Mid the hot sick'ning glare of pomp and light;

And fashion worshipp'd by a gaudy throng
Of heartless idlers—from the jarring world
And all its passions, follies, cares, and crimes—
And bids us gaze, even in the city's heart,
On such a scene as this! O fairest spot!
[Pg 11] If but the pictured semblance, the dead image
Of thy majestic beauty, hath a power
To wake such deep delight; if that bluc lake,
Over whose lifeless breast no breezes play,
Those mimic mountains robed in purple light,
Yon painted verdure that but *seems* to glow,
Those forms unbreathing, and those motionless woods,
A beauteous mockery all—can ravish thus,
What would it be, could we now gaze indeed
Upon thy *living* landscape? could we breathe
Thy mountain air, and listen to thy waves,
As they run rippling past our feet, and see
That lake lit up by dancing sunbeams—and
Those light leaves quivering in the summer air;
Or linger some sweet eve just on this spot
Where now we *seem* to stand, and watch the stars
Flash into splendour, one by one, as night
Steals over yon snow-peaks, and twilight fades
Behind the steeps of Jura! here, O *here*!
'Mid scenes where Genius, Worth and Wisdom dwelt, [D]
Which fancy peopled with a glowing train
Of most divine creations—Here to stray
With *one* most cherished, and in loving eyes
Read a sweet comment on the wonders round—
Would this indeed be bliss? would not the soul
Be lost in its own depths? and the full heart
Languish with sense of beauty unexprest,
And faint beneath its own excess of life?

Saturday.—Quitted Geneva, and slept at St. Maurice. I was ill during the last few days of our stay, and therefore left Geneva with the less regret. I suffer now so constantly, that a day tolerably free from pain seems a blessing for which I can scarce be sufficiently thankful. Such was yesterday.

Our road lay along the south bank of the lake, through Evian, Thonon, St. Gingough: and on the opposite shores we had in view successively, Lausanne, Vevai, Clarens, and Chillon. A rain storm pursued, or almost surrounded us the whole morning; but we had the good fortune to escape it. We travelled faster than it could pursue, and it seemed to retire before us as we approached. The effect was surprisingly beautiful; for while the two extremities of the lake were discoloured and enveloped in gloom, that part opposite to us was as blue and transparent as heaven itself, and almost as bright. Over Vevai, as we viewed it from La Meillerie, rested one end of a glorious rainbow: the other extremity appeared to touch the bosom of the lake, and shone vividly against the dark mountains above Chillon. La Meillerie—Vevai! what magic in those names! and O what a power has genius to hallow with its lovely creations, scenes already so lavishly adorned by Nature! it was not, however, of St. Preux I thought, as I passed [Pg 12] under the rock of the Meillerie. Ah! how much of happiness, of enjoyment, have I lost, in being forced to struggle against my feelings, instead of abandoning myself to them! but surely I have done right. Let me repeat it again and again to myself, and let that thought, if possible, strengthen and console me.

Monday.—I have resolved to attempt no description of scenery; but my pen is fascinated. I *must* note a few of the objects which struck me to-day and yesterday, that I may at will combine them hereafter to my mind's eye, and recall the glorious pictures I beheld, as we travelled through the Vallais to Brig: the swollen and turbid (no longer "blue and arrowy") Rhone, rushing and roaring along; the gigantic mountains in all their endless variety of fantastic forms, which enclosed us round,—their summits now robed in curling clouds, and then, as the winds swept them aside, glittering in the sunshine; the little villages perched like eagles' nests on the cliffs, far, far above our heads; the deep rocky channels through which the torrents had madly broken a way, tearing through every obstacle till they reached the Rhone, and marking their course with devastation; the scene of direful ruin at Martigny; the cataracts gushing, bounding from the living rock and plunging into some unseen abyss below; even the shrubs and the fruit trees which in the wider parts of the valley bordered the road side; the vines, the rich scarlet barberries, the apples and pears which we might have gathered by extending our hands;—all and each, when I recall them, will rise up a vivid picture before my own fancy;—but never could be truly represented to the mind of another—at least through the medium of words.

And yet, with all its wonders and beauties, this day's journey has not enchanted me like Saturday's. The scenery *then* had a different species of beauty, a deeper interest—when the dark blue sky was above our heads, and the transparent lake shone another heaven at our feet, and the recollection of great and glorious names, and visions of poetic fancy, and ideal forms more lovely than ever trod this earth, hovered around us:—and then those thoughts which would intrude—remembrances of the far-off absent, who are or have been loved, mingled with the whole, and shed an imaginary splendour or a tender interest, over scenes which required no extraneous powers to enhance their native loveliness.—no charm borrowed from imagination to embellish the all-beautiful reality.

Duomo d'Ossola.—What shall I say of the marvellous, the miraculous Simplon? Nothing: every body has said already every thing that *can* be said and *exclaimed.*

In our descent, as the valley widened, and the stern terrific features of the scene assumed a gentler character, we came to the beautiful village of Davedro, with its cottages and vineyards spread over a green [Pg 13] slope, between the mountains and the torrent below. This lovely nook struck me the more from its contrast with the region of snows, clouds, and barren rocks to which our eyes had been for several hours accustomed. In such a spot as Davedro I fancied I should wish to *live,* could I in life assemble round me all that my craving heart and boundless spirit desire;—*or die,* when life had exhausted all excitement, and the subdued and weary soul had learned to be content with repose:—but not not till *then.*

We are now in Italy; but have not yet heard the soft sounds of the Italian language. However, we read with great satisfaction the Italian denomination of our Inn, "La grande Alberga della Villa"—called out "Cameriere!" instead of "Garçon!"—plucked ripe grapes as they hung from the treillages above our heads—gathered green figs from the trees, bursting and luscious—panted with the intense heat—intense and overpowering from its contrast with the cold of the Alpine regions we had just left—and fancied we began to feel

> "— —cette vie enivrante,
> Que le solei du sud inspire à tous les sens."

11 at night.—Fatigue and excitement have lately proved too much for me: but I will not sink. I will yet bear up; and when a day thus passed amid scenes like those of a romance, amid all that would once have charmed my imagination, and enchanted my senses, brings no real pleasure, but is ended, as *now* it ends, in tears, in bitterness of heart, in languor, in sickness, and in pain—ah! let me remember the lesson of resignation I have lately learned; and by elevating my thoughts to a better world, turn to look upon the miserable affections which have agitated me *here* as— — [E]

Could I but become as insensible, as regardless of the painful past as I am of the all lovely present! Why was I proud of my victory over passion? alas! what avails it that I have shaken the viper from my hand, if I have no miraculous antidote against the venom which has mingled with my life-blood, and clogged the pulses of my heart! But the antidote of Paul—even faith—may it not be mine if I duly seek it?

Arona, on the banks of the Lago Maggiore.—Rousseau mentions somewhere, that it was once his intention to place the scene of the Heloïse in the Borromean Islands. What a French idea! How strangely incongruous had the pastoral simplicity of his lovers appeared in such a scene! It must have changed, if not the whole plan, [Pg 14] at least the whole colouring of the tale. Imagine *la divine* Julie tripping up and down the artificial terraces of the Isola Bella, among flower pots and statues, and colonnades and grottos; and St. Preux sighing towards her, from some trim fantastic wilderness in the Isola Madre!

The day was heavenly, and I shall never forget the sunset, as we viewed it reflected in the lake, which appeared at one moment an expanse of living fire. This is the first we have seen of those effulgent sunsets with which Italy will make us familiar.

Milan.—Our journey yesterday, through the flat fertile plains of Lombardy, was not very interesting; and the want of novelty and excitement made it fatiguing, in spite of the matchless roads and the celerity with which we travelled.

Whatever we may think of Napoleon in England, it is impossible to travel on the Continent, and more particularly through Lombardy, without being struck with the magnificence and vastness of his public works—either designed or executed. He is more regretted here than in France; or rather he has not been so soon banished from men's minds. In Italy he followed the rational policy of depressing the nobles, and providing occupation and amusement for the lower classes. I spoke to-day with an intelligent artisan, who pointed out to us a hall built near the public walk by Napoleon, for the people to dance and assemble in, when the weather was unfavourable. The man concluded some very animated and sensible remarks on the late events, by adding expressively, that though many had been benefited by the change, there was to him and all others of his class as much difference between the late reign and the present, as between *l'or et le fer*.

The silver shrine of St. Carlo Borromeo, with all its dazzling waste of magnificence, struck me with a feeling of melancholy and indignation. The gems and gold which lend such a horrible splendour to corruption; the skeleton head, grinning ghastly under its invaluable coronet; the skeleton hand supporting a crozier glittering with diamonds, appeared so frightful, so senseless a mockery of the excellent, simple-minded, and benevolent being they were intended to honour, that I could but wonder, and escape from the sight as quickly as possible. The Duomo is on the whole more remarkable for the splendour of the material, than the good taste with which it is employed: the statues which adorn it inside and out, are sufficient of themselves to form a very respectable congregation: they are four thousand in number.

9th, Tuesday.—We gave the morning to the churches, and the evening to the Ambrosian library. The day was, on the whole, more fatiguing than edifying or amusing. I remarked whatever was remarkable, admired all that is usually admired, but brought away few [Pg 15] impressions of novelty or pleasure. The objects which principally struck my capricious and fastidious fancy, were precisely those which passed unnoticed by every one else, and are not worth recording. In the first church we visited, I saw a young girl respectably and even elegantly dressed, in the beautiful costume of the Milanese, who was kneeling on the pavement before a crucifix, weeping bitterly, and at the same time fanning herself most vehemently with a large green fan. Another church (St. Alessandro, I think) was oddly decorated for a Christian temple. A statue of Venus stood on one side of the porch, a statue of Hercules on the other. The two divinities, whose attributes could not be mistaken, had been *converted* from heathenism into two very respectable saints. I forget their *christian names*. Nor is this the most amusing metamorphosis I have seen here. The transformation of two heathen divinities into saints, is matched by the apotheosis of two modern sovereigns into pagan deities. On the frieze of the *salle*, adjoining the amphitheatre, there is a head of Napoleon, which, by the addition of a beard, has been converted into a Jupiter; and on the opposite side, a head of Josephine, which, being already beautiful and dignified, has required no alteration, except in name, to become a creditable Minerva.

10th.—At the Brera, now called the "Palace of the Arts and Sciences," we spent some delightful hours. There is a numerous collection of pictures by Titian, Guido, Albano, Schidone, the three Carraccis, Tintoretto, Giorgione, etc. Some old paintings in fresco, by Luini and others of his age, were especially pointed out to us, which had been cut from the walls of churches now destroyed. They are preserved here, I presume, as curiosities, and specimens of the progress of the arts, for they possess no other merit—none, at least, that I could discover. Here is the "Marriage of the Virgin," by Raffaelle, of which I had often heard. It disappointed me at the first glance, but charmed me at the second, and enchanted me at the third. The unobtrusive grace and simplicity of Raffaelle do not immediately strike an eye so unpractised, and a taste so unformed as mine still is: for though I have seen the best pictures in England, we have there no opportunity of becoming acquainted with the two divinest masters of the Italian art, Raffaelle and Correggio. There are not, I conceive, half a dozen of either in all the collections together, and those we do possess, are far from being among their best efforts. But Raffaelle must not make me forget the Hagar in the Brera: the affecting—the inimitable Hagar! what agony, what upbraiding, what love, what helpless desolation of heart in that countenance! I may well remember the deep pathos of this picture; for the face of Hagar has haunted me sleeping and waking ever since I beheld it. Marvellous power of art! that mere inanimate forms, and colours compounded of gross materials, [Pg 16] should thus live—thus speak—thus stand a soul-felt presence before us, and from the senseless board or canvas, breathe into our hearts a feeling, beyond what the most impassioned eloquence could ever inspire—beyond what mere words can ever render.

Last night and the preceding we spent at the Scala. The opera was stupid, and Madame Bellochi, who is the present primadonna, appeared to me harsh and ungraceful, when compared to Fodor. The new ballet however, amply indemnified us for the disappointment. Our Italian friends condoled with us on being a few days too late to see *La Vestale*, which had been performed for sixty nights, and is one of Vigano's masterpieces. I thought the *Didone Abbandonata* left us nothing to regret. The immense size of the stage, the splendid scenery, the classical propriety and magnificence of the dresses, the fine music, and the exquisite acting (for there is very little dancing), all conspired to render it enchanting. The celebrated cavern scene in the fourth book of Virgil, is rather too closely copied in a most inimitable pas de deux; so closely, indeed, that I was considerably alarmed *pour les bienséances*; but little Ascanius, who is asleep in a corner (Heaven knows how he came there), wakes at the critical moment, and the impending catastrophe is averted. Such a scene, however beautiful, would not, I think, be endured on the English stage. I observed that when it began, the curtains in front of the boxes were withdrawn, the whole audience, who seemed to be expecting it, was hushed; the deepest silence, the most delighted attention prevailed during its performance; and the moment it was over, a third of the spectators departed. I am told this is always the case; and that in almost every ballet d'action, the public are gratified by a scene, or scenes, of a similar tendency.

The second time I saw the *Didone*, my attention, in spite of the fascination of the scene, was attracted towards a box near us, which was occupied by a noble English family just arrived at Milan. In the front of the box sat a beautiful girl apparently not fifteen, with laughing lips and dimpled cheeks, the very personification of blooming, innocent, *English* loveliness. I watched her (I could not help it, when my interest was once awakened) through the whole scene. I marked her increased agitation: I saw her cheeks flush, her eyes glisten, her bosom flutter, as if with sighs I could not overhear, till at length, overpowered with emotion, she turned away her head, and covered her eyes with her hand. Mothers!—English mothers! who bring your daughters abroad to finish their education—do you well to expose them to scenes like these, and *force* the young bud of early feeling in such a precious hot-bed as this? Can a finer finger on the piano,—a finer taste in painting, or any possible improvement in foreign arts and foreign graces, compensate for one taint on that moral purity, which has ever [Pg 17] been (and may it ever be!) the boast, the charm of Englishwomen? But what have I to do with all this?—I came here to be amused and to forget;—not to moralize or to criticise.

Vigano, who is lately dead, composed the *Didone Abbandonata* as well as *La Vestale*, Otello, Nina, and others. All his ballets are celebrated for their classical beauty and interest. This man, though but a dancing-master, must have had the soul of a painter, a musician, and a poet in one. He must have been a perfect master of design, grouping, contrast, picturesque, and scenic effect. He must have had the most exquisite feeling for musical expression, to adapt it so admirably to his purposes; and those gestures and movements with which he has so gracefully combined it, and which address themselves but too powerfully to the senses and the imagination—what are they, but the very "poetry of motion," *la poésie mise en action*, rendering words a superfluous and feeble medium in comparison?

I saw at the Mint yesterday the medal struck in honour of Vigano, bearing his head on one side, and on the other, Prometheus chained; to commemorate his famous ballet of that name. One of these medals, struck in gold, was presented to him in the name of the government:—a singular distinction for a dancing-master;—but Vigano was a dancing-master of *genius;* and this is the land, where genius in every shape is deified.

The enchanting music of the Prometteo by Beethoven, is well known in England, but to produce the ballet on our stage, as it was exhibited here, would be impossible. The entire tribe of our dancers and figurantes, with their jumpings, twirlings, quiverings, and pirouettings, must be first annihilated; and Vigano, or Didelot, or Noverre rise again to inform the whole corps de ballet with another soul and the whole audience with another spirit:—for

—"Poiche paga il volgo sciocco, è giusto
Scioccamente '*ballar*' per dargli gusto."

The Theatre of the Scala, notwithstanding the vastness of my expectations, did not disappoint me. I heard it criticised as being dark and gloomy; for only the stage is illuminated: but when I remember how often I have left our English theatres with dazzled eyes and aching head,—distracted by the multiplicity of objects and faces, and "blasted with excess of light,"—I feel reconciled to this peculiarity; more especially as it heightens beyond measure the splendour of the stage effect.

We have the Countess Bubna's box while we are here. She scarcely ever goes herself, being obliged to hold a sort of military drawing-room almost every evening. Her husband, General Bubna, has the [Pg 18] command of the Austrian forces in the north of Italy: and though the Archduke Reinier is nominal viceroy, all real power seems lodged in Bubna's bands. He it was who suppressed the insurrection in Piedmont during the last struggle for liberty: 'twas his vocation—more the pity. Eight hundred of the Milanese, at the head of them Count Melzi, were connected with the Carbonari and the Piedmontese insurgents. On Count Bubna's return from his expedition, a list of these malcontents being sent to him by the police, he refused even to look at it, and merely saying that it was the business of the police to *surveiller* those persons, but *he* must be allowed to be ignorant of their names, publicly tore the paper. The same night he visited the theatre, accompanied by Count Melzi, was received with acclamations, and has since been deservedly popular.

Bubna is a heavy gross-looking man, a victim to the gout, and with nothing martial or captivating in his exterior. He has talents, however, and those not only of a military cast. He was generally employed to arrange the affairs of the Emperor of Austria with Napoleon. His loyalty to his own sovereign, and the soldier-like frankness and integrity of his character, gained him the esteem of the French emperor; who, when any difficulties occurred in their arrangements, used to say impatiently—"Envoyez-moi donc Bubna!"

The count is of an illustrious family of Alsace, which removed to Bohemia when that province was ceded to France. He had nearly ruined himself by gambling, when the emperor (so it is said) advised him, or, in other words, commanded him to marry the daughter of one Arnvelt or Arnfeldt, a baptized Jew, who had been servant to a Jewish banker at Vienna; and on his death left a million of florins to each of his daughters. He was a man of the lowest extraction, and without any education; but having sense enough to feel its advantages, he gave a most brilliant one to his daughters. The Countess Bubna is an elegant, an accomplished, and has the character of being also an amiable woman. She is here a person of the very first consequence, the wife of the archduke alone taking precedence of her. A propos of the viceroy, when on the Corso to-day with the Countess Bubna, we met him with the *vice-queen*, as she is styled, here, walking in public. The archduke has not (as the countess observed) *la plus jolie tournure du monde*: his appearance is heavy, awkward, and slovenly, with more than the usual Austrian stupidity of countenance: a complete *testa tedesca*. His beautiful wife, the Princess Maria of Savoy, to whom he has been married only a few months, held his arm; and as she moved a little in front, seemed to drag him after her like a mere appendage to her state. I gazed after them, amused by the contrast: he looking like a dull, stiff, old bachelor, the very figure of Moody in [Pg 19] the Country Girl;—she, an elegant, sprightly, captivating creature; decision in her step, laughter on her lips, and pride, intelligence, and mischief in her brilliant eyes.

We visited yesterday the military college, founded by the viceroy, Eugene Beauharnois, for the children of soldiers who had fallen in battle. The original design is now altered; and it has become a mere public school, to which any boys may be admitted, paying a certain sum a year. We went over the whole building, and afterwards saw the scholars, two hundred and eighty in number, sit down to dinner. Every thing appeared nice, clean, and admirably ordered. At the Mint, which interested me extremely, we found them coining silver crowns for the Levant trade, with the head of Maria Theresa, and the date 1780. We were also shown the beautifully engraved die for the medal which the university of Padua presented to Belzoni.

The evening was spent at the Teatro Re, where we saw a bad sentimental comedy (una Commedia di Carattere) exceedingly well acted. One actor I thought almost equal to Dowton, in his own style;—we had afterwards some fine music. Some of the Milanese airs, which the itinerant musicians give us, have considerable beauty and character. There is less monotony, I think, in their general style than in the Venetian music; and perhaps less sentiment, less softness. When left alone to-night, to do penance on the sofa, for my late walks, and recruit for our journey to-morrow,—I tried to adapt English verses to one or two very pretty airs which Annoni brought me to-day, without the Italian words; but it is a most difficult and invidious task. Even Moore, with his unequalled command over the lyric harmonies of our language, cannot perfectly satisfy ears accustomed to the

"Linked sweetness long drawn out"

of the Italian vowels, combined with musical sounds: fancy such dissonant syllables as *ex, pray, what, breaks, strength,* uttered in minim time, hissing and grating through half a bar, instead of the dulcet *anima mia, Catina amabile—Caro mio tesoro,* etc.

STANZAS FOR MUSIC.

All that it hoped
My heart believed,

And when most trusting,
Was most deceived.

A shadow hath fallen
O'er my young years;
And hopes when brightest,
Were quench'd in tears.
[Pg 20]

I make no plaint—
I breathe no sigh—
My lips can smile,
And mine eyes are dry.

I ask no pity,
I hope no cure—
The heart, tho' broken,
Can live, and endure!

We left Milan two days ago, and arrived early the same day at Brescia; there is, I believe, very little to see there, and of that little, I saw nothing,—being too ill and too low for the slightest exertion. The only pleasurable feeling I can remember was excited by our approach to the Alps, after traversing the flat, fertile, uninteresting plains of Lombardy. The peculiar sensation of elevation and delight, inspired by mountain scenery, can only be understood by those who have felt it: at least I never had formed an idea of it till I found myself ascending the Jura.

But Brescia ought to be immortalized in the history of our travels: for there, stalking down the Corso—*le nez en l'air*—we met our acquaintance L— —, from whom we had parted last on the pavé of Piccadilly. I remember that in London I used to think him not remarkable for wisdom,—and his travels have infinitely improved him—in folly. He boasted to us triumphantly that he had run over sixteen thousand miles in sixteen months: that he had bowed at the levée of the Emperor Alexander,—been slapped on the shoulder by the Archduke Constantine,—shaken hands with a Lapland witch,—and been presented in full volunteer uniform at every court between Stockholm and Milan. Yet is he not one particle wiser than if he had spent the same time in walking up and down the Strand. He has contrived, however, to pick up on his tour, strange odds and ends of foreign follies, which stick upon the coarse-grained materials of his own John Bull character like tinfoil upon sackcloth: so that I see little difference between what he was, and what he is, except that from a *simple goose,*—he has become a compound one. With all this, L— — is not unbearable—not *yet* at least. He amuses others as a butt—and me as a specimen of a new genus of fools: for his folly is not like any thing one usually meets with. It is not, *par exemple,* the folly of stupidity, for he talks much; nor of dullness, for he laughs much; nor of ignorance, for he has seen much; nor of wrong-headedness, for he can be guided right; nor of bad-heartedness, for he is good-natured; nor of thoughtlessness, for he is prudent; nor of extravagance, for he can calculate even to the value of half a lira: but it is an essence of folly, peculiar to himself, and like Monsieur Jacques's melancholy, "compounded of many simples, extracted from various objects, and the [Pg 21] sundry contemplation of his travels." So much, for the present, of our friend L— —.

We left Brescia early yesterday morning, and after passing Desenzano, came in sight of the Lago di Garda. I had from early associations a delightful impression of the beauty of this lake, and it did not disappoint me. It is far superior, I think, to the Lago Maggiore, because the scenery is more *resserrè,* lies in a smaller compass, so that the eye takes in the separate features more easily. The mountains to the north are dark, broken, and wild in their forms, and their bases seemed to extend to the water edge: the hills to the south are smiling, beautiful, and cultivated, studded with white flat-roofed buildings, which glitter one above another in the sunshine. Our drive along the promontory of Sirmione, to visit the ruins of the Villa of Catullus, was delightful. The fresh breeze which ruffled the dark blue lake, revived my spirits, and chased away my head-ache. I was inclined to be enchanted with all I saw; and when our guide took us into an old cellar choked with rubbish, and assured us gravely that it was the very spot in which Catullus had written his Odes to Lesbia. I did not laugh in his face; for, after all, it would be as easy to prove that *it is*, as that it is *not*. The old town and castle of Sirmio are singularly picturesque, whether viewed from above or below, and the grove of olives which crowned the steep extremity of the promontory, interested us, being the first we had seen in Italy: on the whole I fully enjoyed the early part of this day.

At Peschiera, which is strongly fortified, we crossed the Mincio.—

> O fountain Arethuse, and thou honoured flood,
> Smooth-flowing Mincius crowned with vocal reeds.

Its waters were exquisitely transparent; but it was difficult to remember its poetical pretensions, in sight of those odious barracks and batteries. The reeds mentioned by Virgil and Milton still flourish upon its banks, and I forgave them for spoiling in some degree the beauty of the shore, when I thought of Adelaïde of Burgundy, who concealed herself among them for three days, when she fled from the dungeon of Peschiera to the arms of her lover. I was glad I had read her story in Gibbon, since it enabled me to add to classical and poetical associations, an interest at once romantic and real.

The rest to-morrow—for I can write no more.

At Verona, Oct. 20.—I had just written the above when I was startled by a mournful strain from a chorus of voices, raised at intervals, and approaching gradually nearer. I walked to the window, and saw a long funeral procession just entering the church, which is opposite to the door of our inn. I immediately threw over me a veil and shawl, followed it, and stood by while the service was chaunted over the dead. The scene, as viewed by the light of about two hundred tapers, which [Pg 22] were carried by the assistants, was as new to me as it was solemn and striking; but it was succeeded by a strange and forlorn contrast. The moment the service was over, the tapers were suddenly extinguished; the priests and the relatives all disappeared in an inconceivably short time, and before I was quite aware of what was going forward: the coffin, stripped of its embroidered pall and garlands of flowers, appeared a mere chest of deal boards, roughly nailed together; and was left standing on tressels, bare, neglected, and forsaken in the middle of the church. I approached it almost fearfully, and with a deeper emotion than I believed such a thing could now excite within me. And here, thought I, rests the human being, who has lived and loved, suffered and enjoyed, and, if I may judge by the splendour of his funeral rites, has been honoured, served, flattered while living:—and now not one remains to shed a last tear over the dead, but a single stranger, a wanderer from a land he perhaps knew not: to whom his very name is unknown! And while thus I moralized, two sextons appeared; and one of them seizing the miserable and deserted coffin, rudely and unceremoniously flung it on his shoulders, and vanished through a vaulted door; and I returned to my room, to write this, and to think how much better, how much more *humanely*, we manage these things in our own England.

Oct. 21.—Verona is a clean and quiet place, containing some fine edifices by Palladio and his pupils. The principal object of interest is the ancient amphitheatre; the most perfect I believe in Italy. The inner circle, with all its ranges of seats, is entire. We ascended to the top, and looked down into the Piazza d'arme, where several battalions of Austrian soldiers were exercising; their arms glittering splendidly in the morning sun. As I have now been long enough in Italy to sympathize in the national hatred of the Austrians, I turned from the sight, resolved not to be pleased. The arena of the amphitheatre is smaller, and less oval in form than I had expected: and in the centre, there is a little paltry gaudy wooden theatre for puppets and tumblers,—forming a grotesque contrast to the massive and majestic architecture around it: but even tumblers and puppets, as Rospo observed, are better than wild beasts and ferocious gladiators.

There are also at Verona a triumphal arch to the Emperor Gallienus; the architecture and inscription almost as perfect as if erected yesterday;—and a most singular bridge of three irregular arches, built, I believe, by the Scaligieri family, who were once princes of Verona.

It is well known that the story of Romeo and Juliet is here regarded as a traditionary and indisputable fact, and the tomb of Juliet is shown in a garden near the town. So much has been written and said on this subject, I can add only one observation. To the reality of the [Pg 23] story it has been objected that the oldest narrator, Masuccio, relates it as having happened at Sienna: but might he not have heard the tradition at Verona, and transferred the scene to Sienna, since he represented it as related by a Siennese?—Della Corte, whose history of Verona I have just laid down, mentions it as a real historical event; and Louis da Porta, in his beautiful novel, la Giulietta, expressly asserts that he has written it down from tradition. If Shakespeare, as it is said, never saw the novel of Da Porta, how came he by the names of Romeo and Juliet, the Montagues and the Capulets: if he *did* meet with it, how came he to depart so essentially from the story, particularly in the catastrophe? I must get some books, if possible, to clear up these difficulties.

23d, at Padua.—We spent yesterday morning pleasantly at Vicenza. Palladio's edifices in general disappointed me; partly because I am not architect enough to judge of their merits, partly because, of most of them the situation is bad, and the materials paltry: but the Olympic theatre, although its solid perspective be a mere trick of the art, surprised and pleased me. It has an air of antique and classic elegance in its decorations, which is very striking. I have heard it criticised as a specimen of bad taste and trickery: but why should its solid scenery be considered more a *trick*, and in bad taste, than a curtain of painted canvas? In both a deception is practised and intended. We saw many things in Vicenza and its neighbourhood, which I have not time nor spirits, to dwell upon.

We arrived here (at Padua) last night, and to-day I am again ill: unable to see or even to wish to see any thing. My eyes are so full of tears that I can scarcely write. I must lay down my pencil, lest I break through my resolution, and be tempted to record feelings I afterwards tremble to see written down.—O bitter and too lasting remembrance! I must sleep it away—even the heavy and drug-bought sleep to which I am now reduced, is better than such waking moments as these.

Venice, October 25th.—I feel while I gaze round me, as if I had seen Venice in my dreams—as if it were itself the vision of a dream. We have been here two days; and I have not yet recovered from my first surprise. All is yet enchantment: all is novel, extraordinary, affecting from the many associations and remembrances excited in the mind. Pleasure and wonder are tinged with a melancholy interest; and while the imagination is excited, the spirits are depressed.

The morning we left Padua was bright, lovely, and cloudless. Our drive along the shores of the Brenta crowned with innumerable villas and gay gardens was delightful; and the moment of our arrival at Fusina, where we left our carriages to embark in gondolas, was the [Pg 24] most auspicious that could possibly have been chosen. It was about four o'clock: the sun was just declining towards the west: the whole surface of the *lagune*, smooth as a mirror, appeared as if paved with fire;—and Venice, with her towers and domes, indistinctly glittering in the distance, rose before us like a gorgeous exhalation from the bosom of the ocean. It is farther from the shore than I expected. As we approached, the splendour faded: but the interest and wonder grew. I can conceive nothing more beautiful, more singular, more astonishing, than the first appearance of Venice, and sad indeed will be the hour when she sinks (as the poet prophesies) "into the slime of her own canals."

The moment we had disembarked our luggage at the inn, we hired gondolas and rowed to the Piazza di San Marco. Had I seen the church of St. Mark any where else, I should have exclaimed against the bad taste which every where prevails in it: but Venice is the proper region of the fantastic, and the church of St. Mark—with its four hundred pillars of every different order, colour, and material, its oriental cupolas, and glittering vanes, and gilding and mosaics—assimilates with all around it: and the kind of pleasure it gives is suitable to the place and the people.

After dinner I had a chair placed on the balcony of our inn, and sat for some time contemplating a scene altogether new and delightful. The arch of the Rialto just gleamed through the deepening twilight; long lines of palaces, at first partially illuminated, faded away at length into gloomy and formless masses of architecture; the gondolas glided to and fro, their glancing lights reflected on the water. There was a stillness all around me, solemn and strange in the heart of a great city. No rattling carriages shook the streets, no trampling of horses echoed along the pavement: the silence was broken only by the melancholy cry of the gondoliers, and the dash of their oars; by the low murmur of human voices, by the chime of the vesper bells, borne over the water, and the sounds of music raised at intervals along the canals. The poetry, the romance of the scene stole upon me unawares. I fell into a reverie, in which visionary forms and recollections gave way to dearer and sadder realities, and my mind seemed no longer in my own power. I called upon the lost, the absent, to share the present with me,—I called upon past feelings to enhance that moment's delight. I did wrong—and memory avenged herself as usual. I quitted my seat on the balcony, with despair at my heart, and drawing to the table, took out my books and work. So passed our first evening at Venice.

Yesterday we visited the Accademia where there are some fine pictures. The famous assumption by Titian is here, and first made me *feel* what connoisseurs mean when they talk of the carnations and draperies of Titian. We were shown two designs for monuments to the [Pg 25] memory of Titian, modelled by Canova. Neither of them has been erected; but the most beautiful, with a little alteration, and the substitution of a lady's bust for Titian's venerable head, has been dedicated, I believe, to the memory of the Archduchess Christina of Austria. I remember also an exquisite Canaletti, quite different in style and subject from any picture of this master I ever saw.

We then rowed to the ducal palace. The council chamber (I thought of Othello as I entered it) is now converted into a library. The walls are decorated with the history of Pope Alexander the Third, and Frederic Barbarossa, painted by the Tintoretti, father and son, Paul Veronese and Palma. Above them, in compartments, hang the portraits of the Doges; among which Marino Faliero is *not*; but his name only, inscribed on a kind of black pall. The Ganymede is a most exquisite little group, attributed to the age of Praxiteles; and not without reason even to the hand of that sculptor.

To-day we visited several churches—rich, on the outside, with all the luxury of architecture,—withinside, gorgeous with painting, sculpture, and many-coloured marbles. The prodigality with which the most splendid and costly materials are lavished here is perfectly amazing: pillars of lapis-lazuli, columns of Egyptian porphyry, and pavements of mosaic, altars of alabaster ascended by steps incrusted with agate and jasper:—but to particularize would be in vain. I will only mention three or four which I wish to recollect: the Church of the Madonna della Salute, so called because erected to the Virgin in gratitude for the deliverance of the city from a pestilence, which she miraculously drove into the Adriatic. It is remarkable for its splendid pictures, most of them by Luca Giordano; and the superb high altar. I think it was the Church of the Gesuata which astonished us most. The whole of the inside walls and columns are encrusted with Carrara marble inlaid with verd antique, in a kind of damask pattern; over the pulpit it fell like drapery, so easy, so graceful, so exquisitely imitated, that I was obliged to touch it to assure myself of the material. Then by way of contrast followed the Church of San Giorgio Maggiore,—one of Palladio's masterpieces. After the dazzling and gorgeous buildings we had left, its beautiful simplicity and correct taste struck me at first with an impression of poverty and coldness. At the Church of St. John and St. Paul is the famous martyrdom, or rather assassination, of St. Peter Martyr, by Titian, one of the most magical pictures in the world. Its tragic horror is redeemed by its sublimity. Here too is a most admirable series of bas-reliefs in white marble, representing the history of our Saviour, the work of a modern sculptor. Here too the Doges are buried; and close to the Church is the equestrian statue of one of the Falieri family: near which Marino Faliero met the conspirators. [Pg 26]

At the Frati is the grave of Titian: a small square slab covers him, with this inscription:—

> "Qui giace il gran Tiziano Vecelli.
> Emulator dei Zeusi e degli Apelli."

there is no monument:—and there needs none.

It was, I think, in the Church of St. John and St. Paul, that I saw a singular and beautiful altar of black touch-stone, used when mass is said for the soul of an executed criminal.

This is all I can remember of to-day. I am fatigued, and my head aches;—my imagination is yet dazzled:—my eyes are tired of admiring, my mind is tired of thinking, and my heart with feeling.—— Now for repose.

27.—To-day we visited the Manfrini Palace, the Casa Pisani, the Palazzo Barberigo, and concluded the morning in the colonnade of St. Mark, and the public gardens. The day has been far less fatiguing than yesterday: for though we have seen an equal variety of objects, they forced the attention less, and gratified the imagination more.

At the Manfrini Palace there is the most valuable and splendid collection of pictures I have yet seen in Italy or elsewhere. I have no intention of turning my little Diary into a mere catalogue of names which I can find in every guide-book; but I cannot pass over Giorgione's beautiful group of himself, and his wife and child, which Lord Byron calls "love at full length and life, not love ideal," and it is indeed exquisite. A female with a guitar by the same master is almost equal to it. There are two Lucretias—one by Guido and one by Giordano: though both are beautiful, particularly the former, there was, I thought, an impropriety in the conception of both pictures: the figure was too voluptuous—too exposed, and did not give me the idea of the matronly Lucretia, who so carefully arranged her drapery before she fell. I remember, too, a St. Cecilia by Carlo Dolci, of most heavenly beauty,—two Correggios—Iphigenia in Aulis, by Padovanino: in this picture the figure of Agamemnon is a complete failure, but the lifeless beauty of Iphigenia, a wonderful effort of art: and a hundred others at least, all masterpieces.

The Barberigo Palace was the school of Titian. We were shown the room in which he painted, and the picture he left unfinished when he died at the age of 99. It is a David—as vigorous in the touch and style as any of his first pictures.

It is now some days since I had time to write; or rather the intervals of excitement and occupation found me too much exhausted to take up my pencil. Our stay at Venice has been rendered most [Pg 27] agreeable by the kindness of Mr. H——, the British Consul, and his amiable and charming wife, and in their society we have spent much of the last few days.

One of our pleasantest excursions was to the Armenian convent of St. Lazaro, where we were received by Fra Pasquale, an accomplished and intelligent monk, and a particular friend of Mr. H——. After we had visited every part of the convent, the printing press—the library—the laboratory—which contains several fine mathematical instruments of English make; and admired the beautiful little tame gazelle which bounded through the corridors, we were politely refreshed with most delicious sweetmeats and coffee; and took leave of Fra Pasquale with regret.

There is no opera at present, but we have visited both the other theatres. At the San Luca, they gave us "Elizabeth, the Exile of Siberia," tolerably acted: but there was one trait introduced very characteristic of the place and people: Elizabeth in a tremendous snow storm, is pursued by robbers; and finding a crucifix, erected by the road side, embraces it for protection. The crucifix flies away with her in a clap of thunder, and sets her down safely at a distance from her persecutors. The audience appeared equally enchanted and edified by this scene: some of the women near me crossed themselves, and put their handkerchiefs to their eyes: the men rose from their seats, clapped with enthusiasm, and shouted "Bravo! Miracolo!"

At the San Benedetto we were gratified by a deep tragedy entitled "Gabrielle Innocente," so exquisitely absurd, and so grotesquely acted, that the best comedy could scarcely have afforded us more amusement,—certainly not more *merriment*. In the course of the evening, coffee and ices were served in our box, as is the custom here.

With Mrs. H—— this evening I had a long and pleasant conversation; she is really one of the most delightful and unaffected women I ever met with: and as there is nothing in my melancholy visage and shrinking reserve to tempt any person to converse with me, I must also set her down as one of the most good-natured. She talked much of Lord Byron, with whom, during his residence here she was on intimate terms. She spoke of him, not conceitedly as one vain of the acquaintance of a great character; nor with affected reserve, as if afraid of committing herself—but with openness, animation, and cordial kindness, as one whom she liked, and had reason to like. She says the style of Lord Byron's conversation is very much that of Don Juan: just in the same manner are the familiar, the brilliant, the sublime, the affecting, the witty, the ludicrous, and the licentious, mingled and contrasted. Several little anecdotes which she related I need not write down; I can scarcely forget them, and it would not be quite fair [Pg 28] as they were told *en confiance.* I am no anecdote hunter, picking up articles for "my pocket book."

A little while ago Captain F. lent me D'Israeli's Essays on the Literary Character, which had once belonged to Lord Byron; and contained marginal notes in his hand-writing. One or two of them are so curiously characteristic that I copy them here.

The first note is on a passage in which D'Israeli, in allusion to Lord Byron, traces his fondness for oriental scenery to his having read Rycaut at an early age. On this Lord Byron observes, that he read *every book* relating to the east before he was ten years old, including De Tott and Cantemir as well as Rycaut: at that age, he says that he *detested* all poetry, and adds, "when I was in Turkey, I was oftener tempted to turn mussulman than poet: and have often regretted since that *I did not.*"

At page 99 D'Israeli says,

"The great poetical genius of our times has openly alienated himself from the land of his brothers" (over the word *brothers* Lord Byron has written *Cains.*) "He becomes immortal in the *language* of a *people* whom he would *contemn,* he accepts with ingratitude the fame he loves more than life, and he is only truly great on that *spot* of *earth,* whose genius, when he is no more, will contemplate his shade in sorrow and in anger."

Lord Byron has underlined several words in this passage, and writes thus in the margin:

"What was rumoured of me in that language, if *true,* I was unfit for England; and if *false,* England was unfit for me. But 'there is a world elsewhere.' I have never for an instant regretted that country,—but often that I ever returned to it. It is not my fault that I am obliged to write in English. If I understood any present language, Italian, for instance, equally well, I would write in it:—but it will require ten years, at least, to form a style. No tongue so easy to acquire a little of, and so difficult to master thoroughly, as Italian."

The next note is amusing; at page 342 is mentioned the anecdote of Petrarch, who when returning to his native town, was informed that the proprietor of the house in which he was born had *often* wished to make alterations in it, but that the town's-people had risen to insist that the house consecrated by his birth should remain unchanged;—"a triumph," adds D'Israeli, "more affecting to Petrarch than even his coronation at Rome."

Lord Byron has written in the margin—"It would have pained *me* more that the proprietor should *often* have wished to make alterations, than it would give me pleasure that the rest of Arezzo rose against [Pg 29] his right (for *right* he had:) the depreciation of the lowest of mankind is more painful, than the applause of the highest is pleasing. The sting of the scorpion is more in *torture* than the possession of any thing short of Venus would be in rapture."

The public gardens are the work of the French, and occupy the extremity of one of the islands. They contain the only trees I have seen at Venice:—a few rows of dwarfish unhappy-looking shrubs, parched by the sea breezes, and are little frequented. We found here a solitary gentleman, who was sauntering up and down with his hands in his pockets, and a look at once stupid and disconsolate. Sometimes he paused, looked vacantly over the waters, whistled, yawned, and turned away to resume his solemn walk. On a trifling remark addressed to him by one of our party, he entered into conversation, with all the eagerness of a man, whose tongue had long been kept in most unnatural bondage. He congratulated himself on having met with some one who would speak English; adding contemptuously, that "he understood none of the outlandish tongues the people spoke hereabouts:" he inquired what was to be seen here, for though he had been four days in Venice, he had spent every day precisely in the same manner; viz. walking up and down the public gardens. We told him Venice was famous for fine buildings and pictures; he knew nothing of *them* things. And that it contained also, "some fine statues and antiques"—he cared nothing about them neither—he should set off for Florence the next morning, and begged to know what was to be seen there? Mr. R—— told him, with enthusiasm, "the most splendid gallery of pictures and statues in the world!" He looked very blank and disappointed. "Nothing else?" then he should certainly not waste his time at Florence, he should go direct to Rome; he had put down the name of that *town* in his pocket-book, for he understood it was a very *convenient* place: he should therefore stay there a week; thence he should go to Naples, a place he had also heard of, where he should stay another week: then he should go to Algiers, where he should stay *three weeks*, and thence to Tunis, where he expected to be very comfortable, and should probably make a long stay; thence he should return home, having seen every thing worth seeing. He scarcely seemed to know how or by what route he had got to Venice—but he assured us he had come "fast enough;"—he remembered no place he had passed through except Paris. At Paris he told us there was a female lodging in the same hotel with himself, who by his description appears to have been a single lady of rank and fashion, travelling with her own carriages and a suite of servants. He had never seen her; but learning through the domestics that she was travelling the same route, he sat down and wrote her a long letter, beginning "Dear Madam," and proposing they should join [Pg 30] company, "for the sake of good fellowship, and the *bit of chat* they might have on their way." Of course she took no notice of this strange billet, "from which," added he with ludicrous simplicity, "I supposed she would rather travel alone."

Truly, "Nature hath framed strange fellows in her time." After this specimen, sketched from life, who will say there are such things as caricatures?

We visited to-day the Giant's Staircase and the Bridge of Sighs, and took a last farewell of St. Mark—we were surprised to see the church hung with black—the festoons of flowers all removed—masses going forward at several altars, and crowds of people looking particularly solemn and devout. It is the "Giorno dei morte," the day by the Roman Catholics consecrated to the dead. I observed many persons, both men and women, who wept while they prayed, with every appearance of the most profound grief. Leaving St. Mark, I crossed the square. On the three lofty standards in front of the church formerly floated the ensigns of the three states subjects to Venice,—the Morea, Cyprus, and Candia: the bare poles remain, but the ensigns of empire are gone. One of the standards was extended on the ground, and being of immense length, I hesitated for a moment whether I should make a circuit, but at last stepped over it. I looked back with remorse, for it was like trampling over the fallen.

We then returned to our inn to prepare for our departure. How I regret to leave Venice! not the less because I cannot help it.

Rovigo, Nov. 3. We left Venice in a hurry yesterday, slept at Padua, and travelled this morning through a most lovely country, among the Enganean hills to Rovigo, where we are very uncomfortably lodged at the Albergo di San Marco.

I have not yet recovered my regret at leaving Venice so unexpectedly; though as a residence, I could scarce endure it; the sleepy canals, the gliding gondolas in their "dusk livery of woe"—the absence of all verdure, all variety—of all *nature,* in short; the silence, disturbed only by the incessant chiming of bells—and, worse than all, the spectacle of a great city "expiring," as Lord Byron says, "before our eyes," would give me the horrors: but as a visitor, my curiosity was not half gratified, and I should have liked to have stayed a few days longer—perhaps after all, I have reason to rejoice that instead of bringing away from Venice a disagreeable impression of satiety, disgust and melancholy, I have quitted it with feelings of admiration, of deep regret, and undiminished interest.

Farewell, then, Venice! I could not have believed it possible that it would have brought tears to my eyes to leave a place merely for its own sake, and unendeared by the presence of any one I loved. [Pg 31]

As Rovigo affords no other amusement I shall scribble a little longer.

Nothing can be more arbitrary than the Austrian government at Venice. As a summary method of preventing robberies during the winter months, when many of the gondoliers and fishermen are out of employ, the police have orders to arrest, without ceremony, every person who has no permanent trade or profession, and keep them in confinement and to hard labour till the return of spring.

The commerce of Venice has so much and so rapidly declined, that Mr. H—— told us when first he was appointed to the consulship, a hundred and fifty English vessels cleared the port, and this year only five. It should seem that Austria, from a cruel and selfish policy, is sacrificing Venice to the prosperity of Trieste: but why do I call that a cruel policy, which on recollection I might rather term poetical and retributive justice?

The grandeur of Venice arose first from its trade in salt. I remember reading in history, that when the king of Hungary opened certain productive salt mines in his dominions, the Venetians sent him a peremptory order to shut them up; and such was the power of the Republic at that time, that he was forced to obey this insolent command, to the great injury and impoverishment of his states. The tables are now turned; the oppressor has become the oppressed.

The principal revenue derived from Venice is from the tax on houses, there being no *land tax*. So rapid was the decay of the place, that in two years seventy houses and palaces were pulled down; the government forbade this by a special law, and now taxes are paid for many houses whose proprietors are too poor to live in them.

There is no *society*, properly so called, at Venice; three old women of rank receive company now and then, and it is any thing rather than select.

Mr. F. told us at Venice, that on entering the states subject to Austria, he had his Johnson's Dictionary taken from him, and could never recover it; so jealous is the government of English principles and English literature, that *all* English books are prohibited until examined by the police.

The whole country from Milan to Padua was like a vast garden, nothing could exceed its fertility and beauty. It was the latter end of the vintage; and we frequently met huge tub-like waggons loaded with purple grapes, reeling home from the vineyards, and driven by men whose legs were stained with treading in the wine-press—now and then, rich clusters were shaken to the ground, as I have seen wisps of straw fall from a hay-cart in England, and were regarded with equal indifference. Sometimes we saw in the vineyards by the road-side, groups of labourers seated among the branches of the trees, [Pg 32] and plucking grapes from the vines, which were trailed gracefully from tree to tree and from branch to branch, and drooped with their luxurious burthen of fruit. The scene would have been as perfectly delightful, as it was new and beautiful, but for the squalid looks of the peasantry; more especially of the women. The principal productions of the country seem to be wine and silk. There were vast groves of mulberry-trees between Verona and Padua; and we visited some of the silk-mills, in which the united strength of men invariably performed those operations which in England are accomplished by steam or water. I saw in a huge horizontal wheel, about a dozen of these poor creatures labouring so hard, that my very heart ached to see them, and I begged that the machine might be stopped that I might speak to them:—but when it W*as* stopped, and I beheld their half savage, half stupified, I had almost said *brutified* countenances, I could not utter a single word—but gave them something, and turned away.

"Compassion is wasted upon such creatures," said R— —; "do you not see that their minds are degraded down to their condition? they do not pity themselves:"—but therefore did I pity them the more.

Bologna, Nov. 5.—I fear I shall retain a disagreeable impression of Bologna, for here I am again ill. I have seen little of what the town contains of beautiful and curious: and that little, under unpleasant and painful circumstances.

Yesterday we passed through Ferrara; only stopping to change horses and dine. We snatched a moment to visit the hospital of St. Anna and the prison of Tasso—the glory and disgrace of Ferrara. Over the iron gate is written "Ingresso alia prigione di Torquato Tasso." The cell itself is miserably gloomy and wretched, and not above twelve feet square. How amply has posterity avenged the cause of the poet on his tyrant!—and as we emerge from his obscure dungeon and descend the steps of the hospital of St. Anna, with what fervent hatred, indignation, and scorn, do we gaze upon the towers of the ugly red brick palace, or rather fortress, which deforms the great square, and where Alphonso feasted while Tasso wept! The inscription on the door of the cell, calling on strangers to venerate the spot where Tasso, "Infermo più di tristezza che delirio," was confined seven years and one month—was placed there by the French, and its accuracy may be doubted; as far as I can recollect. The grass growing in the wide streets of Ferrara is no poetical exaggeration; I saw it rank and long even on the thresholds of the deserted houses, whose sashless windows, and flapping doors, and roofless walls, looked strangely desolate. [Pg 33]

I will say nothing of Bologna;—for the few days I have spent here have been to me days of acute suffering, in more ways than I wish to remember, and therefore dare not dwell upon.

At Covigliajo in the Apennines.—O for the pencil of Salvator, or the pen of a Radcliffe! But could either, or could both united, give to my mind the scenes of to-day, in all their splendid combinations of beauty and brightness, gloom and grandeur? A picture may present to the eye a small portion of the boundless whole—one aspect of the every-varying face of nature; and words, how weak are they!—they are but the elements out of which the quick imagination frames and composes lovely landscapes, according to its power or its peculiar character; and in which the unimaginative man finds only a mere chaos of verbiage, without form, and void.

The scenery of the Apennines is altogether different in character from that of the Alps: it is less bold, less lofty, less abrupt and terrific—but more beautiful, more luxuriant, and infinitely more varied. At one time, the road wound among precipices and crags, crowned with dismantled fortresses and ruined castles—skirted with dark pine forests—and opening into wild recesses of gloom, and immeasurable depths like those of Tartarus profound; then came such glimpses of paradise! such soft sunny valleys and peaceful hamlets—and vine-clad eminences and rich pastures, with here and there a convent half hidden by groves of cypress and cedars. As we ascended we arrived at a height from which, looking back, we could see the whole of Lombardy spread at our feet; a vast, glittering, indistinct landscape, bounded on the north by the summits of the Alps, just apparent above the horizon, like a range of small silvery clouds; and on the east a long unbroken line of bluish light marked the far distant Adriatic; as the day declined, and we continued our ascent (occasionally assisted by a yoke of oxen where the acclivity was very precipitate), the mountains closed around us, the scenery became more wildly romantic, barren, and bleak. At length, after passing the crater of a volcano, visible through the gloom by its dull red light, we arrived at the Inn of Covigliajo, an uncouth dreary edifice, situated in a lonely and desolate spot, some miles from any other habitation. This is the very inn, infamous for a series of the most horrible assassinations, committed here some years ago. Travellers arrived, departed, disappeared, and were never heard of more; by what agency, or in what manner disposed of, could not be discovered. It was supposed for some time that a horde of banditti were harboured among the mountains, and the police were for a long time in active search for them, while the real miscreants remained unsuspected for their seeming insignificance and helplessness; these were the mistress of the inn, the camerière, and the curate of the nearest village, about two leagues off. They [Pg 34] secretly murdered every traveller who was supposed to carry property—buried or burned their clothes, packages, and vehicles, retaining nothing but their watches, jewels, and money. The whole story, with all its horrors, the manner of discovery, and the fate of these wretches, is told, I think, by Forsyth, who can hardly be suspected of romance or exaggeration. I have him not with me to refer to; but I well remember the mysterious and shuddering dread with which I read the anecdote. I am glad no one else seems to recollect it. The inn at present contains many more than it can possibly accommodate. We have secured the best rooms, or rather the *only* rooms—and besides ourselves and other foreigners, there are numbers of native travellers: some of whom arrived on horseback, and others with the Vetturini. A kind of gallery or corridor separates the sleeping rooms, and is divided by a curtain into two parts: the smaller is appropriated to us, as a saloon: the other half, as I contemplate it at this moment through a rent in the curtain, presents a singular and truly Italian spectacle—a huge black iron lamp, suspended by a chain from the rafters, throws a flaring and shifting light around. Some trusses of hay have been shaken down upon the floor, to supply the place of beds, chairs, and tables; and there, reclining in various attitudes, I see a number of dark looking figures, some eating and drinking, some sleeping; some playing at cards, some telling stories with all the Italian variety of gesticulation and intonation; some silently looking on, or listening. Two or three common looking fellows began to smoke their segars, but when it was suggested that this might incommode the ladies on the other side of the curtain, they with genuine politeness ceased directly. Through this motley and picturesque assemblage I have to make my way to my bed-room in a few minutes—I will take another look at them, and then—andiamo!

Florence, Nov. 8.—"La bellisema e famosissima figlia di Roma," as Dante calls her in some relenting moment. Last night we slept in a blood-stained hovel—and to-night we are lodged in a palace. So much for the vicissitudes of travelling.

I am not subject to idle fears, and least of all to superstitious fears—but last night, at Covigliajo, I could not sleep—I could not even lie down for more than a few minutes together. The whispered voices and hard breathing of the men who slept in the corridor, from whom only a slight door divided me, disturbed and fevered my nerves; horrible imaginings were all around me: and gladly did I throw open my window at the first glimpse of the dawn, and gladly did I hear the first well-known voice which summoned me to a hasty breakfast. How reviving was the breath of the early morning, after leaving that close, suffocating, ill-omened inn! how beautiful the blush of light stealing downwards from the illumined summits to the valleys, tinting [Pg 35] the fleecy mists, as they rose from the earth, till all the landscape was flooded with sunshine: and when at length we passed the mountains, and began to descend into the rich vales of Tuscany—when from the heights above Fesole we beheld the city of Florence, and above it the young moon and the evening star suspended side by side; and floating over the whole of the Val d'Arno, and the lovely hills which enclose it, a mist, or rather a suffusion of the richest rose colour, which gradually, as the day declined, faded, or rather deepened into purple; then I first understood all the enchantment of an Italian landscape.—O what a country is this! All that I see, I *feel*—all that I *feel*, sinks so deep into my heart and my memory! the deeper because I suffer—and because I never think of expressing, or sharing, one emotion with those around me, but lock it up in my own bosom; or at least in my little book—as I do now.

Nov. 10.—We visited the gallery for the first time yesterday morning; and I came away with my eyes and imagination so dazzled with excellence, and so distracted with variety, that I retained no distinct recollection of any particular object except the Venus; which of course was the first and great attraction. This morning was much more delightful; my powers of discrimination returned, and my power of enjoyment was not diminished. New perceptions of beauty and excellence seemed to open upon my mind; and faculties long dormant, were roused to pleasurable activity.

I came away untired, unsated; and with a delightful and distinct impression of all I had seen. I leave to catalogues to particularise; and am content to admire and to remember.

I am glad I was not disappointed in the Venus which I half expected. Neither was I surprised: but I felt while I gazed a sense of unalloyed and unmingled pleasure, and forgot the cant of criticism. It has the same effect to the eye, that perfect harmony has upon the ear: and I think I can understand why no copy, cast, or model, however accurate, however exquisite, can convey the impression of tenderness and sweetness, the divine and peculiar charm of the original.

After dinner we walked in the grounds of the Cascine,—a dairy farm belonging to the grand Duke, just without the gates of Florence. The promenade lies along the bank of the river, and is sheltered and beautiful. We saw few native Italians, but great numbers of English walking and riding. The day was as warm, as sunny, as brilliant as the first days of September in England.

To-night, after resting a little, I went out to view the effect of the city and surrounding scenery, by moonlight. It is not alone the brilliant purity of the skies and atmosphere, nor the peculiar character of the scenery which strikes a stranger; but here art harmonizes with nature: the style of the buildings, their flat projecting roofs, white [Pg 36] walls, balconies, colonnades and statues, are all set off to advantage by the radiance of an Italian moon.

I walked across the first bridge, from which I had a fine view of the Ponte della Trinità, with its graceful arches and light balustrade, touched with the sparkling moonbeams and relieved by dark shadow: then I strolled along the quay in front of the Corsini palace, and beyond the colonnade of the Uffizi, to the last of the four bridges; on the middle of which I stood and looked back upon the city—(how justly styled the Fair!)—with all its buildings, its domes, its steeples, its bridges, and woody hills and glittering convents, and marble villas, peeping from embowering olives and cypresses; and far off the snowy peaks of the Apennines, shining against the dark purple sky: the whole blended together in one delicious scene of shadowy splendour. After contemplating it with a kind of melancholy delight, long enough to get it by heart, I returned homewards. Men were standing on the wall along the Arno, in various picturesque attitudes, fishing, after the Italian fashion, with singular nets suspended to long poles; and as I saw their dark figures between me and the moonlight, and elevated above my eye, they looked like colossal statues. I then strayed into the Piazza del Gran Duca. Here the rich moonlight, streaming through the arcade of the gallery, fell directly upon the fine Perseus of Benvenuto Cellini; and illuminating the green bronze, touched it with a spectral and supernatural beauty. Thence I walked round the equestrian statue of Cosmo, and so home over the Ponte Alla Carrajo.

Nov. 11.—I spent about two hours in the gallery, and for the first time saw the Niobe. This statue has been for a long time a favourite of my imagination, and I approached it, treading softly and slowly, and with a feeling of reverence; for I had an impression that the original Niobe would, like the original Venus, surpass all the casts and copies I had seen both in beauty and expression: but apparently expression is more easily caught than delicacy and grace, and the grandeur and pathos of the attitude and grouping easily copied—for I think the best casts of the Niobe are accurate counterparts of the original; and at the first glance I was capriciously disappointed, because the statue did not *surpass* my expectations. It should be contemplated from a distance. It is supposed that the whole group once ornamented the pediment of a temple—probably the temple of Diana or Latona. I once saw a beautiful drawing by Mr. Cockerell, of the manner in which he supposed the whole group was distributed. Many of the figures are rough and unfinished at the back, as if they had been placed on a height, and viewed only in front.

In the same room with the Niobe is a head which struck me more—the *Alexandre mourant.* The title seemed to me misapplied; for [Pg 37] there is something indignant and upbraiding, as well as mournful, in the expression of this magnificent head. It is undoubtedly Alexander—but Alexander reproaching the gods—or calling upon Heaven for new worlds to conquer.

I visited also the gallery of Bronzes: it contains, among other master-pieces, the aërial Mercury of John of Bologna, of which we see such a multiplicity of copies. There is a conceit in perching him upon the bluff cheeks of a little Eolus: but what exquisite lightness in the figure!—how it mounts, how it floats, disdaining the earth! On leaving the gallery, I sauntered about; visited some churches, and then returned home depressed and wearied: and in this melancholy humour I had better close my book, lest I be tempted to write what I could not bear to see written.

Sunday.—At the English ambassador's chapel. To attend public worship among our own countrymen, and hear the praises of God in our native accents, in a strange land, among a strange people; where a different language, different manners, and a different religion prevail, affects the mind, or at least ought to affect it;—and deeply too: yet I cannot say that I felt devout this morning. The last day I visited St. Mark's, when I knelt down beside the poor weeping girl and her dove-basket, my heart was touched, and my prayers, I humbly trust, were not unheard: to-day, in that hot close crowded room, among those fine people flaunting in all the luxury of dress, I felt suffocated, feverish, and my head ached—the clergyman too—
—

Samuel Rogers paid us a long visit this morning. He does not look as if the suns of Italy had *revivified* him—but he is as *amiable* and amusing as ever. He talked long, *et avec beaucoup d'onction*, of ortolans and figs; till methought it was the very poetry of epicurism; and put me in mind of his own suppers—

> "Where blushing fruits through scatter'd leaves invite,
> Still clad in bloom and veiled in azure light.
> The wine as rich in years as Horace sings;"

and the rest of his description, worthy of a poetical Apicius.

Rogers may be seen every day about eleven or twelve in the Tribune, seated opposite to the Venus, which appears to be the exclusive object of his adoration; and gazing, as if he hoped, like another Pygmalion, to animate the statue; or rather perhaps that the statue might animate *him*. A young Englishman of fashion, with as much talent as espieglerie, placed an epistle in verse between the fingers of the statue, addressed to Rogers; in which the goddess entreats him not to come there *ogling* every day;—for though "partial friends might deem him still alive," she knew by his looks that he had come from the other side of the Styx; and retained her *antique* abhorrence of the spectral [Pg 38] dead, etc. etc. She concluded by beseeching him, if he could not desist from haunting her with his *ghostly* presence, at least to spare her the added misfortune of being be-rhymed by his muse.

Rogers, with equal good nature and good sense, neither noticed these lines nor withdrew his friendship and intimacy from the writer.

Carlo Dolce is not one of my favourite masters. There is a cloying sweetness in his style, a general want of power which wearies me: yet I brought away from the Corsini Palace to-day an impression of a head by Carlo Dolce (La Poesia), which I shall never forget. Now I recall the picture, I am at a loss to tell where lies the charm which has thus powerfully seized on my imagination. Here are no "eyes upturned like one inspired"—no distortion—no rapt enthusiasm—no Muse full of the God;—but it is a head so purely, so divinely intellectual, so heavenly sweet, and yet so penetrating,—so full of sensibility, and yet so unstained by earthly passion—so brilliant, and yet so calm—that if Carlo Dolce had lived in our days, I should have thought he intended it for the personified genius of Wordsworth's poetry. There is such an individual reality about this beautiful head, that I am inclined to believe the tradition, that it is the portrait of one of Carlo Dolce's daughters who died young:—and yet

> "Did ever mortal mixture of earth's mould
> Breathe such divine, enchanting ravishment?"

Nov. 15.—Our stay at Florence promises to be far gayer than either Milan or Venice, or even Paris; more diversified by society, as well as affording a wider field of occupation and amusement.

Sometimes in the long evenings, when fatigued and over-excited, I recline apart on the sofa, or bury myself in the recesses of a *fauteuil;* when I am aware that my mind is wandering away to forbidden themes, I force my attention to what is going forward; and often see and hear much that is entertaining, if not improving. People are so accustomed to my pale face, languid indifference and, what M—— calls, my *impracticable* silence, that after the first glance and introduction, I believe they are scarcely sensible of my presence: so I sit, and look, and listen, secure and harboured in my apparent dullness. The flashes of wit, the attempts at sentiment, the affectation of enthusiasm, the absurdities of folly, and the blunders of ignorance; the contrast of characters and the clash of opinions, the scandalous anecdotes of the day, related with sprightly malice, and listened to with equally malicious avidity,—all these, in my days of health and happiness, had power to surprise, or amuse, or provoke me. I could mingle *then* in the conflict of minds; and hear my part with smiles in the social circle; [Pg 39] though the next moment, perhaps, I might contemn myself and others: and the personal scandal, the characteristic tale, the amusing folly, or the malignant wit, were effaced from my mind—

——"Like forms with chalk
Painted on rich men's floors for one feast night."

Now it is different: I can smile yet, but my smile is in pity, rather than in mockery. If suffering has subdued my mind to seriousness, and perhaps enfeebled its powers, I may at least hope that it has not soured or imbittered my temper:—if what could once *amuse*, no longer amuses,—what could once *provoke* has no longer power to irritate: thus my loss may be improved into a gain—*car tout est bien, quand tout est mal.*

It is sorrow which makes our experience; it is sorrow which teaches us to feel properly for ourselves and for others. We must feel deeply, before we can think rightly. It is not in the tempest and storm of passions we can reflect,—but afterwards when *the waters have gone over our soul;* and like the precious gems and the rich merchandize which the wild wave casts on the shore out of the wreck it has made—such are the thoughts left by retiring passions.

Reflection is the result of feeling; from that absorbing, heart-rending compassion for oneself (the most painful sensation, *almost,* of which our nature is capable), springs a deeper sympathy for others; and from the sense of our own weakness, and our own self-upbraiding, arises a disposition to be indulgent—to forbear—and to forgive—so at least it ought to be. When once we have shed those inexpressibly bitter tears, which fall unregarded, and which we forget to wipe away, O how we shrink from inflicting pain! how we shudder at unkindness!—and think all harshness even in thought, only another name for cruelty! These are but common-place truths, I know, which have often been a thousand times better expressed. Formerly I heard them, read them, and thought I believed them: now I feel them; and feeling, I utter them as if they were something new.—Alas! the lessons of sorrow are as old as the world itself.

To-day we have seen nothing new. In the morning I was ill: in the afternoon we drove to the Cascina; and while the rest walked, I spread my shawl upon the bank and basked like a lizard in the sunshine. It was a most lovely day, a summer-day in England. In this paradise of a country, the common air, and earth, and skies, seem happiness enough. While I sat to-day, on my green bank—languid, indeed, but free from pain—and looked round upon a scene which has lost its novelty, but none of its beauty,—where Florence, with its glittering domes and its back-ground of sunny hills, terminated my view on one side, and the Apennines, tinted with rose colour and gold, bounded it [Pg 40] on the other, I felt not only pleasure, but a deep thankfulness that such pleasures were yet left to me.

Among the gay figures who passed and repassed before me, I remarked a benevolent but rather heavy-looking old gentleman, with a shawl hanging over his arm, and holding a parasol, with which he was gallantly shading a little plain old woman from the November sun. After them walked two young ladies, simply dressed; and then followed a tall and very handsome young man, with a plain but elegant girl hanging on his arm. This was the Grand Duke and his family; with the Prince of Carignano, who has lately married one of his daughters. Two servants in plain drab liveries, followed at a considerable distance. People politely drew on one side as they approached; but no other homage was paid to the sovereign, who thus takes his walk in public almost every day. Lady Morgan is merry at the expense of the Grand Duke's taste for brick and mortar: but monarchs, like other men, must have their amusements; some invent uniforms, some stitch embroidery;—and why should not this good-natured Grand Duke amuse himself with his trowel if he likes it? As to the Prince of Carignano, I give him up to her lash—*le traître*—but perhaps he thought he was doing right: and at all events there are not flatterers wanting, to call his perfidy patriotism.

I am told that Florence retains its reputation of being the most devout capital in Italy, and that here love, music, and devotion hold divided empire, or rather are *tria juncta in uno.* The liberal patronage and taste of Lord Burghersh, contribute perhaps to make music so much a *passion* as it is at present. Magnelli, the Grand Duke's Maestra di Cappella, and director of the Conservatorio, is the finest tenor in Italy. I have the pleasure of hearing him frequently, and think the purity of his taste at least equal to the perfection of his voice; rare praise for a singer in these "most brisk and giddy-paced times." He gave us last night the beautiful recitative which introduces Desdemona's song in Othello—

"Nessun maggior dolore,
Che ricordarsi del tempo felice
Nella miseria!"

and the words, the music, and the divine pathos of the man's voice combined, made me feel—as I thought I never could have felt again.

TO – –

As sounds of sweetest music, heard at eve,
When summer dews weep over languid flowers,
When the still air conveys each touch, each tone,
However faint—and breathes it on the ear
[Pg 41] With a distinct and thrilling power, that leaves
Its memory long within the raptur'd soul.—
—Even *such* thou art to me!—and thus I sit
And feel the harmony that round thee lives,
And breathes from every feature. Thus I sit—
And when most quiet—cold—or silent—*then*
Even then, I feel each word, each look, each tone!
There's not an accent of that tender voice,

There's not a day-beam of those sunbright eyes,
Nor passing smile, nor melancholy grace,
Nor thought half utter'd, feeling half betray'd
Nor glance of kindness,—no, nor gentlest touch
Of that dear hand, in amity extended,
That e'er was lost to me;—that treasur'd well,
And oft recall'd, dwells not upon my soul
Like sweetest music heard at summer's eve!

Yesterday we visited the church of San Lorenzo, the Laurentian library, and the Pietra Dura manufactory, and afterwards spent an hour in the Tribune.

In a little chapel in the San Lorenzo are Michel Angelo's famous statues, the Morning, the Noon, the Evening, and the Night. I looked at them with admiration rather than with pleasure; for there is something in the severe and overpowering style of this master, which affects me disagreeably, as beyond my feeling, and above my comprehension. These statues are very ill disposed for effect: the confined *cell* (such it seemed) in which they are placed is so strangely disproportioned to the awful and massive grandeur of their forms.

There is a picture by Michel Angelo, considered a chef-d'œuvre, which hangs in the Tribune, to the right of the Venus: now if all the connaisseurs in the world, with Vasari at their head, were to harangue for an hour together on the merits of this picture, I might submit in silence, for I am no connoisseur; but that it is a disagreeable, a hateful picture, is an opinion which fire could not melt out of me. In spite of Messieurs les Connaisseurs, and Michel Angelo's fame, I would die in it at the stake: for instance, here is the Blessed Virgin, not the "Vergine Santa, d'ogni grazia piena," but a Virgin, whose brick-dust coloured face, harsh unfeminine features, and muscular, masculine arms, give me the idea of a washerwoman, (con rispetto parlando!) an infant Saviour with the proportions of a giant: and what shall we say of the nudity of the figures in the background; profaning the subject and shocking at once good taste and good sense? A little farther on, the eye rests on the divine Madre di

Dio of Correggio: what beauty, what sweetness, what maternal love, and humble adoration are blended in the look and attitude with which she bends over her infant! Beyond it hangs the Madonna del Cardellino of Raffaelle: what heavenly grace, what simplicity, what saint-like purity, in the expression of that face, and that exquisite mouth! And from these must I turn back, on pain of being thought an ignoramus, to admire the [Pg 42] coarse perpetration of Michel Angelo—because it is Michel Angelo's? But I speak in ignorance. [F]

To return to San Lorenzo. The chapel of the Medici, begun by Ferdinand the First, where coarse brickwork and plaster mingle with marble and gems, is still unfinished and likely to remain so: it did not interest me. The fine bronze sarcophagus, which encloses the ashes of Lorenzo the Magnificent, and of his brother Giuliano, assassinated by the Pazzi, interested me far more. While I was standing carelessly in front of the high altar, I happened to look down, and under my feet were these words, "To Cosmo The Venerable, the Father of his Country." I moved away in haste, and before I had decided to my own satisfaction upon Cosmo's claims to the gratitude and veneration of posterity, we left the church.

At the Laurentian library we were edified by the sight of some famous old manuscripts, invaluable to classical scholars. To my unlearned eyes the manuscript of Petrarch, containing portraits of himself and Laura, was more interesting. Petrarch is hideous—but I was pleased with the head of Laura, which in spite of the antique dryness and stiffness of the painting, has a soft and delicate expression not unlike one of Carlo Dolce's Madonnas. Here we saw Galileo's forefinger, pointing up to the skies from a white marble pedestal; and exciting more derision than respect.

At the Pietra Dura, notwithstanding the beauty and durability of some of the objects manufactured, the result seemed to me scarce worth the incredible time, patience, and labour required in the work. *Par exemple*, six months' hard labour spent upon a butterfly in the lid of a snuff-box seems a most disproportionate waste of time. Thirty workmen are employed here at the Grand Duke's expense; for this manufacture, like that of the Gobelins at Paris, is exclusively carried on for the sovereign.

Nov. 20.—I am struck in this place with grand beginnings and mean endings. I have not yet seen a finished church, even the Duomo has no façade.

Yesterday we visited the Palazzo Mozzi to see Benvenuto's picture, "The Night after the Battle of Jena." Then several churches—the Santa Croce, which is hallowed ground: the Annonciata, celebrated for the frescos of Andrea del Sarto; and the Carmine, which pleased me by the light elegance of its architecture, and its fine alto-relievos in white marble. In this church is the chapel of the Madonna del Carmele, painted by Masuccio, and the most ancient frescos extant: they are curious rather than beautiful, and going to decay.

To-day we visited the school of the Fine Arts: it contains a very fine [Pg 43] and ample collection of casts after the antique; and some of the works of modern artists and students are exhibited. Were I to judge from the specimens I have seen here and elsewhere, I should say that a cold, glaring, hard *tea-tray* style prevails in painting, and a still worse taste, if possible, in sculpture. No soul, no grandeur, no simplicity; a meagre insipidity in the conception, a nicety of finish in the detail; affectation instead of grace, distortion instead of power, and prettiness instead of beauty. Yet the artists who execute these works, and those who buy them, have free access to the marvels of the gallery, and the treasures of the Pitti Palace. Are they sans eyes, sans souls, sans taste, sans every thing, but money and self-conceit?

Nov. 22.—Our mornings, however otherwise occupied, are generally concluded by an hour in the gallery or at the Pitti Palace; the evenings are spent in the Mercato Nuovo, in the workshops of artists, or at the Cascina.

To-day at the gallery I examined the Dutch school and the Salle des Portraits, and ended as usual with the Tribune. The Salle des Portraits contains a complete collection of the portraits of painters down to the present day. In general their respective countenances are expressive of their characters and style of painting. Poor Harlow's picture, painted by himself, is here.

The Dutch and Flemish painters (in spite of their exquisite pots and pans, and cabbages and carrots, their birch-brooms, in which you can count every twig, and their carpets, in which you can reckon every thread) do not interest me; their landscapes too, however natural, are mere Dutch nature (with some brilliant exceptions), fat cattle, clipped trees, boors, and windmills. Of course I am not speaking of Vandyke, nor of Rubens, he that "in the colours of the rainbow lived," nor of Rembrandt, that king of clouds and shadows; but for mine own part, I would give up all that Mieris, Netscher, Teniers, and Gerard Douw ever produced, for one of Claude's Eden-like creations, or one of Guido's lovely heads—or merely for the pleasure of looking at Titian's Flora once a day, I would give a whole gallery of Dutchmen, if I had them.

In the daughter of Herodias, by Leonardo da Vinci, there is the same eternal face he always paints, but with a peculiar expression—she turns away her head with the air of a fine lady, whose senses are shocked by the sight of blood and death, while her heart remains untouched either by remorse or pity.

His ghastly Medusa made me shudder while it fascinated me, as if in those loathsome snakes, writhing and glittering round the expiring head, and those abhorred and fiendish abominations crawling into life, there still lurked the fabled spell which petrified the beholder. Poor Medusa! was this the guerdon of thy love? and were those the tresses [Pg 44] which enslaved the ocean's lord? Methinks that in this wild mythological fiction, in the terrific vengeance which Minerva takes for her profaned temple, and in the undying snakes which for ever hiss round the head of her victim—there is a deep moral, if woman would lay it to her heart.

In Guercino's Endymion, the very mouth is asleep: in his Sybil the very eyes are prophetic, and glance into futurity.

The boyish, but divine St. John, by Raffaelle, did not please me so well as some of his portraits and Madonnas; his Leo the Tenth, for instance, his Julius the Second, or even his Fornarina: and I may observe here, that I admire Titian's taste much more than Raffaelle's, *en fait de maîtresse*. The Fornarina is a mere *femme du peuple*, a coarse virago, compared to the refined, the exquisite La Manto, in the Pitti Palace. I think the Flora must have been painted from the same lovely model, as far as I can judge from compared recollections, for I have no authority to refer to. The former is the most elegant, and the latter the most poetical female portrait I ever saw. At Titian's Venus in the Tribune, one hardly ventures to look up; it is the perfection of earthly loveliness, as the Venus de' Medici is all ideal—all celestial beauty. In the multiplied copies and engravings of this picture I see every where the bashful sweetness of the countenance, and the tender languid repose of the figure are made coarse, or something worse: degraded, in short, into a character altogether unlike the original.

I say nothing of the Gallery of the Palazzo Pitti; which is not a collection so much as a *selection* of the most invaluable gems and masterpieces of art. The imagination dazzled and bewildered by excellence can scarcely make a choice—but I think the Madonna Della Seggiola of Raffaelle, Allori's magnificent Judith, Guido's Cleopatra, and Salvator's Catiline, dwell most upon my memory.

Nov. 24.—After dinner, we drove to the beautiful gardens of the Villa Strozzi, on the Monte Ulivetto, and the evening we spent at the Cocomero, where we saw a detestable opera, capitally acted, and heard the most vile, noisy, unmeaning music, sung to perfection.

Nov. 26.—Yesterday we spent some hours at Morghen's gallery, looking over his engravings; and afterwards examined the bronze gates of the Baptistery, which Michel Angelo used to call the gates of Paradise. We then ascended the Campanile or Belfry Tower to see the view from its summit. Florence lay at our feet, diminished to a model of itself, with its walls and gates, its streets and bridges, palaces and churches, all and each distinctly visible; and beyond, the Val d'Arno with its amphitheatre of hills, its villas, and its vineyards—classical Fesole, with its ruined castle, and Monte Ulivetto, with its diadem of cypresses; luxuriant nature and graceful art, blending into [Pg 45] one glorious picture, which no smoky vapours, no damp exhalations, blotted and discoloured; but all was serenely bright and fair, gay with moving life, and rich with redundant fertility.

> "O dell' Etruria gran Città Reina,
> D'arti e di studj e di grand' or feconda;
> Cui tra quanto il sol guarda, e 'l mar circonda,
> Ogn' altra in pregio di belta s' inchina:
> Monti superbi, la cui fronte alpina
> Fa di sè contra i venti argine e sponda:
> Valli beate, per cui d'onda in onda

L'Arno con passo signoril cammina:
Bei soggiorni ove par ch' abbiansi eletto
Le grazie il seggio, e, come in suo confine,
Sia di natura il bel tutto ristretto, &c."

Filicaja will be pardoned for his hyperboles by all who remember that he was himself a Florentine.

28.—"Corinne" I find is a fashionable *vade mecum* for sentimental travellers in Italy; and that I too might be *à la mode*, I brought it from Molini's to-day, with the intention of reading on the spot, those admirable and affecting passages which relate to Florence; but when I began to cut the leaves, a kind of terror seized me, and I threw it down, resolved not to open it again. I know myself weak—I feel myself unhappy; and to find my own feelings reflected from the pages of a book, in language too deeply and eloquently true, is not good for me. I want no helps to admiration, nor need I kindle my enthusiasm at the torch of another's mind. I can suffer enough, feel enough, think enough, without this.

Not being well, I spent a long morning at home, and then strayed into the church of the Santo Spirito, which is near our hotel. There is in this church a fine copy of Michel Angelo's Pietà, which a monk, whom I met in the church, insisted was the original. But I believe the *originalissimo* group is at Rome. There are also two fine pictures, a marriage of the Virgin, in a very sweet Guido-like style, and the woman taken in adultery. This church is the richest in paintings I have seen here. I remarked a picture of the Virgin said to be possessed of miraculous powers; and that part of it visible, is not destitute of merit as a painting; but some of her grateful devotees, having decorated her with a real blue silk gown, spangled with tinsel stars, and two or three crowns, one above another, of gilt foil, the effect is the oddest imaginable. As I was sitting upon a marble step, philosophizing to myself, and wondering at what seemed to me such senseless bad taste, such pitiable and ridiculous superstition, there came up a poor woman leading by the hand a pale and delicate boy, about four years old. She prostrated herself before the picture, while the child knelt beside her, and prayed for some time with fervour; [Pg 46] she then lifted him up, and the mother and child kissed the picture alternately with great devotion; then making him kneel down and clasp his little hands, she began to teach him an Ave Maria, repeating it word for word, slowly and distinctly, so that I got it by heart too. Having finished their devotions, the mother put into the child's hands a piece of money, which she directed him to drop into a box, inscribed, "per i poveri vergognosi"—"for the bashful poor;" they then went their way. I was an unperceived witness of this little scene, which strongly affected me: the simple piety of this poor woman, though mistaken in its object, appeared to me respectable; and the Virgin, in her sky-blue brocade and her gilt tiara, no longer an object to ridicule. I returned home rejoicing in kinder, gentler, happier thoughts; for though I may wish these poor people a purer worship, yet, as Wordsworth says somewhere, far better than I could express it—

"Rather would I instantly decline
To the traditionary sympathies
Of a most rustic ignorance,—
This rather would I do, than see and hear
The repetitions wearisome of sense
Where soul is dead, and feeling hath no place."

The Ave Maria which I learnt, or rather *stole* from my poor woman, pleases me by its simplicity.

AVE MARIA.

Dio ti salvi, O Maria, piena di grazia! Il Signore è teco! tu sei benedetta fra le donne, e benedetto è il frutto del tuo seno, GESU! Santa Maria! madre di Dio! Prega per noi peccatori, adesso, e nell 'ora della nostra morte! e cosi sia. [G]

Sunday.—Attended divine service at the English ambassador's, in the morning, and in the evening, not being well enough to go to the Cascine, I remained at home. I sat down at the window and read Foscolo's beautiful poem, "I sepoleri:" the subject of my book, and the sight of Alfieri's house meeting my eye whenever I looked up, inspired the idea of visiting the Santa Croce again, and I ventured out unattended. The streets, and particularly the Lung' Arno, were crowded with gay people in their holiday costumes. Not even our Hyde Park, on a summer Sunday, ever presented a more lively spectacle or a better dressed mob. I was often tempted to turn back rather than encounter this moving multitude; but at length I found [Pg 47] my way to the Santa Croce, which presented a very different scene. The service was over; and a few persons were walking up and down the aisles, or kneeling at different altars. In a chapel on the other side of the cloisters, they were chanting the Via Crucis; and the blended voices swelled and floated round, then died away, then rose again, and at length sunk into silence. The evening was closing fast, the shadows of the heavy pillars grew darker and darker, the tapers round the high altar twinkled in the distance like dots of light, and the tombs of Michel Angelo, of Galileo, of Machiavelli, and Alfieri, were projected from the deep shadow in indistinct formless masses: but I needed not to see them to image them before me; for with each and all my fancy was familiar. I spent about an hour walking up and down—abandoned to thoughts which were melancholy, but not bitter. All memory, all feeling, all grief, all pain were swallowed up in the sublime tranquillity which was within me and around me. How could I think of myself, and of the sorrow which swells at my impatient heart, while all of genius that could die, was sleeping round me; and the spirits of the glorious dead—they who rose above their fellow men by the might of intellect—whose aim was excellence, the noble end "that made ambition virtue," were, or seemed to me, present?—and if those tombs could have opened their ponderous and marble jaws, what histories of sufferings and persecution, wrongs and wretchedness, might they not reveal! Galileo—

"chi vide
Sotto l'etereo padiglion rotarsi
Piu mondi, e il sole iradiarli immoto."

pining in the dungeons of the inquisition; Machiavelli,

"quel grande,
Che temprando lo scettro a'regnatori,

Gil allor ne sfronda— —"

tortured and proscribed; Michel Angelo, persecuted by envy; and Alfieri perpetually torn, as he describes himself, by two furies—"Ira e Malinconia"—

"La mente e il cor in perpetua lite."

But they fulfilled their destinies: inexorable Fate will be avenged upon the favourites of Heaven and nature. I can remember but one instance in which the greatly gifted spirit was not also the conspicuously wretched mortal—our own divine Shakspeare—and of him we know but little.

In some books of travels I have met with, Boccaccio, Aretino, and Guicciardini, are mentioned among the illustrious dead of the Santa Croce. The second, if his biographers say true, was a wretch, whose ashes ought to have been scattered in the air. He was buried I [Pg 48] believe at Venice—or no matter where. Boccaccio's tomb *is*, or *was*, at Certaldo; and Guicciardini's—I forget the name of the church honoured by his remains—but it is not the Santa Croce.

The finest figure on the tomb of Michel Angelo is architecture. It should be contemplated from the left, to be seen to advantage. The effect of Alfieri's monument depends much on the position of the spectator: when viewed in front, the figure of Italy is very heavy and clumsy; and in no point of view has it the grace and delicacy which Canova's statues generally possess.

There is a most extraordinary picture in this church representing God the Father supporting a dead Christ, by Cigoli, a painter little known in England, though I have seen some admirable pictures of his in the collections here: his style reminds me of Spagnoletto's.

Our departure is fixed for Wednesday next: and though I know that change and motion are good for me, yet I dread the fatigue and excitement of travelling; and I shall leave Florence with regret. For a melancholy invalid like myself, there cannot be a more delightful residence: it is gay without tumult—quiet, yet not dull. I have not mingled in society; therefore cannot judge of the manners of the people. I trust they are not exactly what Forsyth describes: with all his taste he sometimes writes like a caustic old bachelor; and on the Florentines he is peculiarly severe.

We leave our friend L. behind for a few days, and our Venice acquaintance V. will be our *compagnon de voyage* to Rome. Of these two young men, the first amuses me by his follies, the latter rather fatigues *de trop de raison*. The first talks too much, the latter too little: the first speaks, and speaks egregious nonsense; the latter never says any thing beyond common-place: the former always makes himself ridiculous, and the latter never makes himself particularly agreeable: the first is (*con rispetto parlando*) a great fool, and the latter would be pleasanter were he less wise. Between these two *opposites*, I was standing this evening on the banks of the Arno, contemplating a sunset of unequalled splendour. L. finding that enthusiasm was his cue, played off various sentimental antics, peeped through his fingers, threw his head on one side, exclaiming, "Magnificent, by Jove! grand! grandissimo! It just reminds me of what Shakspeare says: 'Fair Aurora'—I forget the rest."

V. with his hands in his pockets, contemplated the superb spectacle—the mountains, the valley, the city flooded with a crimson glory, and the river flowing at our feet like molten gold—he gazed on it all with a look of placid satisfaction, and then broke out—"Well! this does one's heart good!"

L. (I owe him this justice) is not the author of the famous blunder [Pg 49] which is now repeated in every circle. I am assured it was our neighbour, Lord G. though I scarce believe it, who on being presented with the Countess of Albany's card, exclaimed—"The Countess of Albany! Ah!—true—I remember: wasn't she the widow of Charles the Second, who married Ariosto?" There is in this celebrated *beveu*, a glorious confusion of times and persons, beyond even my friend L.'s capacity.

The whole party are gone to the Countess of Albany's to-night to take leave: that being, as L. says, "the correct thing." Our notions of correctness vary with country and climate. What Englishwoman at

Florence would not be *au désespoir*, to be shut from the Countess of Albany's parties—though it is a known and indisputable fact, that she was never married to Alfieri? A propos d'Alfieri—I have just been reading a selection of his tragedies—his Filippo, the Pazzi, Virginia, Mirra; and when I have finished Saul, I will read no more of them for some time. There is a superabundance of harsh energy, and a want of simplicity, tenderness, and repose throughout, which fatigues me, until admiration becomes an effort instead of a pleasurable feeling. Marochesi, a celebrated tragedian, who, Minutti says, understood "*la vera filosofia della comica*," used to recite Alfieri's tragedies with him or to him. Alfieri was himself a bad actor and declaimer. I am surprised that the tragedy of Mirra should be a great favourite on the stage here. A very young actress, who made her debût in this character, enchanted the whole city by the admirable manner in which she performed it; and the piece was played for eighteen nights successively; a singular triumph for an actress, though not uncommon for a singer. In spite of its many beauties and the artful management of the story; it would, I think, be as impossible to make an English audience endure the Mirra, as to find an English actress who would exhibit herself in so revolting a part.

Tuesday.—Our last day at Florence. I walked down to the San Lorenzo this morning early, and made a sketch of the sarcophagus of Lorenzo de' Medici. Afterwards we spent an hour in the gallery, and bid adieu to the Venus—

"O bella Venere!
Che sola sei,
Piacer degli uomini
E degli dei!"

When I went to take a last look of Titian's Flora, I found it removed from its station, and an artist employed in copying it. I could have envied the lady for whom this copy was intended; but comforted myself with the conviction that no hireling dauber in water-colours could [Pg 50] do justice to the heavenly original, which only wants motion and speech to live indeed. We then spent nearly two hours in the Pitti Palace; and the court having lately removed to

Pisa, we had an opportunity of seeing Canova's Venus, which is placed in one of the Grand Duke's private apartments. She stands in the centre of a small cabinet, pannelled with mirrors, which reflect her at once in every possible point of view. This statue was placed on the pedestal of the Venus de' Medicis during her forced residence at Paris; and is justly considered as the triumph of modern art: but though a most beautiful creature, she is not a goddess. I looked in vain for that full divinity, that ethereal *something* which breathes round the Venus of the Tribune. In another private room are two magnificent landscapes by Salvator Rosa.

Every good catholic has a portrait of the Virgin hung at the head of his bed; partly as an object of devotion, and partly to scare away the powers of evil: and for this purpose the Grand Duke has suspended by his bed-side one of the most beautiful of Raffaelle's Madonnas. Truly, I admire the good taste of his piety, though it is rather selfish thus to appropriate such a gem, when the merest daub would answer the same purpose. It was only by secret bribery I obtained a peep at this picture, as the room is not publicly shown.

The lower classes at Florence are in general ill-looking; nor have I seen one handsome woman since I came here. Their costume too is singularly unbecoming; but there is an airy cheerfulness and vivacity in their countenances, and a civility in their manners which is pleasing to a stranger. I was surprised to see the women, even the servant girls, decorated with necklaces of real pearl of considerable beauty and value. On expressing my surprise at this to a shopkeeper's wife, she informed me that these necklaces are handed down as a kind of heir-loom from mother to daughter; and a young woman is considered as dowered who possesses a handsome chain of pearl. If she has no hope of one in reversion, she buys out of her little earnings a pearl at a time, till she has completed a necklace.

The style of swearing at Florence is peculiarly elegant and classical; I hear the vagabonds in the street adjuring Venus and Bacchus; and my shoemaker swore "by the aspect of Diana," that he would not take less than ten pauls for what was worth about three;—yet was the knave forsworn.

JOURNEY TO ROME.

SOFFRI E TACI.

Ye empty shadows of unreal good!
Phantoms of joy!—too long—too far pursued,
Farewell! no longer will I idly mourn
O'er vanished hopes that never can return;
[Pg 51] No longer pine o'er hoarded griefs—nor chide
The cold vain world, whose falsehood I have tried.
Me never more can sweet affections move,
Nor smiles awake to confidence and love:
To *me*, no more can disappointment spring,
Nor wrong, nor scorn one bitter moment bring!
With a firm spirit—though a breaking heart,
Subdu'd to act through life my weary part,
Its closing scenes in patience I await,
And by a stern endurance, conquer fate.

December 8.—In beginning another volume, I feel almost inclined to throw the last into the fire; as in writing it I have generally begun the record of one day by tearing away the half of what was written the day before: but though it contains much that I would rather forget, and some things written under the impression of pain, and sick and irritable feelings, I will not yet *ungratefully* destroy it. I have frequently owed to my little Diary not amusement only, but consolation. It has gradually become not only the faithful depository of my recollections, but the confidante of my feelings, and the sole witness of my tears. I know not if this be wise: but if it be folly, I have the comfort of knowing that a mere act of my will destroys for ever the record of my weakness; and meantime a confidante whose mouth is sealed with a patent lock and key, and whom I can put out of existence in a single moment, is not dangerous; so, as Lord Byron elegantly expresses it, "*Here goes.*"

We left Florence this morning; and saw the sun rise upon a country so enchantingly beautiful, that I dare not trust myself to description; but I felt it, and still feel it—almost in my heart. The blue cloudless sky, the sun pouring his beams upon a land, which even in this wintry season smiles when others languish—the soft varied character of the scenery, comprising every species of natural beauty—the green slope, the woody hill, the sheltered valley,—the deep dales, into which we could just peep, as the carriage whirled us too rapidly by—the rugged fantastic rocks, cultivated plains, and sparkling rivers, and, beyond all, the chain of the Apennines with light clouds floating across them, or resting in their recesses—all this I saw, and felt, and shall not forget.

I write this at Arezzo, the birth-place of Petrarch, of Redi, of Pignotti, and of that Guido who discovered Counter-point. Whether Arezzo is remarkable for any thing else, I am too sleepy to recollect: and as we depart early to-morrow morning, it would only tantalize me to remember. We arrived here late, by the light of a most resplendent moon. If such is this country in winter, what must it be in summer?

9th, at Perugia.—All the beauties of natural scenery have been combined with historical associations, to render our journey of to-day most interesting; and with a mind more at ease, nothing has been [Pg 52] wanting to render this one of the most delightful days I have spent abroad.

At Cortona, Hannibal slept the night before the battle of Thrasymene. Soon after leaving this town on our left, we came in view of the lake, and the old tower on its banks. There is an ancient ruin on a high eminence to the left, which our postilion called the "Forteressa di Annibale il Carthago." Further on, the Gualandra hills seem to circle round the lake; and here was the scene of the battle. The channel of the Sanguinetto, which then ran red with the best blood of Rome and Carthage, was dry when we crossed it—

> "And hooting boys might dry-shod pass,
> And gather pebbles from the naked ford."

While we traversed the field of battle at a slow pace, V. who had his Livy in his pocket, read aloud his minute description of the engagement; and we could immediately point out the different places mentioned by the historian. The whole valley and the hills around are now covered with olive woods; and from an olive tree which grew close to the edge of the lake, I snatched a branch as we passed by, and shall preserve it—an emblem of peace, from the theatre of slaughter. The whole landscape as we looked back upon it from a hill on this side of the Casa del Rano, was exceedingly beautiful. The lake seemed to slumber in the sunshine; and Passignano jutting into the water, with its castellated buildings, the two little woody islands, and the undulating hills enclosing the whole, as if to shut it from the world, made it look like a scene fit only to be peopled by fancy's fairest creations, if the remembrance of its blood-stained glories had not started up, to rob it of half its beauty. Mrs. R— — compared it to the lake of Geneva; but in my own mind, I would not admit the comparison. The lake of Geneva stands alone in its beauty; for there the sublimest and the softest features of nature are united: there the wonderful, the wild, and the beautiful, blend in one mighty scene; and love and heroism, poetry and genius, have combined to hallow its shores. The lake of Perugia is far more circumscribed: the scenery around it wants grandeur and extent; though so beautiful in itself, that if no comparison had been made, no want would have been suggested: and on the bloody field of Thrasymene I looked with curiosity and interest unmingled with pleasure. I have long survived my sympathy with the fighting heroes of antiquity. All this I thought as we slowly walked up the hill, but I was silent as usual: as Jaques says, "I can think of as many matters as other men, but I praise God, and make no boast of it." We arrived here too late to see any thing of the city.

Dec. 10th, at Terni.—The ridiculous *contre-temps* we sometimes meet with would be matter of amusement to me, if they did not affect [Pg 53] others. And in truth, as far as paying well, and scolding well, can go, it is impossible to travel more magnificently, more *à la milor Anglais* than we do: but there is no controlling fate; and here, as our evil destinies will have it, a company of strolling actors had taken possession of the best quarters before our arrival; and our accommodations are, I must confess, tolerably bad.

When we left Perugia this morning, the city, throned upon its lofty eminence, with its craggy rocks, its tremendous fortifications, and its massy gateways, had an imposing effect. Forwards, we looked over a valley, which so resembled a lake, the hills projecting above the glittering white vapour having the appearance of islands scattered over its surface, that at the first glance I was positively deceived; and all my topographical knowledge, which I had conned on the map the night before, completely put to the rout. As the day advanced, this white mist sank gradually to the earth, like a veil dropped from the form of a beautiful woman, and nature stood disclosed in all her loveliness.

Trevi, on its steep and craggy hill, detached from the chain of mountains, looked beautiful as we gazed up at it, with its buildings mingled with rocks and olives—

I had written thus far, when we were all obliged to decamp in haste to our respective bed-rooms; as it is found necessary to convert our salon into a dormitory. I know I shall be tired, and very tired to-morrow,—therefore add a few words in pencil, before the impressions now fresh on my mind are obscured.

After Trevi came the Clitumnus with its little fairy temple; and we left the carriage to view it from below, and drink of the classic stream. The temple (now a chapel) is not much in itself, and was voted in bad taste by some of our party. To me the tiny fane, the glassy river, more pure and limpid than any fabled or famous fountain of old, the beautiful hills, the sunshine, and the associations connected with the whole scene, were enchanting; and I could not at the moment descend to architectural criticism.

The road to Spoleto was a succession of olive grounds, vineyards, and rich woods. The vines with their skeleton boughs looked wintry and miserable; but the olives, now in full fruit and foliage, intermixed with the cypress, the ilex, the cork tree, and the pine, clothed the landscape with a many-tinted robe of verdure.

While sitting in the open carriage at Spoleto, waiting for horses, I saw one of that magnificent breed of "milk white steers," for which the banks of the Clitumnus have been famed from all antiquity, led past me gaily decorated, to be baited on a plain without the city. As the noble creature, serene and unresisting, paced along, followed by a wild, ferocious-looking, and far more brutal rabble, I would have given all I possessed to redeem him from his tormentors: but it was in [Pg 54] vain. As we left the city, we heard his tremendous roar of agony and rage echo from the rocks. I stopped my ears, and was glad when we were whirled out of hearing. The impression left upon my nerves by this rencontre, makes me dislike to remember Spoleto: yet I believe it is a beautiful and interesting place. Hannibal, as I recollect, besieged this city, but was bravely repulsed. I could say much more of the scenes and the feelings of to-day; but my pencil refuses to mark another letter.

Dec. 11th, at Civita Castellana.—I could not write a word to-night in the salon, because I wished to listen to the conversation of two intelligent travellers, who, arriving after us, were obliged to occupy the same apartment. Our accommodations here are indeed deplorable altogether. After studying the geography of my bed, and finding no spot thereon, to which Sancho's couch of pack-saddles and pummels would not be a bed of down in comparison, I ordered a fresh faggot on my hearth: they brought me some ink in a gally-pot—*invisible* ink—for I cannot see what I am writing; and I sit down to scribble, *pour me désennuyer.*

This morning we set off to visit the Falls of Terni (la cascata di Marmore) in two carriages and four: O such equipages!—such rat-like steeds! such picturesque accoutrements! and such poetical looking guides and postilions, ragged, cloaked, and whiskered!—but it was all consistent: the wild figures harmonized with the wild landscape. We passed a singular fortress on the top of a steep insulated rock, which had formerly been inhabited by a band of robbers and their families, who were with great difficulty, and after a regular siege, dislodged by a party of soldiers, and the place dismantled. In its present ruined state, it has a very picturesque effect; and though the presence of the banditti would no doubt have added greatly to the romance of the scene, on the present occasion we excused their absence.

We visited the falls both above and below, but unfortunately we neither saw them from the best point of view, nor at the best season. The body of waters is sometimes ten times greater, as I was assured—but can scarce believe it possible. The words "Hell of waters," used by Lord Byron, would not have occurred to me while looking at this cataract, which impresses the astonished mind with an overwhelming idea of power, might, magnificence, and impetuosity; but blends at the same time all that is most tremendous in sound and motion, with all that is most bright and lovely in forms, in colours, and in scenery.

As I stood close to the edge of the precipice, immediately under the great fall, I felt my respiration gone: I turned giddy, almost faint, and [Pg 55] was obliged to lean against the rock for support. The mad plunge of the waters, the deafening roar, the presence of a power which no earthly force could resist or control, struck me with an awe almost amounting to terror. A bright sunbow stood over the torrent, which, seen from below, has the appearance of a luminous white arch bending from rock to rock. The whole scene was—but how can I say what it was? I have exhausted my stock of fine words; and must be content with silent recollections, and the sense of admiration and wonder unexpressed.

Below the fall, an inundation which took place a year ago, undermined and carried away part of the banks of the Nera, at the same time laying open an ancient Roman bridge, which had been buried for ages. The channel of the river and the depth of the soil must have been greatly altered since this bridge was erected.

When we returned to the inn at Terni, and while the horses were putting to, I took up a volume of Eustace's tour, which some traveller had accidentally left on the table; and turning to the description of Terni, read part of it, but quickly threw down the book with indignation, deeming all his verbiage the merest nonsense I had ever met with: in fact, it *is* nonsense to attempt to image in words an individual scene like this. When we had made out our description as accurately as possible, it would do as well for any other cataract in the world: we can only combine rocks, wood, and water, in certain proportions. A good picture may give a tolerable idea of a particular scene or landscape: but no picture, no painter, not Ruysdael himself, can give a just idea of a cataract. The lifeless, silent, unmoving image is there: but where is the thundering roar, the terrible velocity, the glory of refracted light, the eternity of sound, and infinity of motion, in which essentially its effect consists?

In the valley beneath the Falls of Terni, there is a beautiful retired little villa, which was once occupied by the late Queen Caroline: and in the gardens adjoining it, we gathered oranges from the trees ourselves for the first time. After passing Mount Soracte, of classical fame, we took leave of the Apennines; having lived amongst them ever since we left Bologna.

The costume of this part of the country is very gay and picturesque: the women wear a white head-dress formed of a square kerchief, which hangs down upon the shoulders, and is attached to the hair by a silver pin: a boddice half laced, and decorated with knots of ribbon, and a short scarlet petticoat complete their attire. Between Perugia and Terni I did not see one woman without a coral necklace; and those who have the power, load themselves with trinkets and ornaments.

Rome, December 12.—The morning broke upon us so beautifully between Civita Castellana and Nevi, that we lauded our good fortune, [Pg 56] and anticipated a glorious approach to the "Eternal City." We were impatient to reach the heights of Baccano; from which, at the distance of fifteen miles, we were to view the cross of St. Peter's glittering on the horizon, while the postilions rising in their stirrups, should point forward with exultation, and exclaim "Roma!" But, O vain hope! who can controul their fate? just before we reached Baccano, impenetrable clouds enveloped the whole Campagna. The mist dissolved into a drizzling rain; and when we entered the city, it poured in torrents. Since we left England, this is only the third time it has rained while we were on the road; it seems therefore unconscionable to murmur. But to lose the first view of Rome! the first view of the dome of St. Peter's! no—that lost moment will never be retrieved through our whole existence.

We found it difficult to obtain suitable accommodation for our numerous *cortège*, the Hotel d'Europe, and the Hotel de Londres being quite full: and for the present we are rather indifferently lodged in the Albergo di Parigi.

So here we are, in Rome! where we have been for the last five hours, and have not seen an inch of the city beyond the dirty pavement of the Via Santa Croce; where an excellent dinner cooked *à l'Anglaise*, a blazing fire, a drawing-room snugly carpeted and curtained, and the rain beating against our windows, would almost persuade us that we are in London; and every now and then, it is with a kind of surprise that I remind myself that I am really in Rome. Heaven send us but a fine day to-morrow!

13.—The day arose as beautiful, as brilliant, as cloudless, as I could have desired for the first day in Rome. About seven o'clock, and before any one was ready for breakfast, I walked out; and directing my steps by mere chance to the left, found myself in the Piazza di Spagna and opposite to a gigantic flight of marble stairs leading to the top of a hill. I was at the summit in a moment; and breathless and agitated by a thousand feelings, I leaned against the obelisk, and looked over the whole city. I knew not where I was: nor among the crowded mass of buildings, the innumerable domes and towers, and vanes and pinnacles, brightened by the ascending sun, could I for a while distinguish a single known object; for my eyes and my heart were both too full: but in a few minutes my powers of perception returned; and in the huge round bulk of the castle of St. Angelo, and the immense façade and soaring cupola of St. Peter's, I knew I could not be mistaken. I gazed and gazed as if I would have drunk it all in at my eyes: and then descending the superb flight of steps rather more leisurely than I had ascended, I was in a moment at the door of our hotel.

The rest of the day I wish I could forget—I found letters from England on the breakfast table [Pg 57] —

Until dinner time were we driving through the narrow dirty streets at the mercy of a stupid *laquais de place*, in search of better accommodations, but without success: and, on the whole, I fear I shall always remember too well the disagreeable and painful impressions of my first day in Rome.

Dec. 18.—A week has now elapsed, and I begin to know and feel Rome a little better than I did. The sites of the various buildings, the situations of the most interesting objects, and the bearings of the principal hills, the Capitol, the Palatine, the Aventine, and the Æsquiline, have become familiar to me, assisted in my perambulations by an excellent plan. I have been disappointed in nothing, for I expected that the general appearance of modern Rome would be mean; and that the impression made by the ancient city would be melancholy; and I had been, unfortunately, too well prepared, by previous reading, for all I see, to be astonished by any thing except the Museum of the Vatican.

I entered St. Peter's expecting to be struck dumb with admiration, and accordingly it was so. A feeling of vastness filled my whole mind, and made it disagreeable, almost impossible to speak or exclaim: but it was a style of grandeur, exciting rather than oppressive to the imagination, nor did I experience any thing like that sombre and reverential awe, I have felt on entering one of our Gothic minsters. The interior of St. Peter's is all airy magnificence, and gigantic splendour; light and sunshine pouring in on every side; gilding and gay colours, marbles and pictures, dazzling the eye above, below, around. The effect of the whole has not diminished in a second and third visit; but rather grows upon me. I can never utter a word for the first ten minutes after I enter the church.

For the Museum of the Vatican, I confess I was totally unprepared; and the first and second time I walked through the galleries, I was so amazed—so intoxicated, that I could not fix my attention upon any individual object, except the Apollo, upon which, as I walked along confused and lost in wonder and enchantment, I stumbled accidentally, and stood spell-bound. Gallery beyond gallery, hall within hall, temple within temple, new splendours opening at every step! of all the creations of luxurious art, the Museum of the Vatican may alone defy any description to do it justice, or any fancy to conceive the unimaginable variety of its treasures. When I remember that the French had the audacious and sacrilegious vanity to snatch from these glorious sanctuaries the finest specimens of art, and hide them in their villanous old gloomy Louvre, I am confounded.

I have been told and can well believe, that the whole *giro* of the galleries exceed two miles. [Pg 58]

I have not yet studied the frescos of Raffaelle sufficiently to feel all their perfection; and should be in despair at my own dullness, were I not consoled by the recollection of Sir Joshua Reynolds. At present one of Raffaelle's divine Virgins delights me more than all his camere and logie together; but I can look upon them with due veneration, and grieve to see the ravages of time and damp.

19.—Last night we took advantage of a brilliant full moon to visit the Coliseum by moonlight; and if I came away disappointed of the pleasure I had expected, the fault was not in me nor in the scene around me. In its sublime and heart-stirring beauty, it more than equalled, it surpassed all I had anticipated—but—(there must always be a *but!* always in the realities of this world something to disgust;) it happened that one or two gentlemen joined our party—young men too, and classical scholars, who perhaps thought it fine to affect a well-bred *nonchalance*, a fashionable disdain for all romance and enthusiasm, and amused themselves with *quizzing* our guide, insulting the gloom, the grandeur, and the silence around them, with loud impertinent laughter at their own poor jokes; and I was obliged to listen, sad and disgusted, to their empty and tasteless and misplaced flippancy. The young barefooted friar, with his dark lanthorn, and his black eyes flashing from under his cowl, who acted as our cicerone, was in picturesque unison with the scene; but—more than one murder having lately been committed among the labyrinthine recesses of the ruin, the government has given orders that every person entering after dusk should be attended by a guard of two soldiers. These fellows therefore necessarily walked close after our heels, smoking, spitting, and spluttering German. Such were my companions, and such was my *cortège*. I returned home vowing that while I remained at Rome, nothing should induce me to visit the Coliseum by moonlight again.

To-day I was standing before the Laocoon with Rogers, who remarked that the absence of all parental feeling in the aspect of Laocoon, his self-engrossed indifference to the sufferings of his children (which is noticed and censured, I think, by Dr. Moore) adds to the pathos, if properly considered, by giving the strongest possible idea of that physical agony which the sculptor intended to represent. It may be so, and I thought there was both truth and *tacte* in the poet's observation.

The Perseus of Canova does not please me so well as his Paris; there is more simplicity and repose in the latter statue, less of that theatrical air which I think is the common fault of Canova's figures.

It is absolutely necessary to look at the Perseus before you look at the Apollo, in order to do the former justice. I have gazed with admiration at the Perseus for minutes together, then walked from it to the Apollo and felt instantaneously, but could not have expressed, the difference. [Pg 59] The first is indeed a beautiful statue, the latter "breathes the flame with which 'twas wrought," as if the sculptor had left a portion of his own soul within the marble to half animate his glorious creation. The want of this informing life is strongly felt in the Perseus, when contemplated after the Apollo. It is delightful when the imagination rises in the scale of admiration, when we ascend from excellence to perfection: but excellence after perfection is absolute inferiority; it sinks below itself, and the descent is so disagreeable and disappointing, that we can seldom estimate justly the object before us. We make comparisons involuntarily in a case where comparisons are odious.

The weather is cold here during the prevalence of the tramontana: but I enjoy the brilliant skies and the delicious purity of the air, which leaves the eye free to wander over a vast extent of space. Looking from the gallery of the Belvedere at sunset this evening, I clearly saw Tivoli, Albano, and Frascati, although all Rome and part of the Campagna lay between me and those towns. The outlines of every building, ruin, hill, and wood were so distinctly marked, and *stood out* so brightly to the eye! and the full round moon, magnified through the purple vapour which floated over the Apennines, rose just over Tivoli, adding to the beauty of the scene. O Italy! how I wish I could transport hither all I love! how I wish I were well enough, happy enough, to enjoy all the lovely things I see! but pain is mingled with all I behold, all I feel: a cloud seems for ever before my eyes, a weight for ever presses down my heart. I know it is wrong to repine: and that I ought rather to be thankful for the pleasurable sensations yet spared to me, than lament that they are so few. When I take up my pen to record the impressions of the day, I sometimes turn within myself, and wonder how it is possible that amid the strife of feelings not all subdued, and the desponding of the heart, the mind should still retain its faculties unobscured, and the imagination all its vivacity and its susceptibility to pleasure,—like the beautiful sunbow I saw at the Falls of Terni, bending so bright and so calm over the verge of the abyss which toiled and raged below.

22.—This morning was devoted to the Capitol, where the objects of art are ill arranged and too crowded: the lights are not well managed, and on the whole I could not help wishing, in spite of my veneration for the Capitol, that some at least among the divine master-pieces it contains could be transferred to the glorious halls of the Vatican, and shrined in temples worthy of them.

The objects which most struck me were the dying Gladiator, the Antinous, the Flora, and the statue called (I know not on what authority) the Faun of Praxiteles. [Pg 60]

The dying Gladiator is the chief boast of the Capitol. The antiquarian Nibby insists that this statue represents a Gaul, that the sculpture is Grecian, that it formed part of a group on a pediment, representing the vengeance which Apollo took on the Gauls, when, under their king Brennus, they attacked the temple of Delphi: that the cord round the neck is a twisted chain, an ornament peculiar to the Gauls; and that the form of the shield, the bugles, the style of the hair, and the mustachios, all prove it to be a Gaul. I asked, "why should such faultless, such exquisite sculpture be thrown away upon a high pediment? the affecting expression of the countenance, the head 'bowed low and full of death,' the gradual failure of the strength and sinking of the form, the blood slowly trickling from his side—how could any spectator, contemplating it at a vast height, be sensible of these minute traits—the distinguishing perfections of this matchless statue?" It was replied, that many of the ancient buildings were so constructed, that it was possible to ascend and examine the sculpture above the cornice, and though some statues so placed were unfinished at the back, (for instance, some of the figures which belonged to the group of Niobe,) others (and he mentioned the Ægina marbles as an example) were as highly finished behind as before. I owned myself unwilling to consider the Gladiator a Gaul, but the reasoning struck me, and I am too unlearned to weigh the arguments he used, much less confute them. That the statue being of Grecian marble and Grecian sculpture must therefore have come from Greece, does not appear a conclusive argument, since the Romans commonly employed Greek artists: and as to the rest of the argument,—suppose that in a dozen centuries hence, the charming statue of Lady Louisa Russell should be discovered under the ruins of Woburn Abbey, and that by a parity of reasoning, the production of Chantrey's chisel should be attributed to Italy and Canova, merely because it is cut from a block of Carrara marble? we might smile at such a conclusion.

Among the pictures in the gallery of the Capitol, the one most highly valued pleases me least of all—the Europa of Paul Veronese. The splendid colouring and copious fancy of this master can never reconcile me to his strange anomalies in composition, and his sins against good taste and propriety. One wishes that he had allayed the heat of his fancy with some cooling drops of discretion. Even his colouring so admired in general, has something florid and meretricious to my eye and taste.

One of the finest pictures here is Domenichino's Cumean Sibyl, which, like all other masterpieces, defies the copyist and engraver. The Sibilla Persica of Guercino hangs a little to the left; and with her contemplative air, and the pen in her hand, she looks as if she were recording the effusions of her more inspired sister. The former [Pg 61] is a chaste and beautiful picture, full of feeling and sweetly coloured; but the vicinity of Domenichino's magnificent creation throws it rather into shade. Two unfinished pictures upon which Guido was employed at the time of his death are preserved in the Capitol: one is the Bacchus and Ariadne, so often engraved and copied; the other, a single figure, the size of life, represents the Soul of the righteous man ascending to heaven. Had Guido lived to finish this divine picture, it would have been one of his most splendid productions; but he was snatched away to realize, I trust, in his own person, his sublime conception. The head alone is finished, or nearly so; and has a most extatic expression. The globe of the earth seems to sink from beneath the floating figure, which is just sketched upon the canvass, and has a shadowy indistinctness which to my fancy added to its effect. Guercino's chef-d'œuvre, the Resurrection of Saint Petronilla, (a saint, I believe, of very hypothetical fame,) is also here; and has been copied in mosaic for St. Peters. A magnificent Rubens, the She Wolf nursing Romulus and Remus; a fine copy of Raffaelle's Triumph of Galatea by Giulo Romano; Domenichino's Saint Barbara, with the same lovely inspired eyes he always gives his female saints, and a long et cetera.

From the Capitol we immediately drove to the Borghese palace, where I spent half an hour looking at the picture *called* the Cumean Sibyl of Domenichino, and am more and more convinced that it is a Saint Cecilia and not a Sibyl.

We have now visited the Borghese palace four times; and à-propos to pictures, I may as well make a few memoranda of its contents. It is not the most numerous, but it is by far the most valuable and select private gallery in Rome.

Domenichino's Chase of Diana, with the two beautiful nymphs in the foreground, is a splendid picture. Titian's Sacred and Profane Love puzzles me completely: I neither understand the name nor the intention of the picture. It is evidently allegorical: but an allegory very clumsily expressed. The aspect of Sacred Love would answer just as well for Profane Love. What is that little cupid about, who is groping in the cistern behind? why does Profane Love wear gloves? The picture, though so provokingly obscure in its subject, is most divinely painted. The three Graces by the same master is also here; two heads by Giorgione, distinguished by all his peculiar depth of character and sentiment, some exquisite Albanos; one of Raffaelle's finest portraits—and in short, an endless variety of excellence. I feel my taste become more and more fastidious every day.

This morning we heard mass at the Pope's Chapel; the service was read by Cardinal Fesche, and the venerable old pope himself, robed and mitred *en grand costume,* was present. No females are allowed [Pg 62] to enter without veils, and we were very ungallantly shut up behind a sort of grating, where, though we had a tolerable view of the ceremonial going forward, it was scarcely possible for us to be seen. Cardinal Gonsalvi sat so near us, that I had leisure and opportunity to contemplate the fine intellectual head and acute features of this remarkable man. I thought his countenance had something of the Wellesley cast.

The Pope's Chapel is decorated in the most exquisite taste; splendid at once and chaste. There are no colours—the whole interior being white and gold.

At an unfortunate moment, Lady Morgan's ludicrous description of the twisting and untwisting of the Cardinal's tails came across me, and made me smile very *mal à-propos*: it is certainly from the life. Whenever this lively and clever woman describes what she has actually seen with her own eyes, she is as accurately true as she is witty and entertaining. Her sketches after nature are admirable; but her observations and inferences are coloured by her peculiar and rather unfeminine habits of thinking. I never read her "*Italy*" till the other day, when L., whose valet had contrived to smuggle it into Rome, offered to lend it to me. It is one of the books most rigorously proscribed here; and if the Padre Anfossi or any of his satellites had discovered it in my hands, I should assuredly have been fined in a sum beyond what I should have liked to pay.

We concluded the morning at St. Peter's, where we arrived in time for the anthem.

23.—Our visit to the Barberini palace to-day was solely to view the famous portrait of Beatrice Cenci. Her appalling story is still as fresh in remembrance here, and her name and fate as familiar in the mouths of every class, as if instead of two centuries, she had lived two days ago. In spite of the innumerable copies and prints I have seen, I was more struck than I can express by the dying beauty of the Cenci. In the face the expression of heart-sinking anguish and terror is just not *too* strong, leaving the loveliness of the countenance unimpaired; and there is a woe-begone negligence in the streaming hair and loose drapery which adds to its deep pathos. It is consistent too with the circumstances under which the picture is traditionally said to have been painted—that is, in the interval between her torture and her execution.

A little daughter of the Princess Barberini was seated in the same room, knitting. She was a beautiful little creature; and as my eye glanced from her to the picture and back again, I fancied I could trace a strong family resemblance; particularly about the eyes, and the very peculiar mouth. I turned back to ask her whether she had ever been [Pg 63] told that she was like *that* picture? pointing to Cenci. She shook back her long curls, and answered with a blush and a smile, "Yes, often." [H]

The Barberini Palace contains other treasures beside the Cenci. Poussin's celebrated picture of the Death of Germanicus, Raffaelle's Fornarina, inferior I thought to the one at Florence, and a St. Andrew by Guido, in his very best style of heads, "mild, pale, and penetrating;" besides others which I cannot at this moment recall.

24.—Yesterday, after chapel, I walked through part of the Vatican; and then, about vesper-time, entered St. Peter's, expecting to hear the anthem: but I was disappointed. I found the church as usual crowded with English, who every Sunday convert St. Peter's into a kind of Hyde Park, where they promenade arm in arm, show off their finery, laugh, and talk aloud: as if the size and splendour of the edifice detracted in any degree from its sacred character. I was struck with a feeling of disgust; and shocked to see this most glorious temple of the Deity metamorphosed into a mere theatre. Mr. W. told me this morning, that in consequence of the shameful conduct of the English, in pressing in and out of the chapel, occupying all the seats, irreverently interrupting the service, and almost excluding the natives, the anthem will not be sung in future.

This is not the first time that the behaviour of the English has created offence, in spite of the friendly feeling which exists towards us, and the allowances which are made for our national character. Last year the pope objected to the indecent custom of making St. Peter's a place of fashionable rendezvous, and notified to Cardinal Gonsalvi his desire that English ladies and gentlemen should not be seen arm in arm walking up and down the aisles, during and after divine service. The cardinal, as the best means of proceeding, spoke to the Duchess of Devonshire, who signified the wishes of the Papal Court to a large party, assembled at her house. The hint so judiciously and so delicately given, was at the time attended to, and during a short interval the offence complained of ceased. New comers have since recommenced the same course of conduct: and in fact, nothing *could* be worse than the exhibition of gaiety and frivolity, gallantry and coquetterie at St. Peter's yesterday. I almost wish the pope may interfere, and with rigour; though, individually, I should lose a high gratification, if our visits to St. Peter's were interdicted. It is surely [Pg 64] most ill-judged and unfeeling (to say nothing of the *profanation*, for such it is), to show such open contempt for the Roman Catholic religion in its holiest, grandest temple, and under the very eyes of the head of that church. I blushed for my countrywomen.

On Christmas Eve we went in a large party to visit some of the principal churches, and witness the celebration of the Nativity; one of the most splendid ceremonies of the Romish Church. We arrived at the chapel of Monte Cavallo about half-past nine; but the pope being ill and absent, nothing particular was going forward; and we left it to proceed to the San Luigi dei Francesi, where we found the church hung from the floor to the ceiling with garlands of flowers, blazing with light, and resounding with heavenly music: but the crowd was intolerable, the people dirty, and there was such an effluence of strong perfumes, in which garlic predominated, that our physical sensations overcame our curiosity: and we were glad to make our escape. We then proceeded to the church of the Ara Celi, built on the site of the temple of Jupiter Capitolinus, and partly from its ruins. The scene here from the gloomy grandeur and situation of the church, was exceedingly fine: but we did not stay long enough to see the concluding procession, as we were told it would be much finer at the Santa Maria Maggiore; for there the *real* manger which had received our Saviour at his birth was deposited: and this inestimable relic was to be displayed to the eyes of the devout; and with a waxen figure laid within (called here Il Bambino), was to be carried in procession round the church, "with pomp, with music, and with triumphing."

The *real* cradle was a temptation not to be withstood: and to witness this signal prostration of the human intellect before ignorant and crafty superstition, we adjourned to the Santa Maria Maggiore. For processions and shows I care very little, but not for any thing, not for all I suffered at the moment, would I have missed the scene which the interior of the church exhibited; for it is impossible that any description could have given me the faintest idea of it. This most noble edifice, with its perfect proportions, its elegant Ionic columns, and its majestic simplicity, appeared transformed, for the time being, into the temple of some Pagan divinity. Lights and flowers, incense and music, were all around: and the spacious aisles were crowded with the lowest classes of the people, the inhabitants of the neighbouring hills, and the peasantry of the Campagna, who with their wild ruffianlike figures and picturesque costumes, were lounging about, or seated at the bases of pillars, or praying before the altars. How I wished to paint some of the groups I saw! but only Rembrandt could have done them justice. [Pg 65]

We remained at the Santa Maria Maggiore till four o'clock, and no procession appearing, our patience was exhausted. I nearly fainted on my chair from excessive fatigue; and some of our party had absolutely laid themselves down on the steps of an altar, and were fast asleep; we therefore returned home completely knocked up by the night's dissipation.

27.—"Come," said L. just now, as he drew his chair to the fire, and rubbed his hands with great complacency, "I think we've worked pretty hard to-day; three palaces, four churches—besides odds and ends of ruins we dispatched in the way: to say nothing of old Nibby's lectures in the morning about the Volces, the Saturnines, the Albanians, and the other old Romans—by Jove! I almost fancied myself at school again——

'Armis vitrumque canter,'

as old Virgil or somebody else says. So now let's have a little écarté to put it all out of our heads:—for my brains have turned round like a windmill, by Jove! ever since I was on the top of that cursed steeple on the capitol," etc., etc.

I make a resolution to myself every morning before breakfast, that I will be prepared with a decent stock of good-nature and forbearance, and not laugh at my friend L.'s absurdities; but in vain are my amiable intentions: his blunders and his follies surpass all anticipation, as they defy all powers of gravity. I console myself with the conviction that such is his slowness of perception, he does not see that he is the *butt* of every party; and such his obtuseness of feeling, that if he did see it, he would not mind it; but he is the heir to twenty-five thousand a year, and therefore, as R. said, he can afford to be laughed at.

We "dispatched," as L. says, a good deal to-day, though I did not "work quite so hard" as the rest of the party: in fact, I was obliged to return home from fatigue, after having visited the Doria and Sciarra Palaces (the last for the second time), and the church of San Pietro in Vincoli.

The Doria Palace contains the largest collection of pictures in Rome: but they are in a dirty and neglected condition, and many of the best are hung in the worst possible light: added to this there is such a number of bad and indifferent pictures, that one ought to visit the Doria Gallery half a dozen times merely to select those on which a cultivated taste would dwell with pleasure. Leonardo da Vinci's portrait of Joanna of Naples, is considered one of the most valuable pictures in the collection. It exhibits the same cast of countenance which prevails through all his female heads, a sort of sentimental simpering affectation which is very disagreeable, and not at all [Pg 66] consistent with the character of Joanna. I was much more delighted by some magnificent portraits by Titian and Rubens; and by a copy of the famous antique picture, the Nozze Aldobrandini, executed in a kindred spirit by the classic pencil of Poussin.

The collection at the Sciarra Palace is small but very select. The pictures are hung with judgment, and well taken care of. The Magdalen, which is considered one of Guido's masterpieces, charmed me most: the countenance is heavenly; though full of ecstatic and devout contemplation, there is in it a touch of melancholy, "all sorrow's softness charmed from its despair," which is quite exquisite: and the attitude, and particularly the turn of the arm, are perfectly graceful: but why those odious turnips and carrots in the foreground? They certainly do not add to the sentiment and beauty of the picture.—Leonardo da Vinci's Vanity and Modesty, and Caravaggio's Gamblers, both celebrated pictures in very different styles, are in this collection. I ought not to forget Raffaelle's beautiful portrait of a young musician who was his intimate friend. The Doria and Sciarra palaces contain the only Claudes I have seen in Rome. Since the acquisition of the Altieri Claudes, we may boast of possessing the finest productions of this master in England. I remember but one solitary Claude in the Florentine gallery; and I see none here equal to those at Lord Grosvenor's and Angerstein's. We visited the church of San Pietro in Viscoli, to see Michel Angelo's famous statue of Moses,—of which, who has not heard? I must confess I never was so disappointed by any work of art as I was by this statue, which is easily accounted for. In the first place, I had not seen any model or copy of the original; and, secondly, I *had* read Zappi's sublime sonnet, which I humbly conceive does rather more than justice to its subject. The fine opening—

> "Chi e costui che in dura pietra scolto
> Siede *Gigante*"—

gave me the impression of a colossal and elevated figure: my surprise, therefore, was great to see a sitting statue, not much larger than life, and placed nearly on the level of the pavement; so that, instead of looking up at it, I almost looked down upon it. The "Doppio raggio in fronte," I found in the shape of a pair of horns, which, at the first glance, gave something quite Satanic to the head, which disgusted me. When I began to recover from this first disappointment—although my eyes were opened gradually to the sublimity of the attitude, the grand forms of the drapery, and the lips, which unclose as if about to speak—I still think that Zappi's sonnet (his acknowledged chef-d'œuvre) is a more sublime production than the chef-d'œuvre it celebrates.

The mention of Zappi reminds me of his wife, the daughter of Carlo [Pg 67] Maratti, the painter. She was so beautiful that she was her father's favourite model for his Nymphs, Madonnas, and Vestal Virgins; and to her charms she added virtue, and to her virtue uncommon musical and literary talents. Among her poems, there is a sonnet addressed to a lady, once beloved by her husband, beginning

"Donna! che tanto al mio sol piacesti,"

which is one of the most graceful, most feeling, most delicate compositions I ever read. Zappi celebrates his beautiful wife under the name of Clori, and his first mistress under that of Filli: to the latter he has addressed a sonnet, which turns on the same thought as Cowley's well known song, "Love in thine eyes." As they both lived about the same time, it would be difficult to tell which of the two borrowed from the other; probably they were both borrowers from some elder poet.

The characteristics of Zappi's style, are tenderness and elegance; he occasionally rises to sublimity; as in the sonnet on the Statue of Moses, and that on Good Friday. He never emulates the flights of Guido or Filicaja, but he is more uniformly graceful and flowing than either; his happy thoughts are not spun out too far,—and his *points* are seldom mere *concetti*.

SONETTO.

DI GIAMBATTISTA ZAPPI.

Amor s'asside alia mia Filli accanto,
Amor la segue ovunque i passi gira:
In lei parla, in lei tace, in lei sospira,
Anzi in lei vive, ond'ella ed ei può tanto.

Amore i vezzi, amor le insegna il canto;
E se mai duolsi, o se pur mai s'adira,
Da lei non parte amor, anzi se mira
Amor ne le belle ire, amor nel pianto.

Se avvien che danzi in regolato errore,
Darle il moto al bel piede, amor riveggio,
Come l'auretto quando muove un fiore.

Le veggio in fronte amor come in suo seggio,
Sul crin, negli occhi, su le labbra amore,
Sol d'intorno al suo cuore, amor non veggio. [I]

[Pg 68]

After being confined to the house for three days, partly by indisposition, and partly by a vile sirocco, which brought, as usual, vapours, clouds, and blue devils in its train—this most lovely day tempted me out; and I walked with V. over the Monte Cavallo to the Forum of Trajan. After admiring the view from the summit of the pillar, we went on towards the Capitol, which presented a singular scene: the square and street in front, as well as the immense flight of steps, one hundred and fifty in number, which lead to the church of the Ara Celi, were crowded with men, women, and children, all in their holiday dresses. It was with difficulty we made our way through them, though they very civilly made way for us, and we were nearly a quarter of an hour mounting the steps, so dense was the multitude ascending and descending, some on their hands and knees out of extra-devotion. At last we reached the door of the church, where we understood, from the exclamations and gesticulations of those of whom we inquired, something extraordinary was to be seen. On one side of the entrance was a puppet show, on the other a band of musicians, playing "Di tanti palpati." The interior of the church was crowded to suffocation; and all in darkness, except the upper end, where upon a stage brilliantly and very artificially lighted by unseen lamps, there was an exhibition in wax-work, as large as life, of the Adoration of the Shepherds. The Virgin was habited in the court dress of the last century, as rich as silk and satin, gold lace, and paste diamonds could make it, with a flaxen wig, and high-heeled shoes. The infant Saviour lay in her lap, his head encircled with rays of gilt wire, at least two yards long. The shepherds were very well done, but the sheep and dogs best of all; I believe they were the real animals stuffed. There was a distant landscape, seen between the pasteboard trees, which was well painted, and from the artful disposition of the light and perspective, was almost a deception—but by a blunder very consistent with the rest of the show, it represented a part of the Campagna of Rome. Above all was a profane representation of that Being, whom I dare scarcely allude to, in conjunction with such preposterous vanities, encircled with saints, angels, and clouds; the whole got up very like a scene in a pantomime, [Pg 69] and accompanied by music from a concealed orchestra, which was intended, I believe, to be sacred music, but sounded to me like some of Rossini's airs. In front of the stage there was a narrow passage divided off, admitting one person at a time, through which a continued file of persons moved along, who threw down their contributions as they passed, bowing and crossing themselves with great devotion. It would be impossible to describe the ecstasies of the multitude, the lifting up of hands and eyes, the string of superlatives—the bellissimos, santissimos, gloriosissimos, and maravigliosissimos, with which they expressed their applause and delight. I stood in the back-ground of this strange scene, supported on one of the long-legged chairs which V—— placed for me against a pillar, at once amazed, diverted, and disgusted by this display of profaneness and superstition, till the heat and crowd overcame me, and I was obliged to leave the church. I shall never certainly forget the "Bambino" of the Ara Celi: for though the exhibition I saw afterwards at the San Luigi (where I went to look at Domenichino's fine pictures) surpassed what I have just described, it did not so much surprise me. Something in the same style is exhibited in almost every church, between Christmas day and the Epiphany.

During our examination of Trajan's Forum to-day, I learnt nothing new, except that Trajan levelled part of the Quirinal to make room for it. The ground having lately been cleared to the depth of about twelve feet, part of the ancient pavement has been discovered, and many fragments of columns set upright: pieces of frieze and broken capitals are scattered about. The pillar, which is now cleared to the base, stands in its original place, but not, as it is supposed, at its original level, for the Romans generally raised the substructure of their buildings, in order to give them a more commanding appearance. The antiquarians here are of opinion that both the pavement of the Basilica and the base of the pillar were raised above the level of the ancient street, and that there is a flight of steps, still concealed, between the pillar and the pavement in front. The famous Ulpian Library was on each side of the Basilica, and the Forum differed from other Forums in not being an open space surrounded by buildings, but a building surrounded by an open space.

Dec 31.-Jan. 1.—That hour in which we pass from one year to another, and begin a new account with ourselves, with our fellow creatures, and with God, must surely bring some solemn and serious thoughts to the bosoms of the most happy and most unreflecting among the triflers on this earth. What then must it be to me? The first hour, the first moment of the expiring year was spent in tears, in distress, in bitterness of heart—as it began so it ends. Days, and weeks, [Pg 70] and months, and seasons, came and "passed like visions to their viewless home," and brought no change. Through the compass of the whole year I have not enjoyed one single day—I will not say of happiness—but of health and peace; and what I have endured has left me little to learn in the way of suffering. Would to heaven that as the latest minutes now ebb away while I write, memory might also pass away! Would to heaven that I could efface the last year from the series of time, hide it from myself, bury it in oblivion, stamp it into annihilation, that none of its dreary moments might ever rise up again to haunt me, like spectres of pain and dismay! But this is wrong—I feel it is—and I repent, I recall my wish. That great Being, to whom the life of a human creature is a mere point, but who has bestowed on his creatures such capacities of feeling and suffering, as extend moments to hours and days to years, inflicts nothing in vain, and if I have suffered much, I have also learned much. Now the last hour is past—another year opens; may it bring to those I love all I wish them in my heart! to me it can bring nothing. The only blessing I hope from time is *forgetfulness*—my only prayer to heaven is—*rest, rest, rest.*

Jan. 4.—We *dispatched,* as L** would say, a good deal to-day: we visited the Temple of Vesta, the Church of Santa Maria in Cosmadino, the Temple of Fortune, the Ponte Rotto, and the house of Nicolo Rienzi: all these lie together in a dirty, low, and disagreeable part of Rome. Thence we drove to the Pyramid of Caius Cestus.—As we know nothing of this Caius Cestus, but that he lived, died, and was buried, it is not possible to attach any fanciful or classical interest to his tomb, but it is an object of so much beauty in itself, and from its situation so striking and picturesque, that it needs no additional interest. It is close to the ancient walls of Rome, which stretch on either side as far as the eye can reach in huge and broken masses of brickwork, fragments of battlements and buttresses, overgrown in many parts with shrubs and even trees. Around the base of the Pyramid lies the burying-ground of strangers and heretics. Many of the monuments are elegant, and their frail materials and diminutive forms are in affecting contrast with the lofty and solid pile which towers above them. The tombs lie around in a small space "amicably close," like brothers in exile, and as I gazed I felt a kindred feeling with all; for I, too, am a wanderer, a stranger and a heretic; and it is probable that my place of rest may be among them. Be it so! for methinks this earth could not afford a more lovely, a more tranquil, or more sacred spot. I remarked one tomb, which is an exact model, and in the same material with the sarcophagus of Cornelius Scipio, in the Vatican. One small slab of white marble bore the name of a young girl, an only child, who died at sixteen, and "left her parents disconsolate:" another elegant [Pg 71] and simple monument bore the name of a young painter of genius and promise, and was erected "by his companions and fellow students as a testimony of their affectionate admiration and regret." This part of old Rome is beautiful beyond description, and has a wild, desolate, and poetical grandeur, which affects the imagination like a dream.—The very air disposes one to reverie. I am not surprised that Poussin, Claude, and Salvator Rosa made this part of Rome a favourite haunt, and studied here their finest effects of colour, and their grandest combinations of landscape. I saw a young artist seated on a pile of ruins with his sketch book open on his knee, and his pencil in his hand—during the whole time we were there he never changed his attitude, nor put his pencil to the paper, but remained leaning on his elbow, like one lost in ecstasy.

Jan 5.—To-day we drove through the quarter of the Jews, called the Ghetta degli Ebrei. It is a long street enclosed at each end with a strong iron gate, which is locked by the police at a certain hour every evening (I believe at ten o'clock); and any Jew found without its precincts after that time, is liable to punishment and a heavy fine. The street is narrow and dirty, the houses wretched and ruinous, and the appearance of the inhabitants squalid, filthy, and miserable—on the whole, it was a painful scene, and one I should have avoided, had I followed my own inclinations. If this specimen of the effects of superstition and ignorance was depressing, the next was not less ridiculous. We drove to the Lateran: I had frequently visited this noble Basilica before, but on the present occasion we were to go over it *in form*, with the usual torments of laquais and ciceroni. I saw nothing new but the cloisters, which remain exactly as in the time of Constantine. They are in the very vilest style of architecture, and decorated with Mosaic in a very elaborate manner: but what most amused us was the collection of relics, said to have been brought by Constantine from the Holy Land, and which our cicerone exhibited with a sneering solemnity which made it very doubtful whether he believed himself in their miraculous sanctity. Here is the stone on which the cock was perched when it crowed to St. Peter, and a pillar from the Temple of Jerusalem, split asunder at the time of the crucifixion; it looks as if it had been *sawed* very accurately in half from top to bottom; but this of course only renders it more miraculous. Here is also the column in front of Pilate's house, to which our Saviour was bound, and the very well where he met the woman of Samaria. All these, and various other relics, supposed to be consecrated by our Saviour's Passion, are carelessly thrown into the cloisters—not so the heads of St. Peter and St. Paul, which are considered as the chief treasures in the Lateran, and are deposited in the body of the church in a rich shrine. The beautiful sarcophagus of red porphyry, which once stood in [Pg 72] the Portico of the Pantheon, and contained the ashes of Agrippa, is now in the Corsini chapel here, and encloses the remains of some Pope Clement. The bronze equestrian statue of Marcus Aurelius, which stands on the Capitol, was dug from the cloisters of the Lateran. The statue of Constantine in the portico was found in the baths of Constantine: it is in a style of sculpture worthy the architecture of the cloisters.—Constantine was the first Christian emperor, a glory which has served to cover a multitude of sins; it is indeed impossible to forget that he was the chosen instrument of a great and blessed revolution; but in other respects it is as impossible to look back to the period of Constantine without horror—an era when bloodshed and barbarism, and the general depravity of morals and taste seemed to have reached their climax.

On leaving the Lateran, we walked to the Scala Santa, said to be the very flights of steps which led to the judgment hall at Jerusalem, and transported hither by the Emperor Constantine; but while the other relics which his pious benevolence bestowed on the city of Rome have apparently lost some of their efficacy, the Scala Santa is still regarded with the most devout veneration. At the moment of our approach, an elegant barouche drove up to the portico, from which two well-dressed women alighted, and pulling out their rosaries, began to crawl up the steps on their hands and knees, repeating a Paternoster and an Ave Maria on every step. A poor diseased beggar had just gone up before them, and was a few steps in advance. This exercise, as we are assured, purchases a thousand years of indulgence. The morning was concluded by a walk on the Mont Pincio.

I did not know on that first morning after our arrival, when I ran up the Scalla della Trinità to the top of the Pincian hill, and looked around me with such transport, that I stood by mere chance on that very spot from which Claude used to study his sun sets, and his beautiful effects of evening. His house was close to me on the left, and those of Nicolo Poussin and Salvator Rosa a little beyond. Since they have been pointed out to me, I never pass from the Monte Pincio along the Via Felice without looking up at them with interest: such power has genius, "to hallow in the core of human hearts even the ruin of a wall."

Jan. 6.—Sunday, at the English chapel, which was crowded to excess, and where it was at once cold and suffocating. We had a plain but excellent sermon, and the officiating clergyman, Mr. W., exhorted the congregation to conduct themselves with more decorum at St. Peter's, and to remember what was due to the temple of that God who was equally the God of all Christians. We afterwards went to St. Peter's; where the anthem was performed at vespers as usual, and [Pg 73] the tenor of the Argentino sung. The music was indeed heavenly—but I did not enjoy it: for though the behaviour of the English was much more decent than I have yet seen it, the crowd round the chapel, the talking, pushing, whispering, and movement, were enough to disquiet and discomfort me; I withdrew, therefore, and walked about at a little distance, where I could just hear the swell of the organ. Such is the immensity of the building, that at the other side of the aisle the music is perfectly inaudible.

7.—Visited the Falconieri Palace to see Cardinal Fesche's gallery. The collection is large and contains many fine pictures, but there is such a *mélange* of good, bad, and indifferent, that on the whole I was disappointed. L** attached himself to my side the whole morning—to benefit, as he said, by my "tasty remarks;" he hung so dreadfully heavy on my hands, and I was so confounded by the interpretations and explanations his ignorance required, that I at last found my patience nearly at an end. Pity he is so good-natured and so good-tempered, that one can neither have the comfort of heartily disliking him, nor find nor make the shadow of an excuse to shake him off!

In the evening we had a gay party of English and foreigners: among them— —

A REPLY TO A COMPLAINT

Trust not the ready smile!
'Tis a delusive glow—
For cold and dark the while

The spirits flag below.

With a beam of departed joy,
The eye may kindle yet:
As the cloud in yon wintry sky,
Still glows with the sun that is set,

The cloud will vanish away—
The sun while shine to morrow—
To me shall break no day
On this dull night of sorrow!

A REPLY TO A REPROACH.

I would not that the world should know,
How deep within my panting heart
A thousand warmer feelings glow,
Than word or look could e'er impart.

I would not that the world should guess
At aught beyond this outward show;
What happy dreams in secret bless—
What burning tears in secret flow.
[Pg 74]

And let them deem me cold or vain;
—O there is one who thinks not so!
In one devoted heart I reign,
And what is all the rest below?

9.—We have had two days of truly English weather; cold, damp, and gloomy, with storms of wind and rain. I know not why, but there is something peculiarly deforming and discordant in bad weather here; and we are all rather stupid and depressed. To me, sunshine and warmth are substitutes for health and spirits; and their absence inflicts positive suffering. There is not a single room in our palazzetto which is weather-proof; and as to a good fire, it is a luxury unknown, but not unnecessary, in these regions. In such apartments as contain no fire-place, a stufa, or portable stove, is set, which diffuses little warmth, and renders the air insupportably close and suffocating.

I witnessed a scene last night, which was a good illustration of that extraordinary indolence for which the Romans are remarkable. Our laquais Camillo suffered himself to be turned off, rather than put wood on the fire three times a-day; he would rather, he said, "starve in the streets than break his back by carrying burdens like an ass; and though he was miserable to displease the Onoratissimo Padrone, his first *duty* was to take care of his own health, which, with the blessing of the saints, he was determined to do." R— — threw him his wages, repeating with great contempt the only word of his long speech he understood, "*Asino!*" "Sono Romano, io," replied the fellow, drawing himself up with dignity. He look his wages, however, and marched out of the house.

The impertinence of this Camillo was sometimes amusing, but oftener provoking. He piqued himself on being a profound antiquarian, would confute Nibby, and carried Nardini in his pocket, to whom he referred on all occasions: yet the other day he had the impudence to assure us that Caius Cestus was an English Protestant, who was excommunicated by Pope Julius Cæsar; and took his Nardini out of his pocket to prove his assertion.

V— — brought me to-day the "Souvenirs de Félicie," of Madame de Genlis, which amused me delightfully for a few hours. They contain many truths, many half or whole falsehoods, many impertinent things, and several very interesting anecdotes. They are written with all the graceful simplicity of style, and in that tone of lady-like feeling which distinguishes whatever she writes: but it is clear that though she represents these "Souvenirs" as mere extracts from her journal, they have been carefully composed or re-composed for publication, and were always intended to be seen. Now if my poor little Diary should ever be seen! I tremble but to think of it!—what egotism and vanity, what discontent—repining—caprice—should I be accused of?—neither [Pg 75] perhaps have I always been just to others; *quand on sent, on réfléchit rarement.* Such strange vicissitudes of temper—such opposite extremes of thinking and feeling, written down at the moment, without noticing the intervening links of circumstances and impressions which led to them, would appear like detraction, if they should meet the eye of any indifferent person—but I think I have taken sufficient precautions against the possibility of such an exposure, and the only eyes which will ever glance over this blotted page, when the hand that writes it is cold, will read, not to *criticise,* but to *sympathise.*

10.—A lovely brilliant day, the sky without a cloud and the air as soft as summer. The carriages were ordered immediately after breakfast, and we sallied forth in high spirits—resolved as L** said, with his usual felicitous application of Shakspeare,

"To take the tide in the affairs of men."

The baths of Titus are on the Æsquiline; and nothing remains of them but piles of brickwork, and a few subterranean chambers almost choked with rubbish. Some fragments of exquisite arabesque painting are visible on the ceilings and walls; and the gilding and colours are still fresh and bright. The brickwork is perfectly solid and firm, and appeared as if finished yesterday. On the whole the impression on my mind was, that not the slow and gentle hand of time, but sudden rapine and violence had caused the devastation around us; and looking into Nardini on my return, I found that the baths of Titus were nearly entire in the thirteenth century, but were demolished with great labour and difficulty by the ferocious Senator Brancaleone, who, about the year 1257, destroyed an infinite number of ancient edifices, "per togliere ai Nobili il modo di fortificarsi." The ruins were excavated during the pontificate of Julius the Second, and under the direction of Raffaelle, who is supposed to have taken the idea of the arabesques in the Loggie of the Vatican, from the paintings here. We were shown the niche in which the Laocoon stood, when it was discovered in 1502. After leaving the baths, we entered the neighbouring church of San Pietro in Vincoli, to look again at the beautiful fluted Doric columns which once adorned the splendid edifice of Titus: and on this occasion we were shown the chest in which the fetters of St. Peter are preserved in a triple enclosure of iron, wood, and silver. My unreasonable curiosity not being satisfied by looking at the mere outside of this sacred coffer, I turned to the monk who exhibited it, and civilly requested that he would open it, and show us the miraculous treasure it contained. The poor man looked absolutely astounded and aghast at the audacity of my request, and stammered out, that the coffer was never opened, without a written order from his holiness the pope, and in the presence of a cardinal, and, that this [Pg 76] favour was never granted to a heretic (con rispetto parlando); and with this excuse we were obliged to be satisfied.

The church of San Martino del Monte is built on part of the substructure of the baths of Titus; and there is a door opening from the church, by which you descend into the ancient subterranean vaults. The small, but exquisite pillars, and the pavement, which is of the richest marbles, were brought from the Villa of Adrian at Tivoli. The walls were painted in fresco by Nicolo and Gaspar Poussin, and were once a celebrated study for young landscape painters; almost every vestige of colouring is now obliterated by the damp which streams down the walls. There are some excellent modern pictures in good preservation, I think by Carluccio. This church, though not large, is one of the most magnificent we have yet seen, and the most precious materials are lavished in profusion on every part. The body of Cardinal Tomasi is preserved here, embalmed in a glass case. It is exhibited conspicuously, and in my life I never saw (or smelt) anything so abominable and disgusting.

The rest of the morning was spent in the Vatican.

I stood to-day for some time between those two great masterpieces, the Transfiguration of Raffaelle, and Domenichino's Communion of St. Jerome. I studied them, I examined them figure by figure, and then in the ensemble, and mused upon the different effects they produce, and were designed to produce, until I thought I could decide to my own satisfaction on their respective merits. I am not ignorant that the Transfiguration is pronounced the "grandest picture in the world," nor so insensible to excellence as to regard this glorious composition without all the admiration due to it. I am dazzled by the flood of light which bursts from the opening heavens above, and affected by the dramatic interest of the group below. What splendour of colour! What variety of expression! What masterly grouping of the heads! I see all this—but to me Raffaelle's picture wants unity of interest: it is two pictures in one: the demoniac boy in the foreground always shocks me; and thus from my peculiarity of taste the pleasure it gives me is not so perfect as it ought to be.

On the other hand, I never can turn to the Domenichino without being thrilled with emotion, and touched with awe. The story is told with the most admirable skill, and with the most exquisite truth and simplicity: the interest is one and the same; it all centres in the person of the expiring saint; and the calm benignity of the officiating priest is finely contrasted with the countenances of the group who support the dying form of St. Jerome: anxious tenderness, grief, hope, and fear, are expressed with such deep pathos and reality, that the spectator forgets admiration in sympathy; and I have gazed, till I could almost [Pg 77] have fancied myself one of the assistants. The colouring is as admirable as the composition—gorgeously rich in effect, but subdued to a tone which harmonizes with the solemnity of the subject.

There is a curious anecdote connected with this picture, which I wish I had noted down at length as it was related to me, and at the time I heard it: it is briefly this. The picture was painted by Domenichino for the church of San Girolamo della Carità. At that time the factions between the different schools of painting ran so high at Rome, that the followers of Domenichino and Guido absolutely stabbed and poisoned each other; and the popular prejudice being in favour of the latter, the Communion of St. Jerome was torn down from its place, and flung into a lumber garret. Some time afterwards, the superiors of the convent wishing to substitute a new altar-piece, commissioned Nicolo Poussin to execute it; and sent him Domenichino's rejected picture as old canvas to paint upon. No sooner had the generous Poussin cast his eyes on it, than he was struck, as well he might be, with astonishment and admiration. He immediately carried it into the church, and there lectured in public on its beauties, until he made the stupid monks ashamed of their blind rejection of such a masterpiece, and boldly gave it that character it has ever since retained, of being the second best picture in the world.

11.—A party of four, including L** and myself, ascended the dome of St. Peter's; and even mounted into the gilt ball. It was a most fatiguing expedition, and one I have since repented. I gained, however, a more perfect, and a more sublime idea of the architectural wonders of St. Peter's, than I had before; and I was equally pleased and surprised by the exquisite neatness and cleanliness of every part of the building. We drove from St. Peter's to the church of St. Onofrio, to visit the tomb of Tasso. A plain slab marks the spot, which requires nothing but his name to distinguish it. "After life's fitful fever he sleeps well." The poet Guidi lies in a little chapel close by; and his effigy is so placed that the eyes appear fixed upon the tomb of Tasso.

In the church of Santa Maria Trastevere (which is held in peculiar reverence by the Tresteverini), there is nothing remarkable, except that like many others in Rome, it is rich in the spoils of antique splendour: afterwards to the palazzo Farneze and the Farnesina, to see the frescos of Raffaelle, Giulio Romano, and the Caraccis, which have long been rendered familiar to me in copies and engravings.

12.—I did penance at home for the fatigue of the day before, and to-day (the 13th) I took a delightful drive of several hours attended only by Saccia. Having examined at different times, and in detail, most of the interesting objects within the compass of the ancient city, I wished to generalize what I had seen, by a kind of *survey* of the whole. For [Pg 78] this purpose, making the Capitol a central point, I drove first slowly through the Forum, and made the circuit of the Palatine Hill, then by the arch of Janus (which by a late decision of the antiquarians, has no more to do with Janus than with Jupiter), and the temple of Vesta, back again over the site of the Circus Maximus, between the Palatine and the Aventine (the scene of the Rape of the Sabines), to the baths of Caracalla, where I spent an hour, musing, sketching, and poetizing; thence to the church of San Stefano Rotundo, once a temple dedicated to Claudius by Agrippina; over the Celian Hill, covered with masses of ruins, to the church of St. John and St. Paul, a small but beautiful edifice; then to the neighbouring church of San Gregorio, from the steps of which there is such a noble view. Thence I returned by the arch of Constantine, and the Coliseum, which frowned on me in black masses through the soft but deepening twilight, through the street now called the Suburra, but formerly the Via Scelerata, where Tullia trampled over the dead body of her father, and so over the Quirinal home.

My excursion was altogether delightful, and gave me the most magnificent, and I had almost said, the most *bewildering* ideas of the grandeur and extent of ancient Rome. Every step was classic ground: illustrious names, and splendid recollections crowded upon the fancy—

"And trailing clouds of glory did they come."

On the Palatine Hill were the houses of Cicero and the Gracchi; Horace, Virgil, and Ovid resided on the Aventine; and Mecænas and Pliny on the Æsquiline. If one little fragment of a wall remained, which could with any shadow of probability be pointed out as belonging to the residence of Cicero, Horace, or Virgil, how much dearer, how much more sanctified to memory would it be than all the magnificent ruins of the fabrics of the Cæsars! But no—all has passed away. I have heard the remains of Rome coarsely ridiculed, because, after the researches of centuries, so little is comparatively known—because of the endless disputes of antiquarians, and the night and ignorance in which all is involved; but to the imagination there is something singularly striking in this mysterious veil which hangs like a cloud upon the objects around us. I trod to-day over the shapeless masses of building, extending in every direction as far as the eye could reach. Who had inhabited the edifices I trampled under my feet? What hearts had burned—what heads had thought—what spirits had kindled *there*, where nothing was seen but a wilderness and waste, and heaps of ruins, to which antiquaries—even Nibby himself—dare not give a name? All swept away—buried beneath an ocean of oblivion, above which rise a few great and glorious names, like rocks, over which the billows of time break in vain. [Pg 79]

"Indi esclamo, qual' notte atra, importuua
Tutte l'ampie tue glorie a un tratto amorza?
Glorie di senno, di valor, di forza
Gia mille avesti, or non hai pur una!"

One of the most striking scenes I saw to-day was the Roman forum, crowded with the common people gaily dressed (it is a festa or saint's day); the women sitting in groups upon the fallen columns, nursing or amusing their children. The men were playing at mora, or at a game like quoits. Under the vast side of the Palatine Hill, on the side of the Circus Maximus, I met a woman mounted on an ass, habited in a most beautiful and singular holiday costume, a man walked by her side, leading the animal she rode, with lover-like watchfulness. He was *en veste*, and I observed that his cloak was thrown over the back of the ass as a substitute for a saddle. Two men followed behind with their long capotes hanging from their shoulders, and carrying guitars, which they struck from time to time, singing as they walked along. A little in advance there is a small chapel, and Madona. A young girl approached, and laying a bouquet of flowers before the image, she knelt down, hid her face in her apron, and wrung her hands from time to time as if she was praying with fervor. When the group I have just mentioned came up, they left the pathway, and made a circuit of many yards to avoid disturbing her, the men taking off their hats, and the woman inclining her head, in sign of respect, as they passed.

All this sounds, while I soberly write it down, very sentimental, and picturesque, and poetical. It was exactly what I saw—what I often see: such is the place, the scenery, the people. Every group is a picture, the commonest object has some interest attached to it, the commonest action is dignified by sentiment, the language around us is music, and the air we breathe is poetry.

Just as I was writing the word *music*, the sounds of a guitar attracted me to the window, which looks into a narrow back street, and is exactly opposite a small white house belonging to a vetturino, who has a very pretty daughter. For her this serenade was evidently intended; for the moment the music began, she placed a light in the window as a signal that she listened propitiously, and then retired. The group below consisted of two men, the lover and a musician he had brought with him: the former stood looking up at the window with his hat off, and the musician, after singing two very beautiful airs, concluded with the delicious and popular Arietta "Buona notte, amato bene!" to which the lover *whistled* a second, in such perfect tune, and with such exquisite taste, that I was enchanted. Rome is famous for serenades and serenaders; but at this season they are seldom heard. I remember at Venice being wakened in the dead of the night by such [Pg 80] delicious music, that (to use a hyperbole common in the mouths of this poetical people) I was "transported to the seventh heaven:" before I could perfectly recollect myself, the music ceased, the inhabitants of the neighbouring houses threw open their casements, and vehemently and enthusiastically applauded, clapping their hands, and shouting bravos: but neither at Venice, at Padua, nor at Florence did I hear any thing that pleased and touched me so much as the serenade to which I have just been listening.

14.—To-day was quite heavenly—like a lovely May-day in England: the air so pure, so soft, and the sun so warm, that I would gladly have dispensed with my shawl and pelisse. We went in carriages to the other side of the Palatine, and then dispersing in small parties, as will or fancy led, we lounged and wandered about in the Coliseum, and among the neighbouring ruins till dinner time. I climbed up the western side of the Coliseum, at the imminent hazard of my neck; and looking down through a gaping aperture, on the brink of which I had accidentally seated myself, I saw in the colossal corridor far below me, a young artist, who, as if transported out of his senses by delight and admiration, was making the most extraordinary antics and gestures: sometimes he clasped his hands, then extended his arms, then stood with them folded as in deep thought; now he snatched up his portfolio as if to draw what so much enchanted him, then threw it down and kicked it from him as if in despair. I never saw such admirable dumb show: it was better than any pantomime. At length, however, he happened to cast up his eyes, as if appealing to heaven, and they encountered mine peeping down upon him from above. He stood fixed and motionless for two seconds, staring at me, and then snatching up his portfolio and his hat, ran off and disappeared. I met the same man afterwards walking along the Via Felice, and could not help smiling as he passed: he smiled too, but pulled his hat over his face and turned away.

I discovered to-day (and it is no slight pleasure to make a discovery for one's self), the passage which formed the communication between the Coliseum and the Palace of the Cæsars, and in which the Emperor Commodus was assassinated. I recognized it by its situation, and the mosaic pavement described by Nibby. If I had time I might moralize here, and make an eloquent tirade *à la Eustace* about imperial monsters and so forth,—but in fact I *did* think while I stood in the damp and gloomy corridor, that it was a fitting death for Commodus to die by the giddy playfulness of a child, and the machinations of an abandoned woman. It was not a favourable time or hour to contemplate the Coliseum—the sunshine was too resplendent [Pg 81] —

> It was a garish, broad, and peering day,
> Loud, light, suspicious, full of eyes and ears;
> And every little corner, nook, and hole,
> Was penetrated by the insolent light.

We are told that five thousand animals were slain in the amphitheatre on its dedication—how dreadful! The mutual massacres of the gladiators inspire less horror than this disgusting butchery! To what a pitch must the depraved appetite for blood and death have risen among the corrupted and ferocious populace, before such a sight could be endured!

15.—We drove to-day to the tomb of Cecilia Metella, on the Appian Way, to the Fountain of Egeria, and the tomb of the Scipios near the Porta Cappena.

I wish the tomb of Cecilia Metella had been that of Cornelia or Valeria. There may be little in a name, but how much there is in association! What this massy fabric wanted in classical fame Lord Byron has lately supplied in poetical interest. The same may be said of the Fountain of Egeria, to which he has devoted some of the most exquisite stanzas in his poem, and has certainly invested it with a charm it could not have possessed before. The woods and groves which once surrounded it, have been all cut down, and the scenery round it is waste and bleak; but the fountain itself is pretty, overgrown with ivy, moss, and the graceful capillaire plant (capello di venere) drooping from the walls, and the stream is as pure as crystal. L**, who was with us, took up a stone to break off a piece of the statue, and maimed, defaced, and wretched as it is, I could not help thinking it a profanation to the place, and stopped his hand, calling him a *barbarous Vandyke*: he looked so awkwardly alarmed and puzzled by the epithet I had given him! The identity of this spot (like all other places here) has been vehemently disputed. At every step today we encountered doubt, and contradiction, and cavilling: authorities are marshalled against each other in puzzling array, and the modern unwillingness to be cheated by fine sounds and great names has become a general scepticism. I have no objection to the "shadows, doubts, and darkness" which rest upon all around us; it rather pleases my fancy thus to "dream over the map of things," abandoned to my own cogitations and my own conclusions; but then there are certain points upon which it is very disagreeable to have one's faith disturbed; and the Fountain of Egeria is one of these. So leaving the more learned antiquarians to fight it out, *secundum artem*, and fire each other's wigs if they will, I am determined, and do steadfastly believe, that the Fountain of Egeria I saw to-day is the very identical and original Fountain of Egeria—of Numa's Egeria—and therefore it *is* so. [Pg 82]

The tomb of the Scipios is a dirty dark wine cellar: all the urns, the fine sarcophagus, and the original tablets and inscriptions have been removed to the Vatican. I thought to-day while I stood in the sepulchre, and on the very spot whence the sarcophagus of Publius was removed, if Scipio, or Augustus, or Adrian, could return to this world, how would their Roman pride endure to see their last resting-places, the towers and the pyramids in which they fortified themselves, thus violated and put to ignoble uses, and the urns which contained their ashes stuck up as ornaments in a painted room, where barbarian visitors lounge away their hours, and stare upon their relics with scornful indifference or idle curiosity!

The people here, even the lowest and meanest among them seem to have imbibed a profound respect for antiquity and antiquities, which sometimes produces a comic effect. I am often amused by the exultation with which they point out a bit of old stone, or piece of brick wall, or shapeless fragment of some nameless statue, and tell you it is *antico, molto, antico*, and the half contemptuous tone in which they praise the most beautiful modern production, *é moderna – ma pure non é cativà!*

18.—We had an opportunity of witnessing to-day one of the most splendid ceremonies of the Catholic church. It is one of the four festivals at which the Pope performs mass in state at the Vatican, the anniversary of St. Peter's entrance into Rome, and of his taking possession of the Papal chair; for here St. Peter is reckoned the first Pope. To see the high priest of an ancient and wide-spread superstition publicly officiate in his sacred character, in the grandest temple in the universe, and surrounded by all the trappings of his spiritual and temporal authority, was an exhibition to make sad a reflecting mind, but to please and exalt a lively imagination: I wished myself a Roman Catholic for one half hour only. The procession, which was so arranged as to produce the most striking theatrical effect, moved up the central aisle, to strains of solemn and beautiful music from an orchestra of wind instruments. The musicians were placed out of sight, nor could I guess from what part of the buildings the sounds proceeded; but the blended harmony, so soft, yet so powerful and so equally diffused, as it floated through the long aisles and lofty domes, had a most heavenly effect. At length appeared the Pope, borne on the shoulders of his attendants, and habited in his full Pontifical robes of white and gold; fans of peacocks' feathers were waved on each side of his throne, and boys flung clouds of incense from their censers. As the procession advanced at the slowest possible foot-pace, the Pope from time to time stretched forth his arms which were crossed upon his bosom, and solemnly [Pg 83] blessed the people as they prostrated themselves on each side. I could have fancied it the triumphant approach of an Eastern despot, but for the mild and venerable air of the amiable old Pope, who looked as if more humbled than exalted by the pageantry around him. It might be *acting*, but if so, it was the most admirable acting I ever saw: I wish all his attendants had performed their parts as well. While the

Pope assists at mass, it is not etiquette for him to do anything for himself: one Cardinal kneeling, holds the book open before him, another carries his handkerchief, a third folds and unfolds his robe, a priest on each side supports him whenever he rises or moves, so that he appears among them like a mere helpless automaton going through a certain set of mechanical motions, with which his will has nothing to do. All who approach or address him prostrate themselves and kiss his embroidered slipper before they rise.

When the whole ceremony was over, and most of the crowd dispersed, the Pope, after disrobing, was passing through a private part of the church where we were standing accidentally, looking at one of the monuments. We made the usual obeisance, which he returned by inclining his head. He walked without support, but with great difficulty, and appeared bent by infirmity and age: his countenance has a melancholy but most benevolent expression, and his dark eyes retain uncommon lustre and penetration. During the twenty-one years he has worn the tiara, he has suffered many vicissitudes and humiliations with dignity and fortitude. He is not considered a man of very powerful intellect or very shining talents: he is not a Ganganelli or a Lambertini; but he has been happy in his choice of ministers, and his government has been distinguished by a spirit of liberality, and above all by a partiality to the English, which calls for our respect and gratitude. There were present to-day in St. Peter's about five thousand people, and the church would certainly have contained ten times the number.

19.—We went to-day to view the restored model of the Coliseum exhibited in the Piazza di Spagna; and afterwards drove to the manufactory of the beads called *Roman Pearl,* which is well worth seeing *once.* The beads are cut from thin laminæ of alabaster, and then dipped into a composition made of the scales of a fish (the Argentina). When a perfect imitation of pearl is intended, they can copy the accidental defects of colour and form which occur in the real gem, as well as its brilliance, so exquisitely, as to deceive the most practised eye.

20.—I ordered the open carriage early this morning, and, attended only by Scaccia, partly drove and partly walked through some of the finest parts of ancient Rome. The day has been perfectly lovely;

the [Pg 84] sky intensely blue without a single cloud; and though I was weak and far from well, I felt the influence of the soft sunshine in every nerve: the pure elastic air seemed to penetrate my whole frame, and made my spirits bound and my heart beat quicker. It is true, I had to regret at every step the want of a more cultivated companion, and that I felt myself shamefully—no—not *shamefully,* but *lamentably* ignorant of many things. There is so much of which I wish to know and learn more: so much of my time is spent in hunting books, and acquiring by various means the information with which I ought already to be prepared; so many days are lost by frequent indisposition, that though I enjoy, and feel the value of all I *do* know and observe, I am tantalized by the thoughts of all I must leave behind me unseen—there must necessarily be so much of what I do not even *hear*! Yet, in spite of these drawbacks, my little excursion to-day was delightful. I took a direction just contrary to my last expedition, first by the Quattro Fontane to the Santa Maria Maggiore, which I always see with new delight; then to the ruins called the temple of Minerva Medici, which stand in a cabbage garden near another fine ruin, once called the Trofei di Mario, and now the Acqua Giulia: thence to the Porta Maggiore, built by Claudius; and round by the Santa Croce di Gerusalemme. This church was built by Helena, the mother of Constantine, and contains her tomb, besides a portion of the *True Cross* from which it derives its name. The interior of this Basilica struck me as mean and cold. In the fine avenue in front of the Santa Croce, I paused a few minutes to look round me. To the right were the ruins of the stupendous Claudian Aqueduct with its gigantic arches, stretching away in one unbroken series far into the Campagna: behind me the amphitheatre of Castrense: to the left, other ruins, once called the Temple of Venus and Cupid, and now the Sessorium: in front, the Lateran, the obelisk of Sesostris, the Porta San Giovanni, and great part of the ancient walls; and thence the view extended to the foot of the Apennines. All this part of Rome is a scene of magnificent desolation, and of melancholy yet sublime interest: its wildness, its vastness, its waste and solitary openness, add to its effect upon the imagination. The only human beings I beheld in the compass of at least two miles, were a few herdsmen driving their cattle through the gate of San Giovanni, and two or three strangers who were sauntering about with their note books and portfolios, apparently enthusiasts like myself, lost in the memory of the past and the contemplation of the present.

I spent some time in the Lateran, then drove to the Coliseum, where I found a long procession of penitents, their figures and faces totally concealed by their masks and peculiar dress, chaunting the Via Crucis. I then examined the site of the Temple of Venus and Rome, and satisfied myself by ocular demonstration of the truth of the measurements [Pg 85] which gave sixty feet for the height of the columns and eighteen feet for the circumference. I knew enough of geometrical proportion to prove this to my own satisfaction. On examining the fragments which remain, each fluting measured a foot, that is, eight inches right across. This appears prodigious, but it is nevertheless true. I am forced to believe to-day what I yesterday doubted, and deemed a piece of mere antiquarian exaggeration.

This magnificent edifice was designed and built by the Emperor Adrian, who piqued himself on his skill in architecture, and carried his jealousy of other artists so far, as to banish Apollodorus, who had designed the Forum of Trajan. When he had finished the Temple of Venus and Rome, he sent to Apollodorus a plan of his stupendous structure, challenging him to find a single fault in it. The architect severely criticised some trifling oversights; and the Emperor, conscious of the justice of his criticisms, and unable to remedy the defects, ordered him to be strangled. Such was the fate of Apollodorus, whose misfortune it was to have an Emperor for his rival.

They are now clearing the steps which lead to this temple, from which it appears that the length of the portico in front was three hundred feet, and of the side five hundred feet.

While I was among these ruins, I was struck by a little limpid fountain, which gushed from the crumbling wall and lost itself among the fragments of the marble pavement. All looked dreary and desolate; and that part of the ruin which from its situation must have been the *sanctum sanctorum*, the shrine of the divinity of the place, is now a receptacle of filth and every conceivable abomination.

I walked on to the ruins now called the Basilica of Constantine, once the Temple of Peace. This edifice was in a bad style, and constructed at a period when the arts were at a low ebb: yet the ruins are vast and magnificent. The exact direction of the Via Sacra has long been a subject of vehement dispute. They have now laid open a part of it which ran in front of the Basilica: the pavement is about twelve feet below the present pavement of Rome, and the soil turned up in their excavations is formed entirely of crumbled brickwork and mortar, and fragments of marble, porphyry, and granite. I returned by the Forum and the Capitol, through the Forums of Nerva and Trajan, and so over the Monte Cavallo, home.

23.—Last night we had a numerous party, and Signor P. and his daughter came to sing. *She* is a private singer of great talent, and came attended by her lover or her *fiancé;* who, according to Italian custom, attends his mistress every where during the few weeks which precede their marriage. He is a young artist, a favourite pupil of Camuccini, and of very quiet, unobtrusive manners. La P. has the [Pg 86] misfortune to be plain; her features are irregular, her complexion of a sickly paleness, and though her eyes are large and dark, they appeared totally devoid of lustre and expression. Her plainness, the bad taste of her dress, her awkward figure, and her timid and embarrassed deportment, all furnished matter of amusement and observation to some young people, (English of course,) whose propensities for *quizzing* exceeded their good breeding and good nature. Though La P. does not understand a word of either French or English, I thought she could not mistake the significant looks and whispers of which she was the object, and I was in pain for her, and for her modest lover. I drew my chair to the piano, and tried to divert her attention by keeping her in conversation, but I could get no farther than a few questions which were answered in monosyllables. At length she sang—and sang divinely: I found the pale automaton had a soul as well as a voice. After giving us, with faultless execution, as well as great expression, some of Rossini's finest songs, she sung the beautiful and difficult cavatina in Otello, "*Assisa al piè d'un Salice,*" with the most enchanting style and pathos, and then stood as unmoved as a statue while the company applauded loud and long. A moment afterwards, as she stooped to take up a music book, her lover, who had edged himself by degrees from the door to the piano, bent his head too, and murmured in a low voice, but with the most passionate accent, "O brava, brava cara!" She replied only by a look—but it was such a look! I never saw a human countenance so entirely, so instantaneously changed in character: the vacant eyes kindled and beamed with tenderness: the pale cheek glowed, and a bright smile playing round her mouth, just parted her lips sufficiently to discover a set of teeth like pearls. I could have called her at that moment beautiful; but the change was as transient as sudden—it passed like a gleam of light over her face and vanished, and by the time the book was placed on the desk, she looked as plain, as stupid, and as statue-like as ever. I was the only person who had witnessed this little by-scene; and it gave me pleasant thoughts and interest for the rest of the evening.

Another trait of character occurred afterwards, which amused me, but in a very different style. Our new Danish friend, the Baron B— —, told us he had once been present at the decapitation of nine men, having first fortified himself with a large goblet of brandy. After describing the scene in all its horrible details, and assuring us in his bad German French that it was "*une chose bien mauvaise à voir,*" I could not help asking him with a shudder, how he felt afterwards; whether it was not weeks or months before the impressions of horror left his mind? He answered with smiling naïveté and taking a pinch of snuff, "*Ma foi! madame, je n'ai pas pu manger de la viande toute cette journée-là?*" [Pg 87]

27.—We drove to the Palazzo Spada, to see the famous Spada Pompey, said to be the very statue at the base of which Cæsar fell. I was pleased to find, contrary to my expectations, that this statue has great intrinsic merit, besides its celebrity, to recommend it. The extremities of the limbs have a certain clumsiness which may perhaps be a feature of resemblance, and not a fault of the sculptor; but the attitude is noble, and the likeness of the head to the undisputed bust of Pompey in the Florentine gallery, struck me immediately. The Palazza Spada, with its splendid architecture, dirt, discomfort, and dilapidation, is a fair specimen of the Roman palaces in general. It contains a corridor, which from an architectural deception appears much longer than it really is. I hate tricks—in architecture especially. We afterwards visited the Pantheon, the Church of Santa Maria sopra Minerva, (an odd combination of names,) and concluded the morning at Canova's. It is one of the pleasures of Rome to lounge in the studj of the best sculptors; and it is at Rome only that sculpture seems to flourish as in its native soil. Rome is truly the *city of the soul*, the home of art and artists. With the divine models of the Vatican ever before their eyes, these inspiring skies above their heads, and the quarries of marble at a convenient distance—it is here only they can conceive and execute those works which are formed from the *beau-idéal*; but it is not here they meet with patronage: the most beautiful things I have seen at the various studj have all been executed for English, German, and Russian noblemen. The names I heard most frequently were those of the Dukes of Bedford and Devonshire, Prince Esterhazy, and the King of England.

Canova has been accused of a want of simplicity, and of giving a too voluptuous expression to some of his figures: with all my admiration of his genius, I confess the censure just. It is particularly observable in the Clori svegliata (the Nymph awakened by Love), the Cupid and Psyche, for Prince Yousouppoff, the Endymion, the Graces, and some others.

In some of Thorwaldson's works there is exquisite grace, simplicity, and expression: the Shepherd Boy, the Adonis, the Jason, and the Hebe, have a great deal of antique spirit. I did not like the colossal Christ which the sculptor has just finished in clay: it is a proof that bulk alone does not constitute sublimity: it is deficient in dignity, or rather in *divinity*.

At Rodolf Schadow's, I was most pleased by the Cupid and the Filatrice. His Cupid is certainly the most beautiful Cupid I ever saw, superior, I think, both to Canova's and to Thorwaldson's. The Filatrice, though so exquisitely natural and graceful, a little disappointed me; I had heard much of it, and had formed in my own [Pg 88] imagination an idea different and superior to what I saw. This beautiful figure has repose, simplicity, nature, and grace, but I felt a *want*—the want of some internal sentiment: for instance, if, instead of watching the rotation of her spindle with such industrious attention, the Filatrice had looked careless, or absent, or pensive, or disconsolate, (like Faust's Margaret at her spinning-wheel,) she would have been more interesting—but not perhaps what the sculptor intended to represent.

Schadow is ill, but we were admitted by his order into his private study; we saw there the Bacchante, which he has just finished in clay, and which is to emulate or rival Canova's Dansatrice. He has been at work upon a small but beautiful figure of a piping Shepherd-boy, which is just made out: beside it lay Virgil's Eclogues, and his spectacles were between the leaves. [J]

Almost every thing I saw at Max Laboureur's struck me as vapid and finikin. There were some pretty groups, but nothing to tempt me to visit it again.

30.—We spent the whole morning at the Villa Albani, where there is a superb collection of antique marbles, most of them brought from the Villa of Adrian at Tivoli. To note down even a few of the objects which pleased me would be an endless task. I think the busts interested me most. There is a basso-relievo of Antinous—the beautiful head declined in his usual pensive attitude: it is the most finished and faultless piece of sculpture in relievo I ever saw; and as perfect and as polished as if it came from the chisel yesterday. There is another basso-relievo of Marcus Aurelius, and Faustina, equal to the last in execution, but not in interest.

We found Rogers in the gardens: the old poet was sunning himself—walking up and down a beautiful marble portico, lined with works of art, with his note-book in his hand. I am told he is now writing a poem of which Italy is the subject; and here, with all the Campagna di Roma spread out before him—above him, the sunshine and the cloudless skies—and all around him, the remains of antiquity in a thousand elegant, or venerable, or fanciful forms: he could not have chosen a more genial spot for inspiration. Though we disturbed his poetical reveries rather abruptly, he met us with his usual amiable courtesy, and conversed most delightfully. I never knew him more pleasant, and never saw him so animated.

Our departure from Rome has been postponed from day to day in [Pg 89] consequence of a *trifling* accident. An Austrian colonel was taken by the banditti near Fondi, and carried up into the mountains: ten thousand scudi were demanded for his ransom; and for many days past, the whole city has been in a state of agitation and suspense about his ultimate fate. The Austrians, roused by the insult, sent a large body of troops (some say three thousand men) against about one hundred and fifty robbers, threatening to exterminate them. They were pursued so closely, that after dragging their unfortunate captive over the mountains from one fastness to another, till he was nearly dead from exhaustion and ill-treatment, they either abandoned or surrendered him without terms. The troops immediately marched back to Naples, and the matter rests here: I cannot learn that any thing farther will be done. The robbers being at present panic-struck by such unusual energy and activity, and driven from their accustomed haunts, by these valorous champions of good order and good policy, it is considered that the road is now more open and safe than it has been for some time, and if nothing new happens to alarm us, we set off on Friday next.

I visited to-day the baths of Dioclesian, and the noble church which Michel Angelo has constructed upon, and out of, their gigantic ruins. It has all that grand simplicity, that *entireness* which characterizes his works: it contains, too, some admirable pictures. On leaving the church, I saw on each side of the door, the monuments of Salvator Rosa and Carlo Maratti—what a contrast do they exhibit in their genius, in their works, in their characters, in their countenances, in their lives! Near this church (the Santa Maria dei Angeli) is the superb fountain of the Acqua Felice, the first view of which rather disappointed me. I had been told that it represented Moses striking the rock,—a magnificent idea for a fountain! but the execution falls short of the conception. The water, instead of gushing from the rock, is poured out from the mouths of two prodigious lions of basalt, brought, I believe, from Upper Egypt: they seem misplaced here. A little beyond the Ponta Pia is the Campo Scelerato, where the Vestals were interred alive. We afterwards drove to the Santi Apostoli to see the tomb of the excellent Ganganelli, by Canova. Then to Sant' Ignazio, to see the famous ceiling painted in perspective by the jesuit Pozzo. The effect is certainly marvellous, making the interior appear to the eye, at least twice the height it really is; but though the illusion pleased me as a work of art, I thought the trickery unnecessary and misplaced. At the magnificent church of the Gesuiti (where there are two entire columns of giallo antico) I saw a list of relics for which the church is celebrated, and whose efficacy and sanctity were vouched for by a very respectable catalogue of miracles. Among these relics there are a few [Pg 90] worth mentioning for their oddity, viz. one of the Virgin's *shifts*, three of her hairs, and the skirt of Joseph's coat.

31.—We spent nearly the whole day in the gallery of the Vatican, and in the Pauline and Sistine chapels.

February 1st, at Valletri.—I left Rome this morning exceedingly depressed: Madame de Staël may well call travelling *un triste plaisir*. My depression did not arise from the feeling that I left behind me any thing or any person to regret, but from mixed and melancholy emotions, and partly perhaps from that weakness which makes my hand tremble while I write—which has bound down my mind, and all its best powers, and all its faculties of enjoyment, to a languid passiveness, making me feel at every moment, I am not what I was, or ought to be, or might have been.

We arrived, after a short and most delightful journey by Albano, the Lake Nemi, Gensao, etc. at Velletri, the birth-place of that wretch Octavius, and famous for its wine. The day has been as soft and as sunny as a May-day in England, and the country, through which we travelled but too rapidly, beyond description lovely. The blue Mediterranean spread far to the west, and on the right we had the snowy mountains, with their wild fantastic peaks "rushing on the sky." I felt it all in my heart with a mixture of sadness and delight which I cannot express.

This land was made by nature a paradise: it seems to want no charm, "unborrowed from the eye,"—but how has memory sanctified, history illustrated, and poetry illumined the scenes around us; where every rivulet had its attendant nymph, where every wood was protected by its sylvan divinity; where every tower has its tale of heroism, and "not a mountain lifts its head unsung;" and though the faith, the glory, and the power of the antique time be passed away—still

> A spirit hangs,
> Beautiful region! o'er thy towns and farms,
> Statues and temples, and memorial tombs.

I can allow that one-half, at least, of the beauty and interest we see, lies in our own souls; that it is our own enthusiasm which sheds this mantle of light over all we behold: but, as colours do not exist in the objects themselves, but in the rays which paint them—so beauty is not less real, is not less beauty, because it exists in the medium through which we view certain objects, rather than in those objects themselves. I have met persons who think they display a vast deal of common sense, and very uncommon strength of mind, in rising superior to all prejudices of education and illusions of romance—to whom enthusiasm is only another name for affectation—who, where the cultivated and [Pg 91] the contemplative mind finds ample matter to excite feeling and reflection, give themselves airs of fashionable *nonchalance*, or flippant scorn—to whom the crumbling ruin is so much brick and mortar, no more—to whom the tomb of the Horatii and Curiatii is a *stack of chimneys*, the Pantheon *an old oven*, and the Fountain of Egeria a *pig-sty*. Are such persons aware that in all this there is an affectation, a thousand times more gross and contemptible, than that affectation (too frequent perhaps) which they design to ridicule?

"Whose mind is but the mind of his own eyes,
He is a slave—the meanest we can meet."

2.—Our journey to-day has been long, but delightfully diversified, and abounding in classical beauty and interest. I scarce know what to say, now that I open my little book to record my own sensations: they are so many, so various, so painful, so delicious—my senses and my imagination have been so enchanted, my heart so very heavy—where shall I begin?

In some of the scenes of to-day—at Terracina, particularly, there was beauty beyond what I ever beheld or imagined: the scenery of Switzerland is of a different character, and on a different scale: it is beyond comparison grander, more gigantic, more overpowering, but it is not so poetical. Switzerland is not Italy—is not the enchanting *south*. This soft balmy air, these myrtles, orange-groves, palm-trees; these cloudless skies, this bright blue sea, and sunny hills, all breathe of an enchanted land; "a land of Faery."

Between Velletri and Terracina the road runs in one undeviating line through the Pontine Marshes. The accounts we have of the baneful effects of the malaria here, and the absolute solitude, (not a human face or a human habitation intervening from one post-house to another,) invest the wild landscape with a frightful and peculiar character of desolation. As for the mere exterior of the country, I have seen more wretched and sterile looking spots, (in France, for instance,) but none that so affected the imagination and the spirits. On leaving the Pontine Marshes, we came almost suddenly upon the sunny and luxuriant region near Terracina: here was the ancient city of Anxur; and the gothic ruins of the castle of Theodoric, which frown on the steep above, are contrasted with the delicate and Grecian proportions of the temple below. All the country round is famed in classic and poetic lore. The Promontory (once poetically the *island*) of Circe is still the Monte Circello: here was the region of the Lestrygons, and the scene of part of the Æneid and Odyssey; and Corinne has superadded romantic and charming associations quite as delightful, and quite as *true*.

Antiquarians, who, like politicians, "seem to see the things that are [Pg 92] not," have placed all along this road, the sites of many a celebrated town and fane—"making hue and cry after many a city which has run away, and by certain marks and tokens pursuing to find it:" as some old author says so quaintly. At every hundred yards, fragments of masonry are seen by the road-side; portions of brickwork, sometimes traced at the bottom of a dry ditch, or incorporated into a fence; sometimes peeping above the myrtle bushes on the wild hills, where the green lizards lie basking and glittering on them in thousands, and the stupid ferocious buffalo, with his fierce red eyes, rubs his hide and glares upon us as we pass. No—not the grandest monuments of Rome—not the Coliseum itself, in all its decaying magnificence, ever inspired me with such profound emotions as did those nameless, shapeless vestiges of the dwellings of man, starting up like memorial tombs in the midst of this savage but luxuriant wilderness. Of the beautiful cities which rose along this lovely coast, the colonies of elegant and polished Greece—one after another swallowed up by the "insatiate maw" of ancient Rome, nothing remains—their sites, their very names have passed away and perished. We might as well hunt after a forgotten dream.

Vain was the chief's, the sage's pride,
They had no POET, and they died!

In vain they toil'd, in vain they bled,
They had no POET—and are dead.

I write this a Gaëta—a name famous in the poetical, the classical, the military story of Italy, from the day of Æneas, from whom it received its appellation, down to the annals of the late war. On the site of our inn, (the Albergo di Cicerone,) stood Cicero's Formian Villa; and in an adjoining grove he was murdered in his litter by the satellites of the Triumviri, as he attempted to escape. I stood to-night on a little terrace, which hung over an orange grove, and enjoyed a scene which I would paint, if words were forms, and hues, and sounds—not else. A beautiful bay, enclosed by the Mola di Gaëta, on one side, and the Promontory of Misenum on the other: the sky studded with stars and reflected in a sea as blue as itself—and so glassy and unruffled, it seemed to slumber in the moonlight: now and then the murmur of a wave, not hoarsely breaking on rock and shingles, but kissing the turfy shore, where oranges and myrtles grew down to the water edge. These, and the remembrances connected with all, and a mind to think, and a heart to feel, and thoughts both of pain and pleasure mingling to render the effect more deep and touching.—Why should I write this? O surely I need not fear that I shall *forget*! [Pg 93]

LINES WRITTEN AT MOLA DI GAETA, NEAR THE RUINS OF CICERO'S FORMIAN VILLA.

We wandered through bright climes, and drank the beams
Of southern suns: Elysian scenes we view'd,
Such as we picture oft in those day dreams
That haunt the fancy in her wildest mood.
Upon the sea-heat vestiges we stood,
Where Cicero dwelt, and watch'd the latest gleams
Of rosy light steal o'er the azure flood:
And memory conjur'd up most glowing themes,
Filling the expanded heart, till it forgot
Its own peculiar grief!—O! if the dead
Yet haunt our earth, around this hallow'd spot,
Hovers sweet Tully's spirit, since it fled

The Roman Forum—Forum now no more!
Though cold and silent be the sands we tread,
Still burns the "eloquent air," and to the shore
There rolls no wave, and through the orange shade
There sighs no breath, which doth not speak of him,
The father of his country: and though dim
Her day of empire—and her laurel crown
Torn and defaced, and soiled with blood and tears,
And her imperial eagles trampled down—
Still with a queen-like grace, Italia wears
Her garland of bright names,—her coronal of stars,
(Radiant memorials of departed worth!)
That shed a glory round her pensive brow,
And make her still the worship of the earth!

Naples. Sunday 3rd.—We left Gaëta early. If the scene was so beautiful in the evening—how bright, how lovely it was this morning! The sun had not long risen; and a soft purple mist hung over part of the sea; while to the north and west the land and water sparkled and glowed in the living light. Some little fishing boats which had just put off, rocked upon the glassy sea, which lent them a gentle motion, though itself appeared all mirror-like and motionless. The orange and lemon trees in full foliage literally bent over the water; and it was so warm at half past eight that I felt their shade a relief.

After leaving Gaëta, the first place of note is or *was* Minturnum, where Marius was taken, concealed in the marshes near it. The marshes remain, the city has disappeared. Capua is still a large town; but it certainly does not keep up its ancient fame for luxury and good cheer: for we found it extremely difficult to procure any thing to eat. The next town is Avversa, a name unknown, I believe, in the classical history of Italy: it was founded, if I remember rightly, by the Norman knights. Near this place is or was the convent where Queen Joanna strangled her husband Andrea, with a silken cord of her own weaving. So says the story: *non lo credo io.*

From Avversa to Naples the country is not interesting; but fertile and rich beyond description: an endless succession of vineyards and orange groves. At length we reached Naples; all tired and in a [Pg 94] particularly sober and serious mood: we remembered it was the Sabbath, and had forgotten that it was the first day of the Carnival; and great was our amazement at the scene which met us on our arrival—

> I looked, I stared, I smiled, I laughed: and all
> The weight of sadness was in wonder lost.

The whole city seemed one vast puppet-show; and the noisy gaiety of the crowded streets almost stunned me. One of the first objects we encountered was a barouche full of Turks and Sultanas, driven by an old woman in a tawdry court dress as coachman; while a merry-andrew and a harlequin capered behind as footmen. Owing to the immense size of the city, and the difficulty of making our way through the motley throng of masks, beggars, lazzaroni, eating-stalls, carts and carriages, we were nearly three hours traversing the streets before we reached our inn on the Chiaja.

I feel tired and over-excited: I have been standing on my balcony looking out upon the moonlit bay, and listening to the mingled shouts, the laughter, the music all around me; and thinking—till I feel in no mood to write.

7.—Last night we visited the theatre of San Carlo. It did not strike me as equal to the Scala at Milan. The form is not so fine, the extent of the stage is, or appeared to be, less; but there is infinitely more gilding and ornament; the mirrors and lights, the sky-blue draperies produce a splendid effect, and the coup-d'œil is, on the whole, more gay, more theatre-like. It was crowded in every part, and many of the audience were in dominos and fancy dresses: a few were masked. Rossini's Barbiere di Seviglia, which contains, I think more *melody* than all his other operas put together, (the Tancredi perhaps excepted,) was most enchantingly sung, and as admirably acted; and the beautiful classical ballet of "Niobe and her Children," would have appeared nothing short of perfection, had I not seen the Didone Abbandonata at Milan. But they have no actress here like the graceful, the expressive Pallerini; nor any actor equal to the Æneas of the Scala.

The Austrians, who are paramount here, allow masks only twice a week, Sundays and Thursdays. The people seem determined to indemnify themselves for this restriction on their pleasures by every allowed excess during the two days of merriment, which their despotic conquerors have spared them. I am told by M** and S**, our Italian friends, that the Carnival is now fallen off from its wild spirit of fanciful gaiety; that it is stupid, dull, tasteless, in comparison to what it was formerly, owing to the severity of the Austrian police. I know nothing about the propriety of the measures which have been resorted [Pg 95] to for curbing the excesses of the Carnival: I think if people *will* run away instead of fighting for their national rights, they must be content to suffer accordingly—but I meddle not with politics, and with all my heart abhor them. Whatever the gaities of the Carnival may have been formerly, it is scarce possible to conceive a more fantastic, a more picturesque, a more laughable scene than the Strada di Toledo exhibited to-day; the whole city seemed to wear "one universal grin;" and such an incessant fire of sugar-plums (or what seemed such) was carried on, and with such eagerness and mimic fury, that when our carriage came out of the conflict, we all looked as if a sack of flour had been shaken over us. The implements used in this ridiculous warfare, are, for common purposes, little balls of plaster of Paris and flour, made to resemble small comfits: friends and acquaintances pelted each other with real confetti, and those of the most delicious and expensive kinds. A double file of carriages moved in a contrary direction along the Corso; a space in the middle and on each side being left for horsemen and pedestrians, and the most exact order was maintained by the guards and police; so that if by chance a carriage lost its place in the line it was impossible to recover it, and it was immediately obliged to leave the street, and re-enter by one of the extremities. Besides the warfare carried on below, the balconies on each side were crowded with people in gay or grotesque dresses, who had *sacks* of bon-bons before them, from which they showered vollies upon those beneath, or aimed across the street at each other: some of them filled their handkerchiefs, and then dexterously loosening the corners, and taking a certain aim, flung a volley at once. This was like a cannon loaded with grape-shot, and never failed to do the most terrific execution.

Among the splendid and fanciful equipages of the masqueraders, was one, containing the Duke of Monteleone's family, in the form of a ship, richly ornamented, and drawn by six horses mounted by masks for postilions. The fore part of the vessel contained the Duke's party, dressed in various gay costumes, as Tartar warriors and Indian queens. In the stern were the servants and attendants, *travestied* in the most grotesque and ludicrous style. This magnificent and unwieldly car had by some chance lost its place in the procession, and vainly endeavoured to whip in; as it is a point of honour among the charioteers not to yield the *pas*. Our coachman, however, was ordered (though most unwilling) to draw up and make way for it; and this little civility was acknowledged, not only by a profusion of bows, but by such a shower of delicious sugar plums, that the seats of our carriage were literally covered with them, and some of the gentlemen flung into our laps elegant little baskets, fastened with ribbons, and filled with exquisite sweetmeats. I could not enter into all this with much spirit; "*non son io quel ch'un tempo fui:*" but I was an amused, though a [Pg 96] quiet spectator; and sometimes saw much more than those who were actually engaged in the battle. I observed that to-day our carriage became an object of attention, and a favourite point of attack to several parties on foot, and in carriages; and I was at no loss to discover the reason. I had with me a lovely girl, whose truly English style of beauty, her brilliant bloom, heightened by her eager animation, her lips dimpled with a thousand smiles, and her whole countenance radiant with glee and mischievous archness, made her an object of admiration, which the English expressed by a fixed stare, and the Italians by sympathetic smiles, nods, and all the usual superlatives of delight. Among our most potent and malignant adversaries, was a troop of elegant masks in a long open carriage, the form of which was totally concealed by the boughs of laurel, and wreaths of artificial flowers, with which it was covered. It was drawn by six fine horses, fancifully caparisoned, ornamented with plumes of feathers, and led by grotesque masks. In the carriage stood twelve persons in black silk dominos, black hats, and black masks; with plumes of crimson feathers, and rich crimson sashes. They were armed with small painted targets and tin tubes, from which they shot vollies of confetti, in such quantities, and with such dexterous aim, that we were almost overwhelmed whenever we passed them. It was in vain we returned the compliment; our small shot rattled on their masks, or bounded from their shields, producing only shouts of laughter at our expense.

A favourite style of mask here, is the dress of an English sailor, straw hats, blue jackets, white trowsers, and very white masks with pink cheeks: we saw hundreds in this whimsical costume.

13.—On driving home rather late this evening, and leaving the noise, the crowds, the confusion and festive folly of the Strada di Toledo, we came suddenly upon a scene, which, from its beauty, no less than by the force of contrast, strongly impressed my imagination. The shore was silent, and almost solitary: the bay as smooth as a mirror, and as still as a frozen lake; the sky, the sea, the mountains round were all of the same hue, a soft grey tinged with violet, except where the sunset had left a narrow crimson streak along the edge of the sea. There was not a breeze, not the slightest breath of air, and a single vessel, a frigate with all its white sails crowded, lay motionless as a monument on the bosom of the waters, in which it was reflected as in a mirror. I have seen the bay more splendidly beautiful; but I never saw so peculiar, so lovely a picture. It lasted but a short time: the transparent purple veil became a dusky pall, and night and shadow gradually enveloped the whole. [K]

[Pg 97]

How I love these resplendent skies and blue seas! Nature here seems to celebrate a continual Festa, and to be for ever decked out in holiday costume! A drive along the "*sempre beata Mergellina*" to the extremity of the Promontory of Pausilippo is positive enchantment: thence we looked over a landscape of such splendid and unequalled interest! the shores of Baia, where Cicero, Horace, Virgil, Pliny, Mecænas, lived; the white towers of Puzzuoli and the Islands of Ischia, Procida, and Nisida. There was the Sybil's Cave, Lake Acheron, and the fabled Lethe; there the sepulchre of Misenus, who defied the Triton; and the scene of the whole sixth book of the Æneid, which I am now reading in Annibal Caro's translation: there Agrippina mourned Germanicus; and there her daughter fell a victim to her monster of a son. At our feet lay the lovely little Island of Nisida, the spot on which Brutus and Portia parted for the last time before the battle of Philippi.

To the south of the bay the scenery is not less magnificent, and scarcely less dear to memory: Naples, rising from the sea like an amphitheatre of white palaces, and towers, and glittering domes: beyond, Mount Vesuvius, with the smoke curling from its summits like a silver cloud, and forming the only speck upon the intense blue sky; along its base Portici, Annunziata, Torre del Greco, glitter in the sun; every white building—almost every window in every building, distinct to the eye at the distance of several miles: farther on, and perched like white nests on the mountainous promontory, lie Castel a Mare, and Sorrento, the birth-place of Tasso, and his asylum when the injuries of his cold-hearted persecutors had stung him to madness, and drove him here for refuge to the arms of his sister. Yet, farther on, Capua rises from the sea, a beautiful object in itself, but from which the fancy gladly turns to dwell again upon the snowy buildings of Sorrento.

"O de la liberté vieille et sainte patrie!
Terre autrefois féconde en sublimes vertus!
Sous d'indignes Césars maintenant asservie
Ton empire est tombé! tes héros ne sont plus!
Mais dans son sein l'âme aggrandie
Croit sur leurs monumens respirer leur génie,
Comme on respire encore dans un temple aboli
La Majesté du Dieu dont il était rempli."

De la Martine.

[Pg 98]

THE

SONG OF THE SYREN PARTHENOPE.

A RHAPSODY,

WRITTEN AT NAPLES.

Mine are these waves, and mine the twilight depths
O'er which they roll, and all these tufted isles
That lift their backs like dolphins from the deep,
And all these sunny shores that gird us round!

Listen! O listen to the Sea-maid's shell!
Ye who have wander'd hither from far climes,
(Where the coy summer yields but half her sweets,)
To breathe my bland luxurious airs, and drink
My sunbeams! and to revel in a land
Where Nature—deck'd out like a bride to meet
Her lover—lays forth all her charms, and smiles
Languidly bright, voluptuously gay,
Sweet to the sense, and tender to the heart.

Listen! O listen to the Sea-maid's shell;
Ye who have fled your natal shores in hate
Or anger, urged by pale disease, or want,
Or grief, that clinging like the spectre bat,
Sucks drop by drop the life-blood from the heart,
And hither come to learn forgetfulness,
Or to prolong existence! ye shall find
Both—though the spring Lethean flow no more,
There is a power in these entrancing skies
And murmuring waters and delicious airs,
Felt in the dancing spirits and the blood,
And falling on the lacerated heart
Like balm, until that life becomes a boon,
Which elsewhere is a burthen and a curse.

Hear then—O hear the Sea-maid's airy shell,
Listen, O listen! 'tis the Syren sings,

The spirit of the deep—Parthenope—
She who did once i' the dreamy days of old
Sport on these golden sands beneath the moon,
Or pour'd the ravishing music of her song
Over the silent waters; and bequeath'd
To all these sunny capes and dazzling shores
Her own immortal beauty, and her *name*.

This is the last day of the Carnival, the last night of the opera; the people are permitted to go in masks, and after the performances there will be a ball. To-day, when Baldi was describing the excesses which usually take place during the last few hours of the Carnival, he said, "the man who has but half a shirt will pawn it to-night to buy a good supper and an opera-ticket: to-morrow for fish and soup-maigre—fasting and repentance!"

[Pg 99]

Saturday, 23.—I have just seen a most magnificent sight; one which I have often dreamed of, often longed to behold, and having beheld, never shall forget. Mount Vesuvius is at this moment blazing like a huge furnace; throwing up every minute, or half minute, columns of fire and red-hot stones, which fall in showers and bound down the side of the mountain. On the east, there are two distinct streams of lava descending, which glow with almost a white heat, and every burst of flame is accompanied by a sound resembling cannon at a distance.—

I can hardly write, my mind is so overflowing with astonishment, admiration, and sublime pleasure: what a scene as I looked out on the bay from the Sante Lucia! On one side, the evening star and the thread-like crescent of the new moon were setting together over Pausilippo, reflected in lines of silver radiance on the blue sea; on the other the broad train of fierce red light glared upon the water with a fitful splendour, as the explosions were more or less violent: before me all was so soft, so lovely, so tranquil! while I had only to turn my head to be awe-struck by the convulsion of fighting elements.

I remember, that on our first arrival at Naples, I was disappointed because Vesuvius did not smoke so much as I had been led to expect from pictures and descriptions. The smoke then lay like a scarcely perceptible cloud on the highest point, or rose in a slender white column; to-day and yesterday, it has rolled from the crater in black volumes, mixing with the clouds above, and darkening the sky.

Half-past twelve.—I have walked out again: the blaze from the crater is less vivid; but there are now four streams of lava issuing from it, which have united in two broad currents, one of which extends below the hermitage. It is probable that by to-morrow night it will have reached the lower part of the mountain.

Sunday, 24.—Just returned from chapel at the English ambassador's, where the service was read by a dandy clergyman to a crowd of fine and superfine ladies and gentlemen, crushed together into a hot room. I never saw extravagance in dress carried to such a pitch as it is by my countrywomen here,—whether they dress at the men or against each other, it is equally bad taste. The sermon to-day was very appropriate, from the text, "*Take ye no thought what ye shall eat, or what ye shall drink, or what ye shall put on,*" and, I dare say, it was listened to with singular edification.

5 o'clock.—We have been driving along the Strada Nuova in L**'s britschka, whence we had a fine view of Vesuvius. There are tremendous bursts of smoke from the crater. At one time the whole mountain, down to the very base, was almost enveloped, and the atmosphere round it loaded with the vapour, which seemed to issue in volumes [Pg 100] half as large as the mountain itself. If horses are to be had we go up to-night.

Monday night.—I am not in a humour to describe, or give way to any poetical flights, but I must endeavour to give a faithful, sober, and circumstantial account of our last night's expedition, while the impression is yet fresh on my mind; though there is, I think, little danger of my forgetting. We procured horses, which, from the number of persons proceeding on the same errand with ourselves, was a matter of some difficulty. We set out at seven in the evening in an open carriage, and almost the whole way we had the mountain before us, spouting fire to a prodigious height. The road was crowded with groups of people who had come out from the city and environs to take a nearer view of the magnificent spectacle, and numbers were hurrying to and fro in those little flying *corricoli* which are peculiar to Naples. As we approached, the explosions became more and more vivid, and at every tremendous burst of fire our friend L** jumped half off his seat, making most loud and characteristic exclamations,—"By Jove! a magnificent fellow! now for it, whizz! there he goes, sky high, by George!" The rest of the party were equally enthusiastic in a different style; and I sat silent and quiet from absolute inability to express what I felt. I was almost breathless with wonder, and excitement, and impatience to be nearer the scene of action. While my eyes were fixed on the mountain, my attention was, from time to time, excited by regular rows of small shining lights, six or eight in number, creeping, as it seemed, along the edge of the stream of lava; and, when contrasted with the red blaze which rose behind, and the gigantic black back-ground, looking like a procession of glowworms. These were the torches of travellers ascending the mountain, and I longed to be one of them.

We reached Resina a little before nine, and alighted from the carriage; the ascent being so rugged and dangerous, that only asses and mules accustomed to the road are used. Two only were in waiting at the moment we arrived, which L** immediately secured for me and himself; and though reluctant to proceed without the rest of the party, we were compelled to go on before, that we might not lose time, or hazard the loss of our *monture*. We set off then, each with two attendants, a man to lead our animals and a torch-bearer. The road, as we ascended, became more and more steep at every step, being over a stream of lava, intermixed with stones and ashes, and the darkness added to the difficulty. But how shall I describe the scene and the people who surrounded us; the landscape partially lighted by a fearful red glare, the precipitous and winding road bordered by wild looking gigantic aloes, projecting their huge spear-like leaves almost across our path, and our lazzaroni attendants with their shrill shouts, and strange [Pg 101] dresses, and wild jargon, and striking features, and dark eyes flashing in the gleam of the torches, which they flung round their heads to prevent their being extinguished, formed a scene so new, so extraordinary, so like romance, that my attention was frequently drawn from the mountain, though blazing in all its tumultuous magnificence.

The explosions succeeded each other with terrific rapidity about two in every three minutes; and the noise I can only compare to the roaring and hissing of ten thousand imprisoned winds, mingled at times with a rumbling sound like artillery, or distant thunder. It frequently happened that the guides, in dashing their torches against the ground, set fire to the dried thorns and withered grass, and the blaze ran along the earth like wildfire, to the great alarm of poor L**, who saw in every burning bush a stream of lava rushing to overwhelm us.

Before eleven o'clock we reached the Hermitage, situated between Vesuvius and the Somma, and the highest habitation on the mountain. A great number of men were assembled within, and guides, lazzaroni, servants, and soldiers, were lounging round. I alighted, for I was benumbed and tired, but did not like to venture among those people, and it was proposed that we should wait for the rest of our party a little further on. We accordingly left our donkeys and walked forward upon a kind of high ridge which serves to fortify the Hermitage and its environs against the lava. From this path, as we slowly ascended, we had a glorious view of the eruption; and the whole scene around us, in its romantic interest and terrible magnificence, mocked all power of description. There were, at this time, five distinct torrents of lava rolling down like streams of molten lead; one of which extended above two miles below us and was flowing towards Portici. The showers of red-hot stones flew up like thousands of sky rockets: many of them being shot up perpendicularly fell back into the crater, others falling on the outside bounded down the side of the mountain with a velocity which would have distanced a horse at full speed: these stones were of every size, from two to ten or twelve feet in diameter.

My ears were by this time wearied and stunned by the unceasing roaring and hissing of the flames, while my eyes were dazzled by the glare of the red, fierce light: now and then I turned them for relief to other features of the picture, to the black shadowy masses of the landscape stretched beneath us, and speckled with shining lights, which showed how many were up and watching that night;

and often to the calm vaulted sky above our heads, where thousands of stars (not twinkling as through our hazy or frosty atmosphere, but shining out of "heaven's profoundest azure," with that soft steady brilliance peculiar to a highly rarified medium) looked down upon this frightful turmoil in all their bright and placid loveliness. Nor should I forget one other feature of a scene, on which I looked with a painter's eye. [Pg 102] Great numbers of the Austrian forces, now occupying Naples, were on the mountains, assembled in groups, some standing, some sitting, some stretched on the ground and wrapped in their cloaks, in various attitudes of amazement and admiration: and as the shadowy glare fell on their tall martial figures and glittering accoutrements, I thought I had never beheld any thing so wildly picturesque.

The remainder of our party not yet appearing, we sent back for our asses and guides, and determined to proceed. About half a mile beyond, our companions came up, and here a division took place; some agreeing to go forward, the rest turning back to wait at the Hermitage. I was of course one of those who advanced. My spirits were again raised, and the grand object of all this daring and anxiety was to approach near enough to a stream of lava to have some idea of its consistency, and the manner in which it flowed, or trickled down. The difficulties of our road now increased, "if *road* that might be called, which road was none," but black loose ashes, and masses of scoria and lava heaped in ridges, or broken into hollows in a manner not to be described. Even my animal, though used to the path, felt his footing at every step, and if the torch was by accident extinguished, he stopped, and nothing could make him move. My guide, Andrea, was very vigilant and attentive, and, in the few words of Italian he knew, encouraged me, and assured me there was no danger. I had, however, no fear: in fact, I was infinitely too much interested to have been alive to danger, had it really existed. Salvador, well known to all who have visited Mount Vesuvius, had been engaged by Mr. R. as his guide. He is the principal cicerone on the mountain. It is his business to despatch to the king every three hours, a regular account of the height of the eruption, the progress, extent, and direction of the lava, and, in short, the most minute particulars. He also corresponds, as he assured me, with Sir Humphry Davy; [L] and is employed to inform him of every interesting phenomenon which takes place on the mountain. This man has resided at the foot of it, and been principal guide, for thirty-three years, and knows every inch of its territory.

As the lava had overflowed the usual footpath leading to that conical eminence which forms the summit of the mountain and the exterior of the crater, we were obliged to alight from our sagacious steeds; and, trusting to our feet, walked over the ashes for about a quarter of a mile. The path, or the ground rather, for there was no path, was now dangerous to the inexperienced foot; and Salvador gallantly took me under his peculiar care. He led me on before the rest, and I followed with confidence. Our object was to reach the edge of a stream [Pg 103] of lava, formed of two currents united in a point. It was glowing with an intense heat; and flowing, not with such rapidity as to alarm us, but rather slowly, and by fits and starts. *Trickling*, in short, is the word which expresses its motion: if one can fancy it applied to any object on so large a scale.

At this time the eruption was at its extreme height. The column of fire was from a quarter to a third of a mile high; and the stones were thrown up to the height of a mile and a quarter. I passed close to a rock about four feet in diameter, which had rolled down some time before: it was still red-hot, and I stopped to warm my hands at it. At a short distance from it lay another stone or rock, also red-hot, but six times the size. I walked on first with Salvador, till we were within a few yards of the lava—at this moment a prodigious stone, followed by two or three smaller ones, came rolling down upon us with terrific velocity. The gentlemen and guides all ran; my first impulse was to run too; but Salvador called on me to stop and see what direction the stone would take. I saw the reason of this advice, and stopped. In less than a second he seized my arm and hurried me back five or six yards. I heard the whizzing sound of the stone as it rushed down behind me. A little further on it met with an impediment, against which it bolted with such force, that it flew up into the air to a great height, and fell in a shower of red-hot fragments. All this passed in a moment; I have shuddered since when I thought of that moment; but at the time, I saw the danger without the slightest sensation of terror. I remember the ridiculous figures of the men, as they scrambled over the ridges of scoria; and was struck by Salvador's exclamation, who shouted to them in a tone which would have become Cæsar himself, — "Che tema! — Sono Salvador!" [M]

We did not attempt to turn back again: which I should have done without any hesitation if any one had proposed it. To have come thus far, and be so near the object I had in view, and then to run away at the first alarm! It was a little provoking. The road was extremely dangerous in the descent. I was obliged to walk part of the way, as the guides advised, and but for Salvador, and the interesting information he gave me from time to time, I think I should have been overpowered. He amused and fixed my attention, by his intelligent conversation, his assiduity, and solicitude for my comfort, and the *naïveté* and self-complacency with which his information was conveyed. He told me he had visited Mount Ætna (*en amateur*) during the last great eruption of that mountain, and acknowledged with laudable candour, that Vesuvius, in its grandest moments, was a mere bonfire in comparison: the whole cone of Vesuvius, he said, was not larger than some [Pg 104] of the masses of rock he had seen whirled from the crater of Mount Ætna, and rolling down its sides. He frequently made me stop and look back: and here I should observe that our guides seemed as proud of the performances of the mountain, and as anxious to show it off to the best advantage, as the keeper of a menagerie is of the tricks of his dancing bear, or the proprietor of "Solomon in all his glory" of his raree-show. Their enthusiastic shouts and exclamations would have kept up my interest had it flagged. "O veda, Signora! O bella! O stupenda!" The last great burst of fire was accompanied by a fresh overflow of lava, which issued from the crater, on the west side, in two broad streams, and united a few hundred feet below, taking the direction of Torre del Greco. After this explosion the eruption subsided, and the mountain seemed to repose: now and then showers of stones flew up, but to no great height, and unaccompanied by any vivid flames. There was a dull red light over the mouth of the crater, round which the smoke rolled in dense tumultuous volumes, and then blew off towards the south-west.

After a slow and difficult descent we reached the Hermitage. I was so exhausted that I was glad to rest for a few minutes. My good friend Salvador brought me a glass of *Lachryma Christi* and the leg of a chicken; and with recruited spirits we mounted our animals and again started.

The descent was infinitely more slow and difficult than the ascent, and much more trying to the nerves. I had not Salvador at my side, nor the mountain before me, to beguile me from my fears; at length I prevailed on one of our attendants, a fine tall figure of a man, to sing to me; and though he had been up the mountain *six* times in the course of the day, he sang delightfully and with great spirit and expression, as he strided along with his hand upon my bridle, accompanied by a magnificent rumbling bass from the mountain, which every now and then drowned the melody of his voice, and made me start. It was past three when we reached Resina, and nearly five when we got home: yet I rose this morning at my usual hour, and do not feel much fatigued. About twelve today I saw Mount Vesuvius, looking as quiet and placid as the first time I viewed it. There was little smoke, and neither the glowing lava nor the flames were visible in the glare of the sunshine. The atmosphere was perfectly clear, and as I gazed, almost misdoubting my senses, I could scarcely believe in the reality of the tremendous scene I had witnessed but a few hours before.

26.—The eruption burst forth again to-day, and is exceedingly grand; though not equal to what it was on Sunday night. The smoke rises from the crater in dense black masses, and the wind having veered a few points to the southward, it is now driven in the direction of Naples. At the moment I write this, the skies are obscured by rolling vapours, and the sun, which is now setting just opposite to [Pg 105] Vesuvius, shines, as I have seen him through a London mist, red, and shorn of his beams. The sea is angry and discoloured; the day most oppressively sultry, and the atmosphere thick, sulphureous, and loaded with an almost impalpable dust, which falls on the paper as I write.

March 4.—We have had delicious weather almost ever since we arrived at Naples, but these last three days have been perfectly heavenly. I never saw or felt any thing like the enchantment of the earth, air, and skies. The mountain has been perfectly still, the atmosphere without a single cloud, the fresh verdure bursting forth all around us, and every breeze visits the senses, as if laden with a renovating spirit of life, and wafted from Elysium. Whoever would truly enjoy nature, should see her in this delicious land: "où la plus douce nuit succède au plus beau jour;" for here she seems to keep holiday all the year round. To stand upon my balcony, looking out upon the sunshine and the glorious bay; the blue sea, and the pure skies—and to feel that indefinite sensation of excitement, that *superflu de vie*, quickening every pulse and thrilling through every nerve, is a pleasure peculiar to this climate, where the mere consciousness of existence is happiness enough. Then evening comes on, lighted by a moon and starry heavens, whose softness, richness, and splendour, are not to be conceived by those who have lived always in the vapoury atmosphere of England—dear England! I love, like an Englishwoman, its fireside enjoyments, and home-felt delights: an English drawing-room, with all its luxurious comforts—carpets and hearth-rugs, curtains let down, sofas wheeled round, and a group of family faces round a blazing fire, is a delightful picture; but for the languid frame, and the sick heart, give me this pure elastic air, "redolent of spring;" this reviving sunshine and all the witchery of these deep blue skies!—

Numbers of people set off post-haste from Rome to see the eruption of Mount Vesuvius, and arrived here Wednesday and Thursday; just time enough to be too late. Among them our Roman friend Frattino, who has afforded me more amusement than all our other acquaintance together, and deserves a niche in my gallery of characters.

Frattino is a young Englishman, who, if he were in England, would probably be pursuing his studies at Eton or Oxford, for he is scarce past the age of boyhood; but having been abroad since he was twelve years old, and early plunged into active and dissipated life, he is an accomplished man of fashion, and of the world, with as many airs and caprices as a spoiled child. He is by far the most *beautiful* creature of his sex I ever saw; so like the Antinous, that at Rome he went by that name. The exquisite regularity of his features, the graceful air of his head, his *antique* curls, the faultless proportions of his elegant figure, make him a *thing* to be gazed on, as one looks at a statue. Then he [Pg 106] possesses talents, wit, taste, and information: the most polished and captivating manners, where he wishes to attract,—high honour and generosity, where women are not concerned,—and all the advantages attending on rank and wealth: but under this fascinating exterior, I suspect our Frattino to be a very worthless, as well as a very unhappy being. While he pleases, he repels me. There is a want of heart about him, a want of fixed principles—a degree of profligacy, of selfishness, of fickleness, caprice and ill-temper, and an excess of vanity, which all his courtly address and *savoir faire* cannot hide. What would be insufferable in another, is in him bearable, and even interesting and amusing: such is the charm of manner. But all this cannot last: and I should not be surprised to see Frattino, a few years hence, emerge from his foreign frippery, throw aside his libertine folly, assume his seat in the senate, and his rank in British society; and be the very character he now affects to despise and ridicule—"a true-bred Englishman, who rides a thorough-bred horse."

Our excursion to Pompeii yesterday was "a pic-nic party of pleasure," *à l'Anglaise*. Now a party of pleasure is proverbially a *bore*: and our expedition was in the beginning so unpromising, so mismanaged—our party so numerous, and composed of such a heterogeneous mixture of opposite tempers, tastes, and characters, that I was in pain for the result. The day, however, turned out more pleasant than I expected: exterior polish supplied the want of something better, and our excursion had its pleasures, though they were not such as I should have sought at Pompeii. I felt myself a simple *unit* among many, and found it easier to sympathise with others, than to make a dozen others sympathise with me.

We were twelve in number, distributed in three light barouches, and reached Pompeii in about two hours and a half—passing by the foot of Vesuvius, through Portici, Torre del Greco, and l'Annonziata. The streams of lava, which overwhelmed Torre del Greco in 1794, are still black and barren; but the town itself is rising from its ruins; and the very lava which destroyed it serves as the material to rebuild it.

We entered Pompeii by the street of the tombs: near them are the semicircular seats, so admirably adapted for conversation, that I wonder we have not sofas on a similar plan, and similar scale. I need not dwell on particulars, which are to be found in every book of travels: on the whole, my expectations were surpassed, though my curiosity was not half gratified.

The most interesting thing I saw—in fact the only thing, for which paintings and descriptions had not previously prepared me, was a building which has been excavated within the last fortnight: it is only partly laid open, and labourers are now at work upon it. Antiquarians [Pg 107] have not yet pronounced on its name and design; but I should imagine it to be some public edifice, perhaps dedicated to religious purposes. The paintings on the walls are the finest which have yet been discovered: they are exquisitely and tastefully designed; and though executed merely for *effect*, that effect is beautiful. I remarked one female figure in the act of entering a half-open door: she is represented with pencils and a palette of colours in her hand, similar to those which artists now use: another very graceful female holds a lyre of peculiar construction. These, I presume, were two of the muses: the rest remained hidden. There were two small pannels occupied by sea-pieces, with gallies; and two charming landscapes, so well coloured, and drawn with such knowledge of perspective and effect, that if we may form a comparative idea of the best pictures, from the specimens of taste and skill in mere house-painting, the ancients must have excelled us as much in painting as in sculpture. I remarked on the wall of an entrance or corridor, a dog starting at a wreathed and crested snake, vividly coloured, and full of spirit and expression. While I lingered here a little behind the rest, and most reluctant to depart, a ragged lazzarone boy came up to me, and seizing my dress, pointed to a corner, and made signs that he had something to show me. I followed him to a spot where a quantity of dust and ashes was piled against a wall. He began to scratch away this heap of dirt with hands and nails, much after the manner of an ape, every now and then looking up in my face and grinning. The impediment being cleared away, there appeared on the wall behind, a most beautiful aërial figure with floating drapery, representing either Fame or Victory: but before I had time to examine it, the little rogue flung the earth up again so as to conceal it completely, then pointing significantly at the other workmen, he nodded, shrugged, gesticulated, and held out both his paws for a recompense, which I gave him willingly; at the same time laughing and shaking my head to show I understood his knavery. I rewarded him apparently beyond his hopes, for he followed me down the street, bowing, grinning, and cutting capers like a young savage.

The streets of Pompeii are narrow, the houses are very small, and the rooms, though often decorated with exquisite taste, are constructed without any regard to what *we* should term comfort and convenience; they are dark, confined, and seldom communicate with each other, but have a general communication with a portico, running round a central court. This court is in general beautifully paved with mosaic, having a fountain or basin in the middle, and possibly answered the purpose of a drawing-room. It is evident that the ancient inhabitants of this lovely country lived like their descendants mostly in the open air, and met together in their public walks, or in the forums, and theatres. If they *saw company*, the guests probably assembled under the porticoes, [Pg 108] or in the court round the fountain. The houses seem constructed on the same principle as birds construct their nests; as places of retreat and shelter, rather than of assemblage and recreation: the grand object was to exclude the sunbeams; and this, which gives such gloomy and chilling ideas in our northern climes, must here have been delicious.

Hurried on by a hungry, noisy, merry party, we at length reached the Caserna (the ancient barracks, or as Forsyth will have it, the prætorium). The central court of this building has been converted into a garden: and here, under a weeping willow, our dinner table was spread. Where Englishmen are, there will be good cheer if possible; and our banquet was in truth most luxurious. Besides more substantial cates, we had oysters from Lake Lucrine, and classically excellent they were; London bottled porter, and half a dozen different kinds of wine. Our dinner went off most gaily, but no order was kept afterwards: the purpose of our expedition seemed to be forgotten in general mirth: many witty things were said and done, and many merry ones, and not a few silly ones. We visited the beautiful public walk and the platform of the old temple of Hercules (I call it *old*, because it was a ruin when Pompeii was entire); the Temple of Isis, the Theatres, the Forum, the Basilica, the Amphitheatre, which is in a perfect state of preservation, and more elliptical in form than any of those I have yet seen, and the School of Eloquence, where R** mounted the rostrum, and gave us an oration extempore, equally pithy, classical and comical. About sunset we got into the carriages, and returned to Naples.

Of all the heavenly days we have had since we came to Naples, this has been the most heavenly: and of all the lovely scenes I have beheld in Italy, what I saw to-day has most enchanted my senses and imagination. The view from the eminence on which the old temple stood, and which was anciently the public promenade, was splendidly beautiful, the whole landscape was at one time overflowed with light and sunshine, and appeared as if seen through an impalpable but dazzling veil. Towards evening the outlines became more distinct: the little white towns perched upon the hills, the gentle sea, the fairy island of Rivegliano with its old tower, the smoking crater of Vesuvius, the bold forms of Mount Lactarius and Cape Minerva, stood out full and clear under the cloudless sky: as we returned, I saw the sun sink behind Capri, which appeared by some optical illusion like a glorious crimson transparency suspended above the horizon: the sky, the earth, the sea, were flushed with the richest rose colour, which gradually softened and darkened into purple: the short twilight faded away, and the full moon, rising over Vesuvius, lighted up the scenery with a softer radiance.

Thus ended a day which was not without its pleasures: – yet had I planned a party of pleasure to Pompeii, methinks I could have [Pg 109] managed better. *Par exemple,* I would have deferred it a fortnight later, or till the vines were in leaf; I would have chosen for my companions two or at most three persons whom I could name, whose cultivated minds and happy tempers would have heightened their own enjoyment and mine. After spending a few hours in taking a general view of the whole city, we would have sat down on the platform of the old Greek Temple which commands a view of the mountains and the bay; or, if the heat were too powerful, under the shade of the hill near it. There we would make our cheerful and elegant repast, on bread and fruits, and perhaps a bottle of Malvoisie or Champagne: the rest of the day should be devoted to a minute examination of the principal objects of interest and curiosity: we would wait till the shadows of evening had begun to steal over the scene, purpling the mountains and the sea; we would linger there to enjoy all the splendours of an Italian sunset; and then, with minds softened and elevated by the loveliness and solemnity of the scenes around, we would get into our carriage, and drive back to Naples beneath the bright full moon; and, by the way, we would "talk the flowing heart," and make our recollections of the olden time, our deep impressions of the past, heighten our enjoyment of the present: and this would be indeed a day of *pleasure*, of such pleasure as I think I am capable of feeling—of imparting—of remembering with unmixed delight. Such was *not* yesterday.

M** brought with him this evening, for our amusement, an old man, a native of Cento, who gains his livelihood by a curious exhibition of his peculiar talents. He is blind, and plays well on the violin: he can recite the whole of the Gerusalemme from beginning to end without missing a word: he can repeat any given stanza or number of stanzas either forwards or backwards: he can repeat the last words one after another of any stanzas: if you give him the first word and the last, he can name immediately the particular line, stanza, and book: lastly, he can tell instantly the exact number of words contained in any given stanza. This exhibition was at first amusing; but as I soon found that the man's head was a mere machine, that he was destitute of imagination, and that far from feeling the beauty of the poet, he did not even understand the meaning of the lines he thus repeated up and down, and backwards and forwards, it ceased to interest me after the first sensations of surprise and curiosity were over.

After I had read Italian with Signior B** this evening, he amused me exceedingly by detailing to me the plan of two tragedies he is now writing or about to write. He has already produced one piece on the story of Boadicea, which is rather a drama than a regular tragedy. [Pg 110] It was acted here with great success. After giving his drama due praise, I described to him the plan and characters of Fletcher's Bonduca; and attempted to give him in Italian some idea of the most striking scenes of that admirable play: he was alternately in enchantment and despair, and I thought he would have torn and bitten his Boadicea to pieces, in the excess of his vivacity.

The subject of one of his tragedies is to be the Sicilian Vespers. Casimir Delavigne, who wrote *Les Vêpres Siciliennes*, which obtained some years ago such amazing popularity at Paris, and in which the national vanity of the French is flattered at the expense of the Italians, received a pension from Louis XVIII. B** spoke with contempt of Casimir Delavigne's tragedy, and with indignation of what he called "his wilful misrepresentation of history." He is determined to give the reverse of the picture: the French will be represented as "*gente crudeli—tiranni—oppressori, senza fede;*" Giovanni di Procida, as a hero and patriot, *à l'antique,* and the Sicilians as rising in defence of their freedom and national honour. The other tragedy is to be founded on the history of the famous *Congiura dei Baroni* in the reign of Ferdinand the First, as related by Giannone. The simple facts of this history need not any ornaments, borrowed from invention or poetry, to form a most interesting tale, and furnish ample materials for a beautiful tragedy, in incident, characters, and situations. B** is a little man, dwarfish and almost deformed in person; but full of talent, spirit, and enthusiasm. I asked him why he did not immediately finish these tragedies, which appeared from the sketches he had given me, so admirably calculated to succeed. He replied, that under the present regime, he dared not write up to his own conceptions; and if he curbed his genius, he could do nothing; "Besides," added he mournfully, "I have no time; I am poor—poverissimo! I must work hard all to-day to supply the wants of to-morrow: I am always surveillé by the police, as a known liberal and *literato.*" "*Davvero,*" added he, gaily, "I would soon do, or say, or write something to attract the honour of their more particular notice, if I could be certain they would only imprison me for a couple of years, and ensure me during that time a blanket, bread and water, and the use of pen and ink: then I would write! I would write! *dalla mattina alla sera*; and thank my gaolers as my best friends: but pens are poignards, ink is poison in the eyes of the present government; imprisonment for life, or banishment, is the least I could expect. Now the mere idea of imprisonment for life would kill me in a week, and banishment!—*Ah lungi dallá mia bella Patria, come cantare! come scrivere! come vivere! moriro io anzi nell' momento di partire!*"

[Pg 111]

I drove to-day, tête-à-tête with Laura, to the Lago d'Agnano, about a mile and a half beyond Pausilippo. This lovely fair lake is not more than two miles in circuit; and embosomed in romantic woody hills: innumerable flocks of wild fowl were skimming over its surface, and gave life and motion to the beautiful but quiet landscape. While we were wandering here, enjoying the stillness and solitude, so delightfully contrasted with the unceasing noise, bustle, and crowd of the city, the charm was rudely broken by the appearance of the king; who, attended by a numerous party of his guards and huntsmen, had been wild boar shooting in the neighbouring woods. The waterfowl, scared by the report of fire arms, speedily disappeared, and the guards shouted to each other, and galloped round the smooth sloping banks; cutting up the turf with their horses' hoofs, and deforming the whole scene with uproar, confusion, and affright. Devoutly did I wish them all twenty miles off. The famous Grotto del Cane is on the south bank of the lake, a few yards from the edge of the water. We saw the torch, when held in the vapour, instantaneously extinguished. The ground all around the entrance of the grotto is hot to the touch; and when I plunged my hand into the deleterious gas, which rises about a foot, or a foot and a half, above the surface of the ground, it was so warm I was glad to withdraw it. The disagreeable old woman who showed us this place, brought with her a wretched dog with a rope round his neck, bleared eyes, thin ribs, and altogether of a most pitiful aspect. She was most anxious to exhibit the common but cruel experiment of suspended animation, by holding his head over the mephitic vapour, insisting that he was accustomed to it, and even liked it; of course, we would not suffer it. The poor animal made no resistance; only drooped his head, and put his tail between his legs, when his tyrant attempted to seize him.

Though now so soft, so lovely, and so tranquil, the Lago d'Agnano owes its existence to some terrible convulsion of the elements. The basin is the crater of a sunken volcano, which, bursting forth here, swallowed up a whole city. And the whole region round, bears evident marks of its volcanic origin.

This morning we visited several churches, not one of them worthy of a remark. The architecture is invariably in the vilest taste; and the interior decorations, if possible, still worse: white-washing gilding, and gaudy colours, every where prevail. We saw, however, some good pictures. At the San Gennaro are the famous frescos of Domenichino and Lanfranco: the church itself is hideous. At the Girolomini there is no want of magnificence and ornament; but a barbarous misapplication of both, as usual. The church of the convent of Santa Chiara was painted in fresco by Ghiotto: it is now white-washed [Pg 112] all over. At this church, which I first visited during the merry days of the carnival, I saw a large figure of our Saviour suspended on the cross, dressed in a crimson domino, and blue sash. To what a pitch, thought I, must the love of white-washing and masquerading be carried in this strange city, where the Deity himself is burlesqued, and bad taste is carried to profanation! To-day I saw the same crucifix in a suit of mourning; why should not our South Sea missionaries come and preach here?

The church of San Severo is falling to ruins, owing to some defect in the architecture. It is only remarkable for containing three celebrated statues. The man enveloped in a net, and the Pudicità draped from head to foot, pleased me only as specimens of the patience and ingenuity of the sculptor. The dead Christ covered with a veil, by Corradini, has a merit of a higher class: it is most painful to look upon; and affected me so strongly, that I was obliged to leave the church, and go into the air.

I went to-day with two agreeable and intelligent friends, to take leave of the Studeo and the Museum. I have often resolved not to make my little journal a mere catalogue of objects, which are to be found in my pocket guide, and bought for a few pence; but I cannot resist the temptation of making a few notes of admiration, and commemoration, for my own peculiar use.

The Gallery of Painting contains few pictures; but among them are some master-pieces. The St. John of Leonardo da Vinci (exquisite as it is, considered as a mere painting), provoked me. I am sick of his eternal simpering face: the aspect is that of a Ganymede or a young Bacchus; and if instead of *Ecce Agnus Dei*, they had written over it, *Ecce vinum bonum*, all would have been in character.

How I coveted the beautiful "Carità," the Capo d'Opera of Schidone!—and next to it, Parmegiano's Gouvernante—a delicious picture. A portrait of Columbus, said to be by the same master, is not like him, I am sure; for the physiognomy is vacant and disagreeable. Domenichino's large picture of the Angel shielding Innocence from a Demon pleases me, as all his pictures do—but not perfectly: the devil in the corner, with his fork, and hoofs, and horns, shocks my taste as a ludicrous and vulgar idea, far removed from poetry; but the figure of the angel stretching a shield over the infant, is charming. There are also two fine Claudes, two Holy Families, by Raffaelle, in his sweetest style; and one by Correggio, scarcely less beautiful.

The Gallery of Sculpture is so rich in chef-d'œuvres, that to particularise would be a vain attempt. Passing over those which every one knows by heart, the statue of Aristides struck me most. It was found in Herculaneum; and is marked with ferruginous stains, as if by the action of fire or the burning lava; but it is otherwise uninjured, [Pg 113] and the grave, yet graceful simplicity of the figure and attitude, and the extreme elegance of the drapery, are truly Grecian. It is the union of *power* with *repose*—of perfect *grace* with perfect *simplicity*, which distinguishes the ancient from the modern style of sculpture. The sitting Agrippina, for example, furnished Canova with the model for his statue of Madame Letitia—the two statues are, in point of fact, nearly the same, except that Canova has turned Madame Letitia's head a little on one side; and by this single and trifling alteration has destroyed that quiet and beautiful simplicity which distinguishes the original, and given his statue at once a modern air.

The Flora Farnese is badly placed, in a space too confined for its size, and too near the eye; so that the exquisite harmony and delicacy of the figure are partly lost in its colossal proportions: it should be placed at the end of a long gallery or vista.

There is here a statue of Nero when he was ten years old; from which it would seem that he was not by nature the monster he afterwards became. The features are beautiful; and the expression all candour and sweetness.

One statue struck me exceedingly—not by the choice of the subject, nor the beauty of the workmanship, but from its wonderful force of expression. It is a dying gladiator; but very different from the gladiator of the Capitol. The latter declines gradually, and sickens into death; but memory and feeling are not yet extinct: and what thoughts may pass through that brain while life is thus languishing away! what emotions may yet dwell upon the last beatings of that heart! it is the *sentiment* which gives such profound pathos to that matchless statue: but the gladiator of the Studii has only physical expression: it is sudden death in all its horrors: the figure is still erect, though the mortal blow has been given; the sword has dropt from the powerless hand; the limbs are stiffening in death; the eyes are glazed; the features fixed in an expression of mortal agony; and in another moment you expect the figure to fall at your feet.

The Venus, the Hercules, the Atlas, the Antinous (not equal to that in the Capitol,) the Ganymede, the Apollo, the equestrian statues of the two Balbi, etc. are all familiar to my imagination, from the numerous copies and models I have seen: but the most interesting department of the Museum is the collection of antiques from Herculaneum and Pompeii, which have lately been removed hither from Portici. One room contains specimens of cooking utensils, portable kitchens, tripods, instruments of sacrifice, small bronze Lares, and Penates, urns, lamps, and candelabras of the most elegant forms, and the most exquisite workmanship. Another room contains specimens of ancient armour, children's toys, etc. I remarked here a helmet which I imagine formed part of a trophy; or at least was intended for ornament rather [Pg 114] than use. It is exceedingly heavy; and on it is represented in the most exquisite relievo the War of Troy. Benvenuto Cellini himself never produced any thing equal to the chased work on this helmet.

In a third room is the paraphernalia of a lady's toilette: mirrors of different sizes, fragments of combs, a small crystal box of rouge, etc. Then follow flutes and pipes, all carved out of bone, surgical instruments, moulds for pastry, sculptors' tools, locks and keys, bells, etc.

The room containing the antique glass, astonished me more than any thing else. I knew that glass was an ancient invention: but I thought that its application to domestic purposes was of modern date. Here I found window panes, taken from the Villa of Diomed at Pompeii; bottles of every size and form, white and coloured; pitchers and vases; necklaces; imitations of gems, etc.

There is a little jeu d'esprit of Voltaire's "La Toilette de Madame de Pompadour," in which he wittily exalts the moderns above the ancients, and ridicules their ignorance of the luxuries and comforts of life: but Voltaire had not seen the museum of Portici. We can add few distinct articles to the list of comforts and luxuries it contains:

though it must be confessed that we have improved upon them, and varied them *ad infinitum*. In those departments of the mechanics which are in any way connected with the fine arts, the ancients appear to have attained perfection. To them belongs the invention of all that embellishes life, of all the graceful forms of imitative art, varied with such exquisite taste, such boundless fertility of fancy, that nothing is left to us but to refine upon their ideas, and copy their creations. With all our new invented machines, and engines, we can do little more than what the ancients performed without them.

I ought not to forget one room containing some objects, more curious and amusing than beautiful, principally from Pompeii, such as loaves of bread, reduced to a black cinder, figs in the same state, grain of different kinds, colours from a painter's room, ear-rings and bracelets, gems, specimens of mosaic, etc. etc.

March 7.—Frattinto brought me to-day the last numbers of the Edinburgh and Quarterly Reviews: a great treat so far from home. Both contain some clever essays: among them, an article on prisons, in the Edinburgh, interested me most.

Methinks these two Reviews stalk through the literary world, like the two giants in Pulci's Morgante Maggiore: the one pounding, slaying, mangling, despoiling with blind fury, like the heavy orthodox club-armed Morgante; the other, like the sneering, witty, half-pagan, half-baptized Margutte, slashing and cutting, and piercing through thick and thin; *à tort et à travers*. Truly the simile is more à-propos than I thought when it first occurred to me. [Pg 115]

I went the other day to a circulating library and reading-room kept here by a little cross French-woman, and asked to see a catalogue. She showed me, first, a list of all the books, Italian, French, and English, she was allowed to keep and sell: it was a thin pamphlet of about one hundred pages. She then showed me the catalogue of prohibited books, which was at least as thick as a good sized octavo. The book to which I wished to refer, was the second volume of Robertson's Charles the Fifth. After some hesitation, Madame P** led me into a back room; and opening a sliding pannel, discovered a shelf let into the wall, on which were arranged a number of authors, chiefly English and French. I was not surprised to find Rousseau and Voltaire among them; but am still at a loss to guess what Robertson has done or written to entitle him to a place in such select company.

8th.—Forsyth might well say that Naples has no parallel on earth. Viewed from the sea it appears like an amphitheatre of palaces, temples and castles, raised one above another, by the wand of a necromancer: viewed within, Naples gives me the idea of a vast Bartholomew fair. No street in London is ever so crowded as I have seen the streets of Naples. It is a crowd which has no pause or cessation: early in the morning, late at night, it is ever the same. The whole population seems poured into the streets and squares; all business and amusement is carried on in the open air: all those minute details of domestic life, which, in England, are confined within the sacred precincts of *home*, are here displayed to public view. Here people buy and sell, and work, wash, wring, brew, bake, fry, dress, eat, drink, sleep, etc. etc. all in the open streets. We see every hour, such comical, indescribable appalling sights; such strange figures, such wild physiognomies, picturesque dresses, attitudes and groups—and eyes—no! I never saw such eyes before, as I saw today, half languor and half fire, in the head of a ruffian Lazzarone, and a ragged Calabrian beggar girl. They would have *embrâsé* half London or Paris.

I know not whether it be incipient illness, or the enervating effects of this soft climate, but I feel unusually weak, and the least exertion or excitement is not only disagreeable but painful. While the rest were at Capo di Monte, I stood upon my balcony looking out upon the lovely scene before me, with a kind of pensive dreamy rapture, which if not quite pleasure, had at least a power to banish pain: and thus hours passed away insensibly—

"As if the moving time had been
A thing as stedfast as the scene,
On which we gazed ourselves away." [N]

[Pg 116]

All my activity of mind, all my faculties of thought and feeling and suffering, seemed lost and swallowed up in an indolent delicious reverie, a sort of vague and languid enjoyment, the true "*dolce far niente*" of this enchanting climate. I stood so long leaning on my elbow without moving, that my arm has been stiff all day in consequence.

"How I wish," said I this evening, when they drew aside the curtain, that I might view the sunset from my sofa, and sky, earth and ocean, seemed to commingle in floods of glorious light—"how I wish I could transport those skies to England!" *Cruelle!* exclaimed an Italian behind me, *ôtez-nous notre beau ciel, tout est perdu pour nous.*

THE LAST EVENING AT NAPLES

Yes, Laura! draw the shade aside
And let me gaze—while yet I may,
Upon that gently heaving tide,
Upon that glorious sun-lit bay.

Land of Romance! enchanting shore!
Fair scenes, near which I linger yet!
Never shall I behold ye more,
Never this last—last look forget!

What though the clouds that o'er me lour
Have tinged ye with a mournful hue,
Deep in my heart I felt your power,
And bless ye, while I sigh—Adieu!

Velletri, March 13.—It is now a week since I opened my little book. Ever since the 9th I have been seriously ill: and yesterday morning I left Naples still low and much indisposed, but glad of a change which should substitute any external excitement, however painful, to that unutterable dying away of the heart and paralysis of the mind which I have suffered for some days past. When we turned into the Strada Chiaja, and I gave a last glance at the magnificent bay and the shores all resplendent with golden light, I could almost have exclaimed like Eve, "must I then leave thee, Paradise!" and dropped a few natural tears—tears of weakness, rather than of grief: for what do I leave behind me worthy one emotion of regret? Even at Naples, even in this all-lovely land, "fit haunt for gods," has it not been with me as it has been elsewhere? as long as the excitement of change and novelty lasts, my heart can turn from itself "to luxuriate with indifferent things:" but it cannot last long; and when it is over, I suffer, I am ill: the past returns with tenfold gloom; interposing like a dark shade between me and every object: an evil power seems to [Pg 117] reside in every thing I see, to torment me with painful associations, to perplex my faculties, to irritate and mock me with the perception of what is lost to me: the very sunshine sickens me, and I am forced to confess myself weak and miserable as ever. O time! how slowly you move! how little you can do for me! and how bitter is that sorrow which has no relief to hope but from time alone!

Last night we reached Mola di Gaëta, which looked even more beautiful than before, in the eyes of all but *one*, whose senses were blinded and dulled by dejection, lassitude, and sickness. When I felt myself passively led along the shore, placed where the eye might range at freedom over the living and rejoicing landscape—when I heard myself repeating mechanically the exclamations of others, and felt no ray of beauty, no sense of pleasure penetrate to my heart—shall I own, even to myself, the mixture of anguish and terror with which I shrunk back, conscious of the waste within me? The conviction that now it was all over, that the last and only pleasures hitherto left to me had perished, that my mind was contracted by the selfishness of despondency, and my quick spirit of enjoyment utterly subdued into apathy, gave me for a moment a pang sharper than if a keen knife had cut me to the quick; and then I relapsed into a kind of torpid languor of mind and frame, which I thought was resignation, and as such indulged it.

From my bed this morning I stepped out upon my balcony just as the sun was rising. I wished to convince myself whether the beauty on which I had lately looked with such admiration and delight, had indeed lost all power to touch my heart. The impression made upon my mind at that instant I can only compare to the rolling away of a palpable and suffocating cloud: every thing on which I looked had the freshness and brightness of novelty: a glory beyond its own was again diffused over the enchanting scene from the stores of my own imagination: the sea breeze which blew against my temples new-strung every nerve; and I left Mola with a heart so lightened and so grateful, that not for hours afterwards, not till fatigue and hurry had again wearied down my spirits, did that impression of happy thankfulness pass away.

I am sensible I owed this sudden renovation of health solely to the contemplation of Nature; and a true feeling for all the "maggior pompa" she has poured forth over this glorious region. The shores of Terracina, the azure sea, dancing in the breeze, the waves rolling to our feet, the sublime cliffs, the fleet of forty sail stretching away till lost in the blaze of the horizon, the Circean promontory, even the picturesque fisherman, whom we saw throwing his nets from an insulated rock at some distance from the shore, and whom a very trifling exertion of fancy might have converted into some sea divinity, a Glaucus, [Pg 118] or a Proteus, formed altogether a picture of the most wonderful and luxuriant beauty. In England there is a peculiar charm in the soft aërial perspective, which even in the broadest glare of noonday, blends and masses the forms of the distant landscape; and in that mingling of colours into a cool neutral gray tint so grateful to the eye. Hence it has happened that in some of the Italian pictures I have seen in England, I have often been struck by what appeared to me a violence in the colouring, and a sharp decision in the outline, o'erstepping the modesty of nature—that is, of *English nature*: but there is in this climate a prismatic splendour of tint, a glorious all-embracing light, a vivid distinctness of outline, something in the reality more gorgeous, glowing, and luxuriant, than poetry could dare to express, or painting imitate.

> "Ah that such beauty, varying in the light
> Of living nature, cannot be portrayed
> By words, nor by the pencil's silent skill;
> But is the property of those alone
> Who have beheld it, noted it with care,
> And in their minds recorded it with love."

Wordsworth.

And now we have left the enchanting south; myrtle-hedges, palm-trees, orange-groves, bright Mediterranean, all adieu! How, under other circumstances, should I regret you, with what reluctance should I leave you, thus half explored, half enjoyed! but now other thoughts engross me, the hard struggle to overcome myself, or at least to appear the thing I am not.— —

Man has done what he can to deform this lovely region. The most horrible places we have yet met with are Itri and Fondi, which look like recesses of depravity and dirt, and the houses more like the dens and kennels of wild beasts, than the habitations of civilized human beings. In fact, the populace of these towns consists chiefly of the families of the briganti. The women we saw here were bold coarse Amazons; and the few men who appeared had a slouching gait, and looked at us from under their eyebrows with an expression at once cunning and fierce. We met many begging friars—horrible specimens of their species: altogether I never beheld such a desperate set of canaille as appear to have congregated in these two wretched towns.

At Mola I remarked several beautiful women. Their head-dress is singularly graceful: the hair being plaited round the back of the head, and there fastened with two silver pins, much in the manner of some of the ancient statues. The costume of the peasantry, there, and all the way to Rome, is very striking and picturesque. I remember one woman whom I saw standing at her door spinning with her distaff: [Pg 119] her long black hair, floating down from its confinement, was spread over her shoulders; not hanging in a dishevelled and slovenly style, but in the most rich and luxuriant tresses. Her attitude as she stood suspending her work to gaze at *me*, as I gazed at her with open admiration, was graceful and dignified; and her form and features would have been a model for a Juno or a Minerva. [O]

LINES.

Quenched is our light of youth!
And fled our days of pleasure,

When all was hope and truth,
And trusting—without measure.

Blindly we believed
Words of fondness spoken—
Cruel hearts deceived,
So our peace was broken!

What can charm us more?
Life hath lost its sweetness!
Weary lags the hour—
"Time hath lost its fleetness!"

As the buds in May
Were the joys we cherished,
Sweet—but frail as they,
Thus they passed and perished!

And the few bright hours
Wintry age can number,
Sickly, senseless flowers,
Lingering through December!

Rome, March 15.—We arrived here yesterday morning about one, after a short but delightful journey from Velletri. We have now a suite of apartments in the Hotel d'Europe; and our accommodations are in all respects excellent, almost equal to Schneiderf's at Florence.

On entering Rome through the gate of the Lateran, I was struck by the emptiness and stillness of the streets, contrasted with those of Naples; and still more by the architectural grandeur and beauty which everywhere met the eye. This is as it should be: the merry, noisy, half-naked, merry-andrew set of ragamuffins which crowd the streets and shores of Naples, would strangely misbecome the desolate majesty [Pg 120] of the "Eternal City." Though we now reside in the most fashionable and frequented part of Rome, the sound of carts and carriages is seldom heard. After nine in the evening a profound stillness reigns; and I distinguish nothing from my window but the splashing of the Fountain della Barchetta.

The weather is lovely; we were obliged to close our Venetian blinds against the heat at eight this morning, and afterwards we drove to the gardens of the Villa Borghese, where we wandered about in search of coolness and shade.

26.—I must now descend to the common occurrences of our every-day life.

For the last week we have generally spent the whole or part of the morning, in some of the galleries of art; and the afternoon in the gardens of the neighbouring villas. Those of the Villa Medici have their vicinity to our inn, and their fine air to recommend them. From the Villa Lanti, and the Monte Mario, we have a splendid view of the whole city and Campagna of Rome. The Pope's gardens on the Monte Cavallo, are pleasant, accessible, and very private: the gardens of the Villa Pamfili, are enchanting; but our usual haunt is the garden of the Villa Borghese. In this delightful spot we find shade and privacy, or sunshine and society, as we may feel inclined. To-day it was intensely hot; but we found the cool sequestered walks and alleys of cypress and ilex, perfectly delicious. I spread my shawl upon a green bank carpeted with violets, and lounged in most luxurious indolence. I had a book with me, but felt no inclination to read. The soft air, the trickling and murmuring of innumerable fountains, the urns, the temples, the statues—the localities of the scene—all dispose the mind to a kind of vague but delightful reverie to which we "find no end, in wandering mazes lost."

In these gardens we frequently meet the Princess Pauline: sometimes alone, but oftener surrounded by a cortège of beaux. She is no longer the "Venere Vincitrice" of Canova; but her face, though faded, is pretty and intelligent; and she still preserves the "andar celeste," and all the distinguished elegance of her petite and graceful figure. Of the stories told of her, I suppose one half *may* be true—and that half is quite enough. She is rather more famous for her gallantries, than for her bon-gout in the choice of her favourites; but it is justice to Pauline to add, that her native benevolence of heart seems to have survived all her frailties; and every one who speaks of her here, even those who must condemn her, mention her in a tone of kindness, and even of respect. She is still in deep mourning for the Emperor.

The Villa Pamfili is about two miles from Rome on the other side of the Monte Gianicolo. The gardens are laid out in the artificial style [Pg 121] of Italian gardening, a style which in England would horrify me as in the vilest and most old-fashioned taste—stiff, cold, unnatural, and altogether detestable. Through what inconsistency or perversity of taste is it then, that I am enchanted with the fantastic elegance, and the picturesque gaiety of the Pamfili gardens; where sportive art revels and runs wild amid the luxuriance of nature? Or is it, as I would rather believe, because these long arcades of verdure, these close *walls* of laurel, pervious to the air, but impervious to the sunshine, these broad umbrageous avenues and marble terraces, these paved grottoes and ever trickling fountains, these gods and nymphs, and urns and sarcophagi, meeting us at every turn with some classical or poetical association, harmonize with the climate and the country, and the minds of the people; and are *comfortable* and consistent as a well carpeted drawing-room and a warm chimney-corner would be in England?

"But it is all so artificial and unnatural"—Agreed;—so are our yellow unsheltered gravel walks, meandering through smooth shaven lawns, which have no other beauty than that of being dry when every other place is wet; our shapeless flower-beds so elaborately irregular, our clumps and dots of trees, and dwarfish shrubberies. I have seen some over-dressed grounds and gardens in England, the perpetrations of Capability Brown and his imitators, the landscape gardeners, quite as bad as any thing I see here, only in a different style, and certainly more adapted to England and English taste. I must confess, that in these enchanting gardens of the Villa Pamfili, a little less "ingenuity and artifice" would be better. I hate *mere* tricks and gimcrackery, of which there are a few instances, such as their hydraulic music, jets-d'eau—water-works that play occasionally to the astonishment of children and the profit of the gardeners—but how different, after all, are these Italia gardens to the miserable grandeur, and senseless, tasteless parade of Versailles!

In these gardens an interesting discovery has just been made; an extensive burial place, or columbarium, in singular preservation. The skeletons and ashes have not been removed. Some of the tombs are painted in fresco, others floored with very pretty mosaic. The disposition of the urns is curious: they are imbedded in the masonry of the wall with moveable lids. On a tile I found the name of Sextus Pompeius, in letters beautifully formed, and deeply and distinctly cut, and an inscription which I was not Latinist enough to translate accurately, but from which it appears that these columbaria belonged to a branch of the Pompey family.

27.—To-day, after English chapel, I look a walk to the San Gregorio, on the other side of the Palatine, which since I first came to Rome has been to me a favourite and chosen spot. I sat down on the steps of the church to rest, and enjoy at leisure the fine view of the [Pg 122] hill and ruins opposite. Arches on arches, a wilderness of desolation! and mingled with massive fragments of the halls and towers of the Cæsars, were young shrubs just putting on their brightest green, and the almond-trees covered with their gay blossoms, and the cloudless and resplendent skies bending over all.

I tried to sketch the scene before me, but could not form a stroke. I cannot now take a short walk without feeling its ill effects; and my hand shook so much from nervous weakness, that after a few vain efforts to steady it, I sorrowfully gave up the attempt. On returning home by the Coliseum, and through the Forum and Capitol, I met many things I should wish to remember. After all, what place is like Rome, where it is impossible to move a step without meeting with some incident or object to excite reflection, to enchant the eye, or interest the imagination? Rome may yield to Naples or Florence in mere external beauty; but every other spot on earth, Athens perhaps alone excepted, must yield to Rome in interest.

28.—This morning we walked down to the studio of Mr. Wagenal, to see the Ægina marbles; which, as objects of curiosity, interested me extremely. These statues are on a smaller scale than I expected, being not much more than half the size of life, but of better workmanship, and in a style of sculpture altogether different from any thing I ever saw before. They formed the ornaments of the pediment of the Temple of Jupiter in the island of Ægina, and represented a group of fighting and dying warriors, with an armed Pallas in the centre: but the subject is not known.

The execution of these statues must evidently be referred to the earliest ages of Grecian art; to a period when sculpture was confined to the exact imitation of natural forms. Several of the figures were extremely spirited, and very correct both in design and execution; but there is no attempt at grace, and a total deficiency of ideal beauty: in the Pallas, especially, the drapery and forms are but one remove from the cold formal Etruscan style, which in its turn is but one remove from the yet more tasteless Egyptian. I think it was at the Villa Albani, I saw the singular Etruscan basso-relievo which I was able to compare mentally with what I saw to-day; and the resemblance in *manner* struck me immediately. Thorwaldson is now restoring these marbles in the most admirable style for the King of Bavaria, to whom they were sold by Messrs. Cockerel and Linkh (the original discoverers) for 8000*l*.

Gibson, the celebrated English sculptor, joined us while looking at the Ægina marbles, and accompanied us to the studio of Pozzi, the Florentine statuary. Here I saw several instances of that affected and meretricious taste which prevails too much among the foreign sculptors. [Pg 123] I remember one example almost ludicrous, a female Satyr with her hair turned up behind and dressed in the last Parisian fashion; as if she had just come from under the hands of Monsieur Hyppolite. By the same hand which committed this odd solecism, I saw a statue of Moses, now modelling in clay, which, if finished in marble in a style worthy of its conception, and if not spoiled by some affected niceties in the execution, will be a magnificent and sublime work of art.

Gibson afterwards showed us round his own studio: his exquisite group of Psyche borne away by the Zephyrs enchanted me. The necessity which exists for supporting all the figures has rendered it impossible to give them the same aërial lightness I have seen in paintings of the same subject, yet they are all *but* aërial. Psyche was criticised by two or three of our party; but I thought her faultless: she is a lovely timid girl; and as she leans on her airy supporters, she seems to contemplate her flight down the precipice, half-shrinking, though secure. Mr. W** told me that in the original design, the left foot of one of the Zephyrs rested upon the ground: and that Canova, coming in by chance while Gibson was working on the model, lifted it up, and this simple and masterly alteration has imparted the most exquisite lightness to the attitude.

Gibson was Canova's favourite pupil: he has quite the air of a genius: plain features, but a countenance all beaming with fire, spirit, and intelligence. His Psyche remains still in the model, as he has not yet found a patron munificent enough to order it in marble; at which I greatly wonder. Could I but afford to bestow seven hundred pounds on my own gratification, I would have given him the order on the spot. [P]

30.—Yesterday we dined *al fresco* in the Pamfili gardens: and though our party was rather too large, it was well assorted, and the day went off admirably. The queen of our feast was in high good humour, and irresistible in charms; Frattino very fascinating, T** was caustic and witty, W** lively and clever, Sir J** mild, intelligent, and elegant, V**, as usual, quiet, sensible, and self-complacent, L** as absurd and assiduous as ever. Every body played their part well, each by a tacit convention sacrificing to the *amour propre* of the rest. Every individual really occupied with his own particular *rôle*, but all apparently happy, and mutually pleased. Vanity and selfishness, indifference and ennui, were veiled under a general mask of good humour and good breeding, and the flowery bonds of politeness and gallantry held together those who knew no common tie of thought or interest; and when parted (as they soon will be, north, south, east, [Pg 124] and west), will probably never meet again in this world; and whether they do or not, who thinks or cares!

Our luxurious dinner, washed down by a competent proportion of Malvoisie and Champagne, were spread upon the grass, which was literally *flowery turf*, being covered with violets, iris, and anemones of every dye. Instead of changing our plates, we washed them in a beautiful fountain which murmured near us, having first, by a libation, propitiated the presiding nymph for this pollution of her limpid waters. For my own peculiar taste there were too many servants (who on these occasions are always *de trop*), too many luxuries, too much fuss; but considering the style and number of our party, it was all consistently and admirably managed: the grouping of the company, picturesque because unpremeditated, the scenery round, the arcades, and bowers, and columns, and fountains, had an air altogether quite poetical and romantic; and put me in mind of some of Watteau's beautiful garden-pieces, and Stothard's fêtes-champêtres.

To me the day was not a day of pleasure; for the small stock of strength and spirits with which I set out was soon exhausted, and the rest of the day was wasted in efforts to appear cheerful and support myself to the end, lest I should spoil the general mirth: on all I looked with complacency tinged with my habitual melancholy. What I most admired was the delicious view, from an eminence in the wildest part of the gardens, over the city and Campagna to the blue Apennines, where Frascati and Albano peeped forth like nests of white buildings glittering upon a rich back ground, tinted with blue and purple; the hill where Cato's villa stood, and still called the Portian Hill, and on the highest point the ruined temple of Jupiter Latialis visible at the distance of seventeen miles, and shining in the setting sun like burnished gold. What I most felt and enjoyed was the luxurious temperature of the atmosphere, the purity and brilliance of the skies, the delicious security with which I threw myself down on the turf without fear of damp and cold, and the thankful consciousness, that neither the light or worldly beings round me, nor the sadness which weighed down my own heart, had quite deadened my once quick sense of pleasure, but left me still some perception of the splendour and classical interest of the glorious scenes around me, combined as it was with all the enchantment of natural beauty—

> "— —The music and the bloom
> And all the mighty ravishment of spring."

[Pg 125]

TOLSE AI MARTIRI OGNI CONFIN, CHI AL CORE TOGLIER POTEO LA LIBERTA DEL PIANTO!

O ye blue luxurious skies!
Sparkling fountains,
Snow-capp'd mountains,
Classic shades that round me rise!

Towers and temples, hills and groves,
Scenes of glory,
Fam'd in story,
Where the eye enchanted roves!

O thou rich embroider'd earth!
Opening flowers,
Leafy bowers,
Sights of gladness, sounds of mirth!

Why to my desponding heart,
Darkly thinking,
Sadly sinking,
Can ye no delight impart? [Q]

Sunday, 31.—To-day the Holy week begins, and a kind of programma of the usual ceremonies of each day was laid on my toilette this morning. The bill of fare for this day runs thus:—

"Domenica delle Palme, nel Capella Papale nel Palazzo Apostolico, canta messa un Cardinal Prete. Il Sommo Pontefice fa la benedizione delle Palme, con processione per la Sala Regia."

I gave up going to the English service accordingly, and consented to accompany R** and V** to the Pope's Chapel. We entered just as the ceremony of blessing the palms was going on: a cardinal officiated for the poor old pope, who is at present ill.

After the palms had been duly blessed, they were carried in procession round the splendid anti-chamber, called the Sala Regia; meantime the chapel doors were closed upon them, and on their return, they (not the palms, but the priests) knocked and demanded entrance in a fine recitative; two of the principal voices replied from within; the choir without sung a response, and after a moment's silence the doors were opened, and the service went on.

This was very trivial and tedious. Rospo said, very truly, that the procession in Blue Beard was much better *got up*. All these processions sound very fine in mere description, but in the reality there is always something to disappoint or disgust; something which leaves either a ludicrous or a painful impression on the mind. The old priests and cardinals to-day looking like so many old beggar women dressed up in the cast-off finery of a Christmas pantomime, the [Pg 126] assistants smirking and whispering, the singers grinning at each other between every solemn strain of melody, and blowing their noses and spitting about like true Italians—in short, the want of keeping in the *tout ensemble* shocked my taste and my imagination, and, I may add, better, more serious feelings. It is well to see these things once, that we may not be cheated with fine words, but judge for ourselves. I foresee, however, that I shall not be tempted to encounter any of the more crowded ceremonies.

I remarked that all the Italians wore black to-day.

We spent the afternoon at the Vatican. We found St. Peter's almost deserted; few people, no music, the pictures all muffled, and the altars hung with black drapery. The scaffolding was preparing for the ceremonies of the week; and, on the whole, St. Peter's appeared, for the first time, disagreeable and gloomy.

Monday, April 1.—Non riconosco oggi la mia bella Italia! Clouds, and cold, and rain, to which we have been so long unaccustomed, seem unnatural; and deform that peculiar character of sunny loveliness which belongs to this country: and, à-propos to climate, I may as well observe now, that since the 1st of February, when we left Rome for Naples, up to this present 1st of April, not one day has been so rainy as to confine us to the house: and on referring to my memoranda of the weather, I find that at Naples it rained one day for a few hours only, and for about two hours on the morning we left it: since then, not a drop of rain has fallen: all hot, cloudless, lovely weather. We have been for the last three weeks in summer costume, and guard against the heat as we should in England during the dog-days. To have an idea of an Italian summer, Mr. W** says we must fancy the present heat *quadrupled*.

The day, notwithstanding, has been unusually pleasant, the afternoon, though not brilliant, was clear and soft; and we drove in the open carriage first to the little church of Santa Maria della Pace, to see Raffaelle's famous fresco, the Four Sybils. It is in the finest preservation, and combines all his peculiar graces of design and expression. The colouring has not suffered from time and damp like that of the frescos in the Vatican, but it is at once brilliant and delicate. Nothing can exceed the exquisite grace of the Sibilla Persica, nor the beautiful drapery and inspired look of the Cumana. Fortunately, I had never seen any copy or engraving of this master piece: its beauty was to me enhanced by surprise and all the charm of novelty: and my gratification was complete.

We afterwards spent half an hour in the gardens of the Villa Lanti, on the Monte Gianicolo. The view of Rome from these gardens is superb: though the sky was clouded, the atmosphere was perfectly pure and clear: the eye took in the whole extent of ancient and [Pg 127] modern Rome; beyond it the Campagna, the Alban Hills, and the Apennines, which appeared of a deep purple, with pale clouds floating over their summits. The city lay at our feet, silent, and clothed with the daylight as with a garment—no smoke, no vapour, no sound, no motion, no sign of life: it looked like a city whose inhabitants had been suddenly petrified, or smitten by a destroying angel; and such was the effect of its strange and solemn beauty, that, before I was aware, I felt my eyes fill with tears as I looked upon it.

I saw Naples from the Castle of Saint Elmo—setting aside the sea and Mount Vesuvius, those unequalled features in that radiant picture—the view of the *city* of Naples is not so fine as the view of Rome: it is, comparatively, deficient in sentiment, in interest, and in dignity. Naples wears on her brow the voluptuous beauty of a syren—Rome sits desolate on her seven-hilled throne, "*the Niobe of Nations*."

I wish I could have painted what I saw to-day *as* I saw it. Yet no—the reality was perhaps too much like a picture to please in a picture: the exquisite harmony of the colouring, the softness of the lights and shades, the solemn death-like stillness, the distinctness of every form and outline, and the classic interest attached to every noble object, combined to form a scene, which hereafter, in the silence of my own thoughts, I shall often love to recall and to dwell upon.

To-night I read with Incoronati, the Fourth book of Dante, and two of Petrarch's Canzoni "I' vo pensando," and "Verdi panni," making notes from his explanations and remarks as I went along. These two Canzoni I had selected as being among the most *puzzling* as well as the most beautiful. Those are strangely mistaken, who from a superficial study of a few of his amatory sonnets, regard Petrarch as a mere love-sick poet, who spent his time in be-rhyming an obdurate mistress; and those are equally mistaken who consider him as the poetical votarist of an imaginary fair one. I know but little, even of the little that is known of his life; for I remember being as much terrified by the ponderous quartos of the Abbé de Sade, as I was discomfited and disappointed by the flimsy octavo of Mrs. Dobson. I am now studying Petrarch in his own works; and it seemeth to me, in my simple wit, that such exquisite touches of truth and nature, such depth and purity of feeling, such felicity of expression, such vivid yet delicate pictures of female beauty, could spring only from a real and heartfelt passion. We know too little of Laura: but it is probable, if she had always preserved a stern and unfeeling indifference, she would not have so entirely commanded the affections of a feeling heart; and had she yielded she would not so long have preserved her influence.

Think you if Laura had been Petrarch's wife,
He would have written sonnets all his life?

[Pg 128]

In truth she appears to have been the most finished coquette of her own or any other age. [R]

3.—What a delight it would be, if, at the end of a day like this, I had *somebody* with whom I could talk over things—with whose feelings and impressions I could compare my own—who would direct my judgment, and assist me in arranging my ideas, and double every pleasure by sharing it with me! What would have become of me if I had not thought of keeping a Diary? I should have died of a sort of mental repletion! What a consolation and employment has it been to me to let my overflowing heart and soul exhale themselves on paper! When I have neither power nor spirits to join in common-place conversation, I open my dear little Diary, and feel, while my pen thus swiftly glides along, much less as if I were writing than as if I were speaking—yes! speaking to one who perhaps will read this when I am no more—but not till *then*.

I was well enough to *walk* up to the Rospigliosi Palace this morning to see Guido's Aurora: it is on the ceiling of a pavilion: would it were not! for I looked at it till my neck ached, and my brain turned round "like a parish top." I can only say that it far surpassed my expectations: the colouring is the most brilliant, yet the most harmonious, in the world: and there is a depth, a strength, a richness in the tints, not common to Guido's style. The whole is as fresh as if painted yesterday; though Guido must have died sometime about 1640.

On each side of the hall or pavilion adorned by the Aurora, there is a small room, containing a few excellent pictures. The Triumph of David, by Domenichino, a fine rich picture; an exquisite Andromeda, by Guido, painted with his usual delicacy and sentiment; the twelve Apostles, by Rubens, some of them very fine; "the Five Senses," said to be by Carlo Cignani, but if so he has surpassed himself: it is like Domenichino. The Death of Samson, by L. Carracci, wearies the eye by the number and confusion of the figures: it has no principal group upon which the attention can rest. There is also a fine portrait of Nicolo Poussin, by himself, and an interesting head of Guido.

At three o'clock we went down to the Capella Sistina to hear the Miserere. In describing the effect produced by this divine music, the time, the place, the scenic contrivance should be taken into account: the time—solemn twilight, just as the shades begin to fall around: the place—a noble and lofty hall where the terrors of Michel Angelo's Last Judgment are rendered more terrible by the gathering gloom, and his sublime Prophets frown dimly upon us from the walls above. The extinguishing of the tapers, the concealed choir, the angelic voices [Pg 129] chosen from among the finest in the world, and blended by long practice into the most perfect unison, were combined to produce that overpowering effect which has so often been described. Many ladies wept, and one fainted. Unassisted vocal music is certainly the finest of all: no power of instruments could have thrilled me like the blended stream of melancholy harmony, breathed forth with such an expression of despairing anguish, that it was almost too much to bear.

Good-Friday.—I saw more new, amusing, and delightful things yesterday, than I can attempt to describe or even enumerate: but I think there is no danger of my forgetting general impressions: if my memory should fail me in particulars, my imagination can always recall the whole.

In the morning I declined going to see the ceremonies at the Vatican. The procession of the host from the Sistine to the Pauline Chapel; the washing of the Pilgrims' feet, etc.—all these things are less than indifferent to me; and the illness and absence of the poor old pope rendered them particularly uninteresting. Every body went but myself; and it was agreed that we should all meet at the door of the Sistine Chapel at five o'clock. I remained quietly at home on my sofa till one; and then drove to the Museum of the Vatican, where I spent the rest of the day; it was a grand festa, and the whole of the Vatican, including the immense suite of splendid libraries, was thrown open to the public. All the foreigners in Rome having crowded to St. Peter's, or the chapels, to view the ceremonies going on, I was the only stranger amidst an assemblage of the common people and peasantry, who had come to lounge there till the lighting up of the Cross. I walked on and on, hour after hour, lost in amazement, and wondering where and when this glorious labyrinth was to end; successive galleries fitted up with the gay splendour of an Oriental Haram, in which the books and manuscripts are all arranged and numbered in cases; the beautiful perspective of hall beyond hall vanishing away into immeasurable distance; the refulgent light shed overall; and add to this, the extraordinary visages and costumes of the people, who with their families wandered along in groups or singly, all behaving with the utmost decorum, and making emphatic exclamations on the beauties around them.

"*Ah! che bella cosa! Cosa rara! O bella assai!*" all furnished me with such ample matter for amusement, and observation, and admiration, that I was insensible to fatigue, and knew not that in five hours I had scarcely completed the circuit of the Museum.

One room (the Camera del Papiri) struck me particularly: it is a small octagon, the ceiling and ornaments painted by Raffaelle Mengs with exquisite taste. The group on the ceiling represents the Muse of History writing, while her book reposes on the wings of Time, and a Genius supplies her with materials: the pannels of this room are formed [Pg 130] of old manuscripts, pasted up against the walls and glazed. The effect of the whole is as singular as beautiful.

A new gallery of marbles has lately been opened by the Pope, called from its form the *Sala della Croce*: in splendid, classical, and tasteful decoration, it equals any of the others, but is not, perhaps, so remarkable for the intrinsic value of its contents.

I never more deeply felt my own ignorance and deficiencies than I did to-day. I saw so many things I did not understand, so much which I wished to have explained to me, I longed so inexpressibly for someone to talk to, to exclaim to, to help me to wonder, to admire, to be *extasiée*! but I was alone: and I know not how it is, or why, but when I am alone, not only my powers of enjoyment seem to fail me in a degree, but even my mental faculties; and the multitude of my own ideas and sensations confuse, oppress, and irritate me.

I walked through the whole gyro of the Museum, examining the busts and pictures particularly, with the help of Este's admirable catalogue raisonnée, and at half-past five I reached the Sistine just in time to hear the second Miserere: neither the music nor the effort were equal to the first evening. The music, though inferior to Allegri's, was truly beautiful and sublime; but the scenic pageantry did not strike so much on repetition: the chapel was insufferably crowded, I was sick and stupid from heat and fatigue, and to crown all, just in the midst of one of the most overpowering strains, the cry of condemned souls pleading for mercy, which made my heart pause, and my flesh creep—a lady behind me whispered loudly, "Do look what lovely broderie Mrs. L** has on her white satin spencer!"

After the Miserere, we adjourned to St. Peter's, to see the illumination of the Girandola. I confess the first glance disappointed me; for the cross, though more than thirty feet in height, looks trivial and diminutive, compared with the immensity of the dome in which it is suspended; but just as I was beginning to admire the sublime effect of the whole scene, I was obliged to leave the church, being unable to stand the fatigue any longer.

To-day we have remained quietly at home, recruiting after the exertions of yesterday. After dinner, Colonel —— and Mr. W** began to discuss the politics of Italy, and from abusing the governments they fell upon the people; and being of very opposite principles and parties, they soon began an argument which ended in a warm dispute, and sent me to take refuge in my own room. How I detest politics and discord! How I hate the discussion of politics in Italy! and, above all, the discussion of Italian politics, which offer no point upon which the mind can dwell with pleasure. I have not wandered to Italy—"this land of sun-lit skies and fountains clear," as Barry [Pg 131] Cornwall calls it, only to scrape together materials for a quarto tour, or to sweep up the leavings of the "fearless" Lady Morgan; or to dwell upon the heart-sickening realities which meet me at every turn; evils of which I neither understand the cause nor the cure. And yet say not to Italy

"Caduta è la tua gloria—e tu nol' vedi!"

She does see it,—she does feel it. A spirit is silently and gradually working its way beneath the surface of society, which must, erelong, break forth either for good or for evil. Between a profligate and servile nobility, and a degraded and enslaved populace, a middle class has lately sprung up; the men of letters, the artists, the professors in the sciences, who have obtained property, or distinction at least, in the commotions which have agitated their country, and those who have served at home or abroad in the revolutionary wars. These all seem impelled by one and the same spirit; and make up for their want of numbers by their activity, talents, enthusiasm, and the secret but increasing influence which they exert over the other classes of society. But on subjects like these, however interesting, I have no means of obtaining information at once general and accurate: and I would rather not think, nor speak, nor write, upon "matters which are too high for me." Let the modern Italians be what they may,—what I hear them styled six times a day at least—a dirty, demoralized, degraded, unprincipled race,—centuries behind our thrice-blessed, prosperous, and comfort-loving nation in civilization and morals; if I were come among them as a resident, this picture might alarm me; situated as I am, a nameless sort of person, a mere bird of passage, it concerns me not. I am not come to spy out the nakedness of the land, but to implore from her healing airs and lucid skies the health and peace I have lost, and to worship as a pilgrim at the tomb of her departed glories.—I have not many opportunities of studying the national character; I have no dealings with the lower classes, little intercourse with the higher. No tradesmen cheat me, no hired menials irritate me, no innkeepers fleece me, no postmasters abuse me. I love these rich delicious skies; I love this genial sunshine, which, even in December, sends the spirits dancing through the veins; this pure elastic atmosphere, which not only brings the distant landscape, but almost heaven itself nearer to the eye; and all the treasures of art and nature which are poured forth around me; and over which my own mind, teeming with images, recollections, and associations, can fling a beauty even beyond their own. I willingly turn from all that excites the spleen and disgust of others; from all that may so easily be despised, derided—reviled, and abandon my heart to that state of calm benevolence towards all around me, which leaves me undisturbed, to enjoy, [Pg 132] admire, observe, reflect, remember, with pleasure, if not with profit, and enables me to look upon the glorious scenes with which I am surrounded, not with the impertinent inquisition of a bookmaker, nor the gloomy calculations of a politician, nor the sneering selfism of a Smelfungus—but with the eye of the painter, and the feeling of the poet.

A-propos to poets!—Lady C** has just sent us tickets for Sestini's Accademia to-morrow night. So far from the race of Improvvisatori being extinct, or living only in the pages of Corinne, or in the memory of the Fantastici, and the Bandinelli, the Gianas, and the Corillas of other days,—there is scarcely a small town in Italy, as I am informed, without its Improvvisatore; and I know several individuals in the higher classes of society, both here, and at Florence more particularly, who are remarkable for possessing this extraordinary talent—though, of course, it is only exercised for the gratification of a private circle. Of those who make a public exhibition of their powers, Sgricci and Sestini are the most celebrated—and of these Sgricci ranks first. I never heard him; but Signior Incoronati, who knows him well, described to me his talents and powers as almost supernatural. A wonderful display of his art was the *improvvisazione*—we have no English word for a talent which in England is unknown,—of a regular tragedy on the Greek model, with the choruses and dialogue complete. The subject proposed was from the story of Ulysses, which afforded him an opportunity of bringing in the whole sonorous nomenclature of the Heathen Mythology,—which, says Forsyth, enters in the web of every improvvisatore, and assists the poet both with rhymes and ideas. Most of the celebrated improvvisatori have been Florentines: Sgricci is, I believe, a Neapolitan, and his rival Sestini a Roman.

April 7.—Any public exhibition of talent in the Fine Arts is here called an *Accademia*. Sestini gave his Accademia in an anti-chamber of the Palazzo ——, I forget its name, but it was much like all the other *palaces* we are accustomed to see here; exhibiting the same strange contrast of ancient taste and magnificence, with present meanness and poverty. We were ushered into a lofty room of noble size and beautiful proportions, with its rich fresco-painted walls and ceiling faded and falling to decay; a common brick floor, and sundry window panes broken, and stuffed with paper. The room was nearly filled by the audience, amongst whom I remarked a great number of English. A table with writing implements, and an old shattered jingling piano, occupied one side of the apartment, and a small space was left in front for the poet. Whilst we waited with some impatience for his appearance, several persons present walked up to the table and wrote down various subjects; which on Sestini's coming forward, he [Pg 133] read aloud, marking those which were distinguished by the most general applause. This selection formed our evening's entertainment. A lady sat down in her bonnet and shawl to accompany him; and when fatigued, another fair musician readily supplied her place. It is seldom that an improvvisatore attempts to recite without the assistance of music.

When Dr. Moore heard Corilla at Florence, she sung to the accompaniment of two violins. [S] La Fantastici preferred the guitar; and I should have preferred either to our jingling harpsichord. However, a few chords struck at intervals were sufficient to support the voice, and mark the time. Several airs were tried, and considered before the poet could fix on one suited to his subject and the measure he intended to employ. In general they were pretty and simple, consisting of very few notes, and more like a chant or recitative, than a regular air: one of the most beautiful I have obtained, and shall bring with me to England.

The moment Sestini had made his choice, he stepped forward, and without further pause or preparation, began with the first subject upon his list,—"*Il primo Navigatore.*"

Gesner's beautiful Idyl of "*The First Navigator,*" supplied Sestini with the Story, in all its details; but he versified it with surprizing facility: and, as far as I could judge, with great spirit and elegance. He added, too, some trifling circumstances, and several little *traits,* the naïveté of which afforded considerable amusement. When an accurate rhyme, or apt expression, did not offer itself on the instant it was required, he knit his brows and clenched his fingers with impatience; but I think he never hesitated more than half a second. At the moment the chord was struck, the rhyme was ready. In this manner he poured forth between thirty and forty stanzas, with still increasing animation; and wound up his poem with some beautiful images of love, happiness, and innocence. Of his success I could form some idea by the applauses he received from better judges than myself.

After a few minutes' repose and a glass of water, he next called on the company to supply him with rhymes for a sonnet. These, as fast as they were suggested by various persons, he wrote down on a slip of paper. The last rhyme given was "*Ostello,*"—(a common alehouse)—at which he demurred, and submitting to the company the difficulty of introducing so vulgar a word into an heroic sonnet, respectfully begged that another might be substituted. A lady called out "*Avello*" the poetical term for a grave, or a sepulchre, which expression [Pg 134] bore a happy analogy to the subject proposed. The poet smiled, well pleased;—and stepping forward with the paper in his hand, he immediately, without even a moment's preparation, recited a sonnet on the second subject upon his list,—"*La Morte di Alfieri.*"—I could better judge of the merit of this effusion, because he spoke it unaccompanied by music; and his enunciation was remarkably distinct. The subject was popular, and treated with much feeling and poetic fervour. After lamenting Alfieri as the patriot, as well as the bard, and as the glory of his country, he concluded, by indignantly repelling the supposition that "the latest sparks of genius and freedom were buried in the tomb of Vittorio Alfieri." A thunder of applause followed; and cries of "O bravo Sestini! bravo Sestini!" were echoed from the Italian portion of the audience, long after the first acclamations had subsided. The men rose simultaneously from their seats; and I confess I could hardly keep mine. The animation of the poet, and the enthusiasm of the audience, sent a thrill through every nerve and filled my eyes with tears.

The next subject was "*La Morte di Beatrice Cenci;*"—and this, I think, was a failure. The frightful story of *Cenci* is too well known in England since the publication of Shelley's Tragedy. Here it is familiar to all classes; and though two centuries have since elapsed, it seems as fresh in the memory, or rather in the imagination of these people, as if it had happened but yesterday. The subject was not well chosen for a public and mixed assembly; and Sestini, without adverting to the previous details of horror, confined himself most scrupulously, with propriety, to the subject proposed. He described Beatrice led to execution,—"*con baldanza casta e generosa*"—and the effect produced on the multitude by her youth:—not forgetting to celebrate "*those tresses like threads of gold whose wavy splendour dazzled all beholders,*" as they are described by a contemporary writer. He put into her mouth a long and pious dying speech, in which she expressed her trust in the blessed Virgin, and her hopes of pardon from eternal justice and mercy. To my surprise, he also made her in one stanza confess and repent the murder, or rather sacrifice, [T] which she had perpetrated; which is contrary to the known fact, that Beatrice *never* confessed to the last moment of existence, nor gave any reason to suppose that she repented. The whole was drawn out to too great a length, and, with the exception of a few happy touches, and pathetic sentiments, went off flatly. It was very little applauded.

The next subject was the "*Immortality of the Soul,*" on which the poet displayed amazing pomp and power of words, and a wonderful [Pg 135] affluence of ideas. He showed, too, an intimate acquaintance with all that had ever been said, or sung, upon the same subject, from Plato to Thomas Aquinas. I confess I derived little benefit from all this display of poetry and erudition; for, after the first few stanzas, finding himself irretrievably perplexed by the united difficulties of the language and the subject, I withdrew my attention, and amused myself with the paintings on the walls, and with reveries on the past and present, till I was roused by the acclamations that followed the conclusion of the poem; which excited very general admiration and applause.

The company then furnished the *bouts-rimés* for another sonnet: the subject was "*L'Amor della Patria.*" The title, even before he began, was hailed by a round of plaudits; and the sonnet itself was excellent and spirited. *Excellent* I mean in its general effect, as an *improvvisazione*:—how it would stand the test of cool criticism I cannot tell; nor is that any thing to the purpose: these extemporaneous effusions ought to be judged merely as what they are,—not as finished or correct poems, but as wonderful exercises of tenacious memory, ready wit, and that quickness of imagination which can soar

> ——"al bel cimento
> Sulle ali dell' momento."

To return to Sestini. It may be imagined, that on such a subject as "*L'Amor della Patria,*" the ancient Roman worthies were not forgotten, and accordingly, a Brutus, a Scipio, a Fabius, or a Fabricius, figured in every line. And surely on no occasion could they have been more appropriately introduced:—in Rome, and when addressing Romans, who showed, by their enthusiastic applause, that though the spirit of their forefathers may be extinct, their memory is not.

The next subject, which formed a sort of *pendant* to the Cenci, was the "*Parricide of Tullia.*" In this again his success was complete. The stanza in which Tullia ordered her charioteer to "drive on," was given with such effect as to electrify us: and a sudden burst of approbation which caused a momentary interruption, evidently lent the poet fresh spirits and animation.

The evening concluded with a lively burlesque, entitled "*Il Mercato d'Amore*" which represented Love as setting up a shop to sell "*la Mercanzia della Gioventù*." The list of his stock in trade, though it could not boast of much originality, was given with admirable wit and vivacity. In conclusion, Love being threatened with a bankruptcy, took shelter, as the poet assured us, in the bright eyes of the ladies present. This farewell compliment was prettily turned, and intended, of course, to be general: but it happened, luckily for Sestini, that just opposite to him, and fixed upon him at the moment, were two of the brightest eyes in the world. Whether he owed any of his inspiration to [Pg 136] their beams I know not; but the *à-propos* of the compliment was seized immediately, and loudly applauded by the gentlemen round us.

Sestini is a young man, apparently about five-and-twenty: of a slight and delicate figure, and in his whole appearance, odd, wild, and picturesque. He has the common foreign trick of running his fingers through his black bushy hair; and accordingly it stands on end in all directions. A pair of immense whiskers, equally black and luxuriant, meet at the point of his chin, encircling a visage of most cadaverous hue, and features which might be termed positively ugly, were it not for the "*vago spirito ardento*" which shines out from his dark eyes, and the fire and intelligence which light up his whole countenance, till it almost kindles into beauty. Though he afterwards conversed with apparent ease, and replied to the compliments of the company, he was evidently much exhausted by his exertions. I should fear that their frequent repetition, and the effervescence of mind, and nervous excitement they cannot but occasion, must gradually wear out his delicate frame and feeble temperament, and that the career of this extraordinary genius will be short as it is brilliant. [U]

April 8.—As Maupertuis said after his journey to Lapland—for the universe I would not have missed the sights and scenes of yesterday; but, for the whole universe, I would not undergo such another day of fatigue, anxiety, and feverish excitement.

In the morning about ten o'clock, we all went down to St. Peter's, to hear high mass. The absence of the Pope (who is still extremely ill) detracted from the interest and dignity of the ceremony: there was no general benediction from the balcony of St. Peter's; and nothing pleased me, except the general *coup d'œil;* which in truth was splendid. The theatrical dresses of the mitred priests, the countless multitude congregated from every part of Christendom, in every variety of national costume, the immensity and magnificence of the church, and the glorious sunshine—all these enchanted the eye; but I could have fancied myself in a theatre. I saw no devotion, and I felt none. The whole appeared more like a triumphal pageant acted in honour of a heathen deity, than an act of worship and thanksgiving to the Great Father of all.

I observed an immense number of pilgrims, male and female, who had come from various parts of Italy to visit the shrine of St. Peter on this grand occasion. I longed to talk to a man who stood near me, with a very singular and expressive countenance, whose cape and looped hat were entirely covered with scallop shells and reliques, and his long staff surmounted by a death's head. [Pg 137]

I was restrained by a feeling which I now think rather ridiculous: I feared, lest by conversing with him, I should diminish the effect his romantic and picturesque figure had made on my imagination.

The exposition of the relics was from a balcony half way up the dome, so high and distant that I could distinguish nothing but the impression of our Saviour's face on the handkerchief of St. Veronica, richly framed—at the sight whereof the whole multitude prostrated themselves to the earth: the other relics I forget, but they were all equally marvellous and equally credible.

We returned after a long fatiguing morning to an early dinner; and then drove again to the Piazza of St. Peter's, to see the far-famed illumination of the church. We had to wait a considerable time; but the scene was so novel and beautiful, that I found ample amusement in my own thoughts and observations. The twilight rapidly closed round us: the long lines of statues along the roof and balustrades, faintly defined against the evening sky, looked like spirits come down to gaze; a prodigious crowd of carriages, and people on foot, filled every avenue: but all was still, except when a half-suppressed murmur of impatience broke through the hushed silence of suspense and expectation. At length, on a signal, which was given by the firing of a cannon, the whole of the immense façade and dome, even up to the cross on the summit, and the semi-circular colonnades in front, burst into a blaze, as if at the touch of an enchanter's wand; adding the pleasure of surprise to that of delight and wonder. The carriages now began to drive rapidly round the piazza, each with a train of running footmen, flinging their torches round and dashing them against the ground. The shouts and acclamations of the crowd, the stupendous building with all its architectural outlines and projections, defined in lines of living flame, the universal light, the sparkling of the magnificent fountains—produced an effect far beyond any thing I could have anticipated, and more like the gorgeous fictions of the Arabian Nights, than any earthy reality.

After driving round the piazza, we adjourned to a balcony which had been hired for us overlooking the Tiber, and exactly opposite to the Castle of St. Angelo. Hence we commanded a view of the fire-works, which were truly superb, but made me so nervous and giddy with noise and light and wonder, that I was rejoiced when all was over. A flight of a thousand sky-rockets sent up at once, blotting the stars and the moonlight—dazzling our eyes, stunning our ears, and amazing all our senses together, concluded the Holy Week at Rome.

To-morrow morning we start for Florence, and to-night I close this second volume of my Diary. Thanks to my little ingenious Frenchmen in the Via Santa Croce, I have procured a lock for a third volume, [Pg 138] almost equal to my patent *Bramah* in point of security, though very unlike it in every other respect.

Viterbo, April 9.—"In every bosom Italy is the *second* country in the world, the surest proof that it is in reality the *first.*"

This elegant and just observation occurs, I think, in Arthur Young's travels; I am not sure I quote the words correctly, but the sense will come home to every cultivated mind with the force of a proverbial truism.

One leaves Naples as a man parts with an enchanting mistress, and Rome as we would bid adieu to an old and dear-loved friend. I love it, and grieve to leave it for its own sake; it is painful to quit a place where we leave behind us many whom we love and regret; and almost or quite as painful, I think, to quit a place in which we leave behind us no one to regret, or think of us more; a feeling like this mingled with the sorrow with which I bade adieu to Rome this morning.

Our journey has been fatiguing, *triste*, and tedious.

Radicofani, 10th.—I could almost regret at this moment that I am past the age of romance, for I am in a fine situation for mysterious and imaginary horrors, could I but feel again as I did at gay sixteen; but, alas! *ces beaux jours sont passés*! and here I am on the top of a dreary black mountain, in a rambling old inn which looks like a ci-devant hospital or dismantled barracks, in a bed-room which resembles one of the wards of a poor-house, one little corner lighted by my lamp, and the other three parts all lost in black ominous darkness; while a tempest rages without as if it would break in the rattling casements, and burst the roof over our heads; and yet, insensible that I am! I can calmly take up my pen to amuse myself by scribbling, since sleep is impossible. I can look round my vast and solitary room without fancying a ghost or an assassin in every corner, and listen to the raving and lamenting of the storm, without imagining I hear in every gust the shrieks of wailing spirits, or the groans of murdered travellers; only wishing that the wind were rather less cold, or my fire a little brighter, or my dormitory less *infinitely* spacious; for at present its boundaries are invisible.

The first part of our journey this morning was delightful and picturesque; we passed the beautiful lake of Bolsena and Montepulciano, so famous for its wine (*il Rei di Vino*, as Redi calls it in the *Bacco in Toscana*). Later in the day we entered a gloomy and desolate country; and after crossing the rapid and muddy torrent of Rigo, which, as our *Guide des Voyageurs* wittily informs us, we shall have to cross [Pg 139] *four* times if we are not drowned the *third* time, we began to ascend the mountainous region which divides the Tuscan from the Roman states—a succession of wild barren hills, intersected in every direction by deep ravines, and presenting a scene, sublime indeed from its waste and wild grandeur, but destitute of all beauty, interest, magnificence and variety.

I remember the strange emotion which came across me, when—on the horses stopping to breathe on the summit of a lofty ridge, where all around, as far as the eye could reach, nothing was to be seen but the same unvarying, miserable, heart-sinking barrenness, without a trace of human habitation, except the black fort or the highest point of Radicofani—a soft sound of bells came over my ear as if brought upon the wind. There is something in the sound of bells in the midst of a solitude which is singularly striking, and may be cheering or melancholy, according to the mood in which we may happen to be.

Florence, April 14.—I have not written a word since we arrived at Sienna. What would it avail me to keep a mere journal of suffering? O that I could change as others do, could forget that such things have been which can never be again! that there were not this tenacity in my heart and soul which clings to the shadow though the substance be gone!

This is not a mere effusion of low spirits; I was never more cheerful. I have just left a gay party, where Mr. Rogers (whom by special good fortune we meet at every resting-place, and who dined with us to-day) has been entertaining us delightfully. I disdain low spirits as a mere disease which comes over us, generally from some physical or external cause; to prescribe for them is as easy as to disguise them is difficult: but the hopeless, cureless sadness of a heart which droops with regret, and throbs with resentment, is easily, very easily disguised, but not so easily banished. I hear every body round me congratulating themselves, and *me* more particularly, that we have at last reached Florence, that we are so far advanced on our road homewards, that soon we shall be at Paris, and Paris is to do wonders—Paris and Dr. R** are to *set me up* again, as the phrase is. But I shall never be set up again, I shall never live to reach Paris; none can tell how I sicken at the very name of that detested place; none seem aware how fast, how very fast the principle of life is burning away within me: but why should I speak? and what earthly help can now avail me? I can suffer in silence, I can conceal the weakness which increases upon me, by retiring, as if from choice and not necessity, from all exertion not absolutely inevitable; and the change is so gradual, none will [Pg 140] perceive it till the great change of all comes, and then I shall be at rest.

Florence looked most beautiful as we approached it from the south, girt with her theatre of verdant hills, and glittering in the sunshine. All the country from Sienna to Florence is richly cultivated; diversified with neat hamlets, farms and villas. I was more struck with the appearance of the Tuscan peasantry on my return from the Papal dominions than when we passed through the country before: no where in Tuscany have we seen that look of abject negligent poverty, those crowds of squalid beggars which shocked us in the Ecclesiastical States. In the towns where we stopped to change horses, we were presently surrounded by a crowd of people: the women came out spinning, or sewing and plaiting the Leghorn hats; the children threw flowers into our barouche, the men grinned and gaped, but there was no vociferous begging, no disgusting display of physical evils, filth, and wretchedness. The motive was merely that idle curiosity for which the Florentines in all ages have been remarked. I remember an amusing instance which occurred when I was here in December last. I was standing one evening in the Piazza del Gran Duca, looking at the group of the Rape of the Sabines: in a few minutes a dozen people gathered round me, gaping at the statue, and staring at that and at me alternately, either to enjoy my admiration, or find out the cause of it: the people came out of the neighbouring shops, and the crowd continued to increase, till at length, though infinitely amused, I was glad to make my escape.

I suffered from cold when first we arrived at Florence, owing to the change of climate, or rather to mere weakness and fatigue: today I begin to doubt the possibility of outliving an Italian summer. The blazing atmosphere which depresses the eyelids, the enervating heat, and the rich perfume of the flowers all around us, are almost too much.

April 20.—During our stay at Florence, it has been one of my favourite occupations to go to the Gallery or the Pitti Palace, and placing my portable seat opposite to some favourite pictures, minutely study and compare the styles of the different masters. By the style of any particular painter, I presume we mean to express the combination of two separate essentials—first, his peculiar conception of his subject; secondly, his peculiar method of executing that conception, with regard to colouring, drawing, and what artists call handling. The former department of style lies in the mind, and will vary according to the feelings, the temper, the personal habits, and previous education of the painter: the latter is merely mechanical, and is technically [Pg 141] termed the *manner* of a painter; it may be cold or warm, hard, dry, free, strong, tender: as we say the cold manner of Sasso Ferrato, the warm manner of Giorgione, the hard manner of Holbein, the dry manner of Perugino, the free manner of Rubens, the strong manner of Carravaggio, and so forth; I heard an amateur once observe, that one of Morland's Pig-sties was painted with great *feeling*: all this refers merely to mechanical execution.

I am no connaisseur; and I should have lamented, as a misfortune, the want of some fixed principles of taste and criticism to guide my judgment; some nomenclature by which to express certain effects, peculiarities, and excellencies which I felt, rather than understood; if my own ignorance had not afforded considerable amusement to myself, and perhaps to others. I have derived some gratification from observing the gradual improvement of my own taste: and from comparing the decisions of my own unassisted judgment and natural feelings, with the fiat of profound critics and connaisseurs: the result has been sometimes mortifying, sometimes pleasing. Had I visited Italy in the character of a ready-made connaisseur, I should have lost many pleasures; for as the eye becomes more practised, the taste becomes more discriminative and fastidious; and the more extensive our acquaintance with the works of art, the more limited is our sphere of admiration; as if the circle of enjoyment contracted round us, in proportion as our sense of beauty became more intense and exquisite. A thousand things which once had power to charm, can charm no longer; but, *en revanche*, those which *do* please, please a thousand times more: thus what we lose on one side, we gain on the other. Perhaps, on the whole, a technical knowledge of the arts is apt to divert the mind from the general effect, to fix it on petty details of execution. Here comes a connaisseur, who has found his way, good man! from Somerset House, to the Tribune at Florence: see him with one hand passed across his brow, to shade the light, while the other extended forwards, describes certain indescribable circumvolutions in the air, and now he retires, now advances, now recedes again, till he has hit the exact distance from which every point of beauty is displayed to the best possible advantage, and there he stands—gazing, as never gazed the moon upon the waters, or love-sick maiden upon the moon! We take him perhaps for another Pygmalion? We imagine that it is those parted and half-breathing lips, those eyes that *seem* to float in light; the pictured majesty of suffering virtue, or the tears of repenting loveliness; the divinity of beauty, or "*the beauty of holiness,*" which have thus transfixed him? No such thing: it is *fleshiness* of the tints, the *vaghezza* of the colouring, the brilliance of the carnations, the fold of a robe, or the fore-shortening of a little finger. O! [Pg 142] whip me such connaisseurs! the critic's stop-watch was nothing to this.

Mere mechanical excellence, and all the tricks of art have their praise as long as they are subordinate and conduce to the general effect. In painting as in her sister arts it is necessary

> "Che l'arte che tutto fa nulla si scuopre."

Of course I do not speak here of the Dutch school, whose highest aim, and highest praise, is exquisite mechanical precision in the representation of common nature and still life: but of those pictures which are the productions of mind, which address themselves to the understanding, the fancy, the feelings, and convey either a moral or a poetical pleasure.

In taking a retrospective view of all the best collections in Italy and of the Italian school in particular, I have been struck by the endless multiplication of the same subjects, crucifixions, martyrdoms, and other scripture horrors;—virgins, saints, and holy families. The prevalence of the former class of subjects is easily explained, and has been ingeniously defended; but it is not so easily reconciled to the imagination. The mind and the eye are shocked and fatigued by the succession of revolting and sanguinary images which pollute the walls of every palace, church, gallery, and academy, from Milan to Naples. The splendour of the execution only adds to their hideousness; we at once seek for nature, and tremble to find it. It is hateful to see the loveliest of the arts degraded to such butcher-work. I have often gone to visit a famed collection with a secret dread of being led through a sort of intellectual shambles, and returned with the feeling of one who had supped full of horrors. I do not know how *men* think, and feel, though I believe many a man, who with every other feeling absorbed in overpowering interest, could look unshrinking upon a real scene of cruelty and blood, would shrink away disgusted and sickened from the cold, obtrusive, *painted* representation of the same object; for the truth of this I appeal to men. I can only see with woman's eyes, and think and feel as I believe every woman *must*, whatever may be her love for the arts. I remember that in one of the palaces at Milan—(I think it was in the collection of the Duca Litti)—we were led up to a picture defended from the air by a plate of glass, and which being considered as the gem of the collection, was reserved for the last as a kind of *bonne bouche*. I gave but one glance, and turned away loathing, shuddering, sickening. The cicerone looked amazed at my bad taste, he assured me it was *un vero Correggio* (which by the way I can never believe), and that the duke had refused for it I know not how many thousand scudi. It would be difficult to say what was most execrable in this picture, the appalling nature of the subject, the [Pg 143] depravity of mind evinced in its conception, or the horrible truth and skill with which it was delineated. I ought to add that it hung up in the family dining-room and in full view of the dinner-table.

There is as picture among the chefs-d'œuvres in the Vatican, which, if I were pope (or Pope Joan) for a single day, should be burnt by the common hangman, "with the smoke of its ashes to poison the air," as it now poisons the sight by its unutterable horrors. There is another in the Palazzo Pitti, at which I shiver still, and unfortunately there is no avoiding it, as they have hung it close to Guido's lovely Cleopatra. In the gallery there is a Judith and Holofernes which irresistibly strikes the attention—if any thing would add to the horror inspired by the sanguinary subject, and the atrocious fidelity and talent with which it is expressed, it is that the artist was a *woman*. I must confess that Judith is not one of my favourite heroines; but I can more easily conceive how a woman inspired by vengeance and patriotism could execute such a deed, than that she could coolly sit down, and day after day, hour after hour, touch after touch, dwell upon and almost realize to the eye such an abomination as this.

We can study anatomy, if (like a certain princess) we have a taste that way, in the surgeon's dissecting-room; we do not look upon pictures to have our minds agonized and contaminated by the sight of human turpitude and barbarity, streaming blood, quivering flesh, wounds, tortures, death, and horrors in every shape, even though it should be all very *natural*. Painting has been called the handmaid of nature; is it not the duty of a handmaid to array her mistress to the best possible advantage? At least to keep her infirmities from view and not to expose her too undressed?

But I am not so weak, so cowardly, so fastidious, as to shrink from every representation of human suffering, provided that our sympathy be not strained beyond a certain point. To *please* is the genuine aim of painting, as of all the fine arts; when pleasure is conveyed through deeply excited interest, by affecting the passions, the senses, and the imagination, painting assumes a higher character, and almost vies with tragedy: in fact, it *is* tragedy to the eye, and is amenable to the same laws. The St. Sebastians of Guido and Razzi; the St. Jerome of Domenichino; the sternly beautiful Judith of Allori; the Pietà of Raffaelle; the San Pietro Martire of Titian; are all so many tragic *scenes* wherein whatever is revolting in circumstances or character is judiciously kept from view, where human suffering is dignified by the moral lesson it is made to convey, and its effect on the beholder at once softened and heightened by the redeeming grace which genius and poetry have shed like a glory round it.

Allowing all this, I am yet obliged to confess that I am wearied with this class, of pictures, and that I wish there were fewer of them. [Pg 144]

But there is one subject which never tires, at least never tires *me*, however varied, repeated, multiplied. A subject so lovely in itself that the most eminent painter cannot easily embellish it, or the meanest degrade it; a subject which comes home to our own bosoms and dearest feelings; and in which we may "lose ourselves in all delightfulness," and indulge unreproved pleasure. I mean the *Virgin and Child*, or in other words, the abstract personification of what is loveliest, purest, and dearest, under heaven—maternal tenderness, virgin meekness, and childish innocence, and the *beauty of holiness* over all.

It occurred to me to-day, that if a gallery could be formed of this subject alone, selecting one specimen from among the works of every painter, it would form not only a comparative index to their different styles, but we should find, on recurring to what is known of the lives and characters of the great masters, that each has stamped some peculiarity of his own disposition on his Virgins; and that, after a little consideration and practice, a very fair guess might be formed of the character of each artist, by observing the style in which he has treated this beautiful and favourite subject.

Take Raffaelle for example, whose delightful character is dwelt upon by all his biographers; his genuine nobleness of soul, which raised him far above interest, rivalship, or jealousy, the gentleness of his temper, the suavity of his manners, the sweetness of his disposition, the benevolence of his heart, which rendered him so deeply loved and admired, even by those who pined away at his success, and died of his superiority [V]—are all attested by contemporary writers: where but in his own harmonious character, need Raffaelle have looked for the prototypes of his half-celestial creations?

His Virgins alone combine every grace which the imagination can require—repose, simplicity, meekness, purity, tenderness; blended without any admixture of earthly passion, yet so varied, that though all his Virgins have a general character, distinguishing them from those of every other master, no two are exactly alike. In the Madonna del Seggiola, for instance, the prevailing expression is a serious and pensive tenderness; her eyes are turned from her infant, but she clasps him to her bosom, as if it were not necessary to *see* him, to *feel* him in her heart. In another Holy Family in the Pitti Palace, the predominant expression is maternal rapture: in the Madonna di Foligno, it is a saintly benignity becoming the Queen of Heaven: in the Madonna del Cardellino, it is a meek and chaste simplicity: it is the "*Vergine dolce [Pg 145] e pia*" of Petrarch. This last picture hangs close to the Fornarina in the Tribune,—a strange contrast! Raffaelle's love for that haughty and voluptuous virago, had nothing to do with his conception of ideal beauty and chastity; and could one of his own Virgins have walked out of her frame, or if her prototype could have been found on earth, he would have felt, as others have felt—that to look upon such a being with aught of unholy passion would be profanation indeed.

Next to Raffaelle, I would rank Correggio, as a painter of Virgins. Correggio was remarkable for the humility and gentleness of his deportment, for his pensive and somewhat anxious disposition, and kindly domestic feelings: these are the characteristics which have poured themselves forth upon his Madonnas. They are distinguished generally by the utmost sweetness, delicacy, grace, and devotional feeling. I remember reading somewhere that Correggio had a large family, and was a particularly fond father; and it is certain, that in the expression of maternal tenderness, he is superior to all but Raffaelle: his Holy Family in the Studii at Naples, and his lovely Virgin in the gallery, are instances.

Guido ranks next in my estimation, as a painter of Virgins. He is described as an elegant and accomplished man, remarkable for the modesty of his disposition, and the dignity and grace of his manner; as delicate in his personal habits, and sumptuous in his dress and style of living. He had unfortunately contracted a taste for gaming, which latterly plunged him into difficulties, and tinged his mind with bitterness and melancholy. All his heads have a peculiar expression of elevated beauty, which has been called Guido's air. His Madonnas are all but heavenly: they are tender, dignified, lovely:—but when compared with Raffaelle's, they seem more touched with earthly feeling, and have less of the pure ideal: they are, if I may so express myself, too *sentimental*: sentiment is, in truth, the distinguishing characteristic of Guido's style. It is remarkable, that towards the end of his life, Guido more frequently painted the Mater Dolorosa, and gave to the heads of his Madonnas a look of melancholy, disconsolate resignation, which is extremely affecting.

Titian's character is well known: his ardent cheerful temper, his sanguine enthusiastic mind, his love of pleasure, his love of women; and true it is, that through all his glowing pictures, we trace the voluptuary. His Virgins are rather "*des jeunes épouses de la veille*"—far too like his Venuses and his mistresses: they are all luxuriant *human* beauty; with that peculiar air of blandishment which he has thrown into all his female heads, even into his portraits, and his old women.

Witness his lovely Virgin in the Vatican, his Mater Sapientiæ, and his celebrated Assumption at Venice, in which the eyes absolutely float in rapture. There is nothing ideal in Titian's conception of beauty: he [Pg 146] paints no saints and goddesses *fancy-bred*: his females are all true, lovely women; not like the heavenly creation of Raffaelle, looking as if a touch, a breath would profane them; but warm flesh and blood—heart and soul—with life in their eyes, and love upon their lips: even over his Magdalenes, his beauty-breathing pencil has shed a something which says,

A misura che amò—
Piange i suoi falli!

But this is straying from my subject; as I have embarked in this fanciful hypothesis, I shall multiply my proofs and examples, as far as I can, from memory.

In some account I have read of Murillo, he is emphatically styled *an honest man*: this is all I can remember of his character; and *truth* and nature prevail through all his pictures. In his Virgins, we can trace nothing elevated, poetical or heavenly: they have not the *ideality* of Raffaelle's, nor the tender sweetness of Correggio's; nor the glowing loveliness of Titian's; but they have an individual reality about them, which gives them the air of portraits. That chef-d'œuvre, in the Pitti Palace, for instance, call it a beautiful peasant girl and her baby, and it is faultless: but when I am told it is the "*Vergine gloriosa, del Re Eterno Madre, Figliuola, e Sposa,*" I look instantly for something far beyond what I see expressed. All Murillo's Virgins are so different from each other, that it is plain the artist did not paint from any preconceived idea of his own mind, but from different originals; they are all impressed with that general air of truth, nature, and common life, which stamps upon them a peculiar and distinct character.

Andrea del Sarto, who is in style as in character the very reverse of Murillo, fascinated me at first by his enchanting colouring, and the magical aërial depths of his chiaro-oscuro; but on a further acquaintance with his works, I was struck by the predominance of external form and colour over mind and feeling. His Virgins look as if they had been born and bred in the first circles of society, and have a particular air of elegance, an artificial grace, an attraction, which may be entirely traced to exterior; to the cast of the features, the contour of the form, the disposition of the draperies, the striking attitudes, and, above all, the divine colouring: beauty and dignity, and powerful effect, we always find in his pictures: but no *moral* pathos—no poetry—no sentiment—above all, a strange and total want of devotional expression, simplicity and humility. His Virgin with St. Francis and St. John, which hangs behind the Venus in the Tribunes, is a wonderful picture; and there are two charming Madonnas in the Borghese Palace at Rome. In the first we are struck by the grouping and colouring; in the last, by a certain graceful *lengthiness* of the limbs and [Pg 147] fine animated drawing in the attitudes. But we look in vain for the "sacred and the sweet," for heart, for soul, for countenance.

Andrea del Sarto had, in his profession, great talents rather than genius and enthusiasm. He was weak, dissipated, unprincipled; without elevation of mind or generosity of temper; and that his moral character was utterly contemptible, is proved by one trait in his life. A generous patron who had relieved him in his necessity, afterwards entrusted him with a considerable sum of money, to be laid out in certain purchases; Andrea del Sarto perfidiously embezzled the whole, and turned it to his own use. This story is told in his life, with the addition that "he was persuaded to it by his wife, as profligate and extravagant as himself."

Carlo Dolce's gentle, delicate, and melancholy temperament, are strongly expressed in his own portrait, which is in the Gallery of Paintings here. All his pictures are tinged by the morbid delicacy of his constitution, and the refinement of his character and habits. They have exquisite finish, but a want of power, degenerating at times into coldness and feebleness; his Madonnas are distinguished by regular feminine beauty, melancholy, devotion, or resigned sweetness: he excelled in Mater Dolorosa. The most beautiful of his Virgins is in Pitti Palace, of which picture there is a duplicate in the Borghese Palace at Rome.

Carlo Marratti, without distinguished merit of any kind—unless it was a distinguished merit to be the father of Faustina Zappi,—owed his fortune, his title of *Cavaliere*, and the celebrity he once enjoyed, not to any superiority of genius, but to his successful arts as a courtier, and his assiduous flattery of the great. What can be more characteristic of the man, than his simpering Virgins, fluttering in tasteless, many-coloured draperies, with their sky blue backgrounds, and golden clouds?

Caravaggio was a gloomy misanthrope and a profligate ruffian: we read, that he was banished from Rome, for a murder committed in a drunken brawl; and that he died at last of debauchery and want. Caravaggio was perfect in his gamblers, robbers, and martyrdoms, and should never have meddled with Saints and Madonnas. In his famous *Pietà* in the Vatican, the Virgin is an old beggar-woman, the two Maries are fish-wives, in "maudlin sorrow," and St. Peter and St. John, a couple of bravoes, burying a murdered traveller: *dipinse ferocemente sempre perche feroce era il suo carrattere*, says his biographer; an observation, by the way, in support of my hypothesis.

Rubens, with all his transcendent genius, had a coarse imagination: he bore the character of an honest, liberal, but not very refined man. Rubens painted Virgins—would he had let them alone! fat, comfortable [Pg 148] farmers' wives, nursing their chubby children. Then follows Vandyke in the opposite extreme. Vandyke was celebrated in his day, for his personal accomplishments: he was, says his biographers, a complete scholar, courtier and gentleman. His beautiful Madonnas are, accordingly, what we might expect—rather too intellectual and lady-like: they all look as if they had been polished by education.

The grand austere genius of Michel Angelo was little calculated to portray the dove-like meekness of the *Vergine dolce e pia*, or the playfulness of infantine beauty. In his Mater Amabilis, sweetness and beauty are sacrificed to expression; and dignity is exaggerated into masculine energy. In the Mater Dolorosa, suffering is tormented into agony: the anguish is too human: it is not sufficiently softened by resignation; and makes us turn away with a too painful sympathy. Such is the admirable head in the Palazzo Litti at Milan; such his sublime *Pietà* in the Vatican—but the last, being in marble, is not quite a case in point.

I will mention but two more painters of whose lives and characters I know nothing yet, and may therefore fairly make their works a test of both, and judge of them in their Madonnas, and afterwards measure my own penetration and the truth of my hypothesis, by a reference to the biographical writers.

In the few pictures I have seen of Carlo Cignani, I have been struck by the predominance of mind and feeling over mere external form: there is a picture of his in the Rospigliosi Palace—or rather, to give an example which is nearer at hand, and fresh in my memory, there is in the gallery *here*, his Madonna del Rosario. It represents a beautiful young woman, evidently of plebeian race: the form of the face is round, the features have nothing of the beau-ideal, and the whole head wants dignity: yet has the painter contrived to throw into this lovely picture an inimitable expression which depends on nothing external, which in the living prototype we should term *countenance*; as if a chastened consciousness of her high destiny and exalted character shone through the natural rusticity of her features, and touched them with a certain grace and dignity, emanating from the mind alone, which only mind could give, and mind perceive. I have seen within the last few days, three copies of this picture, in all of them the charming simplicity and rusticity, but in none the exquisite expression of the original: even the hands are expressive, without any particular delicacy or beauty of form. An artist who was copying the picture to-day while I looked at it, remarked this; and confessed he had made several unsuccessful attempts to render the fond pressure of the fingers as she clasps the child to her bosom.

Were I to judge of Carlo Cignani by his works, I should pronounce [Pg 149] him a man of elevated character, noble by instinct, if not by descent, but simple in his habits, and a despiser of outward show and ostentation.

The other painter I alluded to, is Sasso Ferrato, a great and admired manufacturer of Virgins, but a mere copyist, without pathos, power, or originality; sometimes he resembles Guido, sometimes Carlo Dolce; but the graceful harmonious delicacy of the former becomes coldness and flatness in his hands, and the refinement and sweetness of the latter sink into feebleness and insipidity. Were I to judge of his character by his Madonnas, I should suppose that Sasso Ferrato had neither original genius nor powerful intellect, nor warmth of heart, nor vivacity of temper; that he was, in short, a mere mild, inoffensive, good sort of man, studious and industrious in his art, not without a feeling for the excellence he wanted power to attain. [W]

I might pursue this subject further, but my memory fails, my head aches, and my pen is tired for to-night.

Both here and at Rome, I have found considerable amusement in looking over the artists who are usually employed in copying or studying from the celebrated pictures in the different galleries; but I have been taught discretion on such occasions by a ridiculous incident which occurred the other day, as absurdly comic as it was unlucky and vexatious. A friend of mine observing an artist at work in the Pitti palace, whom, by his total silence and inattention to all around, she supposed to be a native Italian who did not understand a word of English, went up to him, and peeping over his shoulder, exclaimed with more truth than discretion, "Ah! what a hideous attempt! that will never be like, I'm sure!" "I am very sorry you think so, ma'am," replied the painter, coolly looking up in her face. He must have read in that beautiful face an expression which deeply avenged the cause of his affronted picture.

We have been twice to the opera since we arrived here. At the Pergola, Bassi, though a woman, is the *Primo Uomo*; the rare quality of her voice, which is a kind of rich deep counter-tenor, unfitting her for female parts. Her voice and science are so admirable, that it would be delicious to hear her blindfold; but her large clumsy figure disguised, or rather *exposed*, in masculine attire, is quite revolting.

At the Cocomero we had the "Italiana in Algieri:" the Prima Donna, who is an admired singer, gave the comic airs with great power and effect, but her bold execution and her ungraceful unliquid voice disgusted me, and I came away fatigued and dissatisfied. The dancing is execrable at both theatres. [Pg 150]

From one end of Italy to the other, nothing is listened to in the way of music but Rossini and his imitators. The man must have a transcendant genius, who can lead and pervert the taste of his age as Rossini has done; but unfortunately those who have not his talent, who cannot reach his beauties nor emulate his airy brilliance of imagination, think to imitate his ornamented style by merely crowding note upon note, semi-quavers, demi-semi-quavers, and semi-demi-semi-quavers in most perplexed succession; and thus all Italy, and thence all Europe, is deluged with this busy, fussy, hurry-skurry music, which means nothing, and leaves no trace behind it either on the fancy or the memory. Must it be ever thus? are Paesiello, and Pergolesi, and Cimarosa—and those divine German masters, who formed themselves on the Italian school and surpassed it—Winter and Mozart [X] and Gluck—are they eternally banished? must sense and feeling be for ever sacrificed to mere sound, the human organ degraded into a mere instrument, [Y] and the ear tickled with novelty and meretricious ornament, till the taste is utterly diseased?

There was a period in the history of Italian literature, when the great classical writers were decried and neglected, and the genius of one man depraved the taste of the age in which he lived. Marini introduced, or at least rendered general and fashionable, that far-fetched wit, that tinsel and glittering style, that luxurious pomp of words, which was easily imitated by talents of a lower order: yet in the Adonis there are many redeeming passages, some touches of real pathos, and some stanzas of natural and beautiful description: and thus it is with Rossini; his best operas contain some melodies among the finest ever composed, and even in his worst, the ear is every now and then roused and enchanted by a few bars of graceful and beautiful melody, to be in the next moment again bewildered in the maze of unmeaning notes, and the clash of overpowering accompaniments.

Lucca, April 23.—Lucca disappoints me in every respect: it was once, when a republic, one of the most flourishing, rich, and populous cities in Italy; it is now consigned over to the Ex-queen of Etruria; and its fate will be perhaps the same as that of Venice, Pisa, and Sienna, which, when they lost their independence, lost also their public spirit, their public virtue, and their prosperity.

It is impossible to conceive any thing more rich and beautiful, than [Pg 151] the country between Florence and Lucca, though it can boast little of the elevated picturesque, and is destitute of poetical associations. The road lay through valleys, with the Apennines (which are here softened down into gently sunny hills) on each side. Every spot of ground is in the highest state of cultivation; the boundaries between the small fields of wheat or lupines, were rows of olives or mulberries, with an interminable treillage of vines flung from tree to tree. In England we should be obliged to cut them all down for fear of depriving the crops of heat and sunshine, but here they have no such fears. The style of husbandry is exquisitely neat, and in general performed by manual labour. The only plough I saw would have excited the amusement and amazement of an English farmer: I should think it was exactly similar to the ploughs of Virgil's time: it was drawn by an ox and an ass yoked together, and guided by a woman. The whole country looked as if it had been laid out by skilful gardeners, and the hills in many parts were cut into terraces, that not one available inch of soil might be lost. The products of this luxuriant country are corn, silk, wine, and principally oil: potteries abound, the making of jars and flasks being an immense and necessary branch of trade.

The city of Lucca has an appearance in itself of stately solemn dulness, and bears no trace of the smiling prosperity of the adjacent country: the shops are poor and empty, there are no signs of business, and the streets swarm with beggars. The interior of the Duomo is a fine specimen of Gothic: the exterior is Greek, Gothic, and Saracenic jumbled together in vile taste: it contains nothing very interesting. The palace is like other palaces, very fine and so forth; and only remarkable for not containing one good picture, or one valuable work of art.

Pisa, April 25.—Pisa has a look of elegant tranquillity, which is not exactly *dulness*, and pleases me particularly: if the thought of its past independence, the memory of its once proud name in arts, arms, and literature, came across the mind, it is not accompanied by any painful regret caused by the sight of present misery and degradation, but by that philosophic melancholy with which we are used to contemplate the mutability of earthly greatness.

The Duomo, the Baptistry, the Leaning Tower, and the Campo Santo, stand altogether in a fine open elevated part of the city. The Duomo is a magnificent edifice in bad taste. The interior, with its noble columns of oriental granite, is grand, sombre, and very striking. As to the style of architecture, it would be difficult to determine what name to give it: it is not Greek, nor Gothic, nor Saxon, and exhibits a strange mixture of Pagan and Christian ornaments, not very unfrequent in Italian churches. The Leaning Tower should be contemplated from the portico of the church to heighten its effect: when the [Pg 152] perpendicular column cuts it to the eye like a plumb line, the obliquity appears really terrific.

The Campo Santo is an extraordinary place: it affects the mind like the cloisters of one of our Gothic cathedrals which it resembles in effect. Means have lately been taken to preserve the singular frescos on the walls, which for five hundred years have been exposed to the open air.

I remarked the tomb of that elegant fabulist Pignotti; the last personage of celebrity buried in the Campo Santo.

The university of Pisa is no longer what it was when France and Venice had nearly gone to war about one of its law professors, and its colleges ranked next to those of Padua: it has declined in fame, in riches, and in discipline. The Botanic Garden was a few years ago the finest in all Europe, and is still maintained with great cost and care: it contains a lofty magnolia, the stem of which is as bulky as a good sized tree: the gardener told us rather poetically, that when in blossom it perfumed the whole city of Pisa.

Leghorn, April 26.—So different from any thing we have yet seen in Italy! busy streets—gay shops—various costumes—Greeks, Turks, Jews, and Christians, mingled on terms of friendly equality—a crowded port, and all the activity of prosperous commerce.

Leghorn is in every sense a *free* port: all kinds of merchandise enter exempt from duty, all religions are equally tolerated, and all nations trade on an equal footing.

The Jews, who are in every other city a shunned and degraded race, are among the most opulent and respectable inhabitants of Leghorn: their quarter is the richest, and, I may add, the *dirtiest* in the city: their synagogue here is reckoned the finest in Europe, and I was induced to visit it yesterday at the hour of worship. I confess I was much disappointed; and, notwithstanding my inclination to respect always what is respectable in the eyes of others, I never felt so strong a disposition to smile. An old Rabbi with a beard of venerable length, a pointed bonnet, and a long white veil, got up into a superb marble pulpit and chanted in strange nasal tones, something which was repeated after him in various and discordant voices by the rest of the assembly. The congregation consisted of an uncouth set of men and boys, many of them from different parts of the Levant, in the dresses of their respective countries: there was no appearance of devotion, no solemnity; all wore their hats, some were poring over ragged books, some were talking, some sleeping, or lounging, or smoking. While I stood looking about me, without exciting the smallest attention, I heard at every pause a prodigious chattering and whispering, which seemed to come from the regions above, and looking up I saw a row of latticed and skreened galleries where the women were caged [Pg 153] up like the monkies at a menagerie, and seemed as noisy, as restless, and as impatient of confinement: the door-keeper offered to introduce me among them, but I was already tired and glad to depart.

We have visited the pretty English burial-ground, and the tomb of Smollet, which in the true English style is cut and scratched all over with the names of fools, who think thus to link their own insignificance to his immortality. We have also seen whatever else is to be seen, and what all travellers describe: to-morrow we leave Leghorn—for myself without regret: it is a place with which I have no sympathies, and the hot, languid, damp atmosphere, which depresses the spirits and relaxes the nerves, has made me suffer ever since we arrived.

Lucca.—Had I never visited Italy I think I should never have understood the word *picturesque*. In England we apply it generally to rural objects or natural scenery, for nothing else in England *can* deserve the epithet. Civilization, cleanliness, and comfort are excellent things, but they are sworn enemies to the picturesque: they have banished it gradually from our towns, and habitations, into remote countries, and little nooks and corners, where we are obliged to hunt after it to find it; but in Italy the picturesque is every where, in every variety of form; it meets us at every turn, in town and in country, at all times and seasons; the commonest objects of every-day life here become picturesque, and assume from a thousand causes a certain character of poetical interest it cannot have elsewhere. In England, when travelling in some distant county, we see perhaps a craggy hill, a thatched cottage, a mill on a winding stream, a rosy milkmaid, or a smock-frocked labourer whistling after his plough, and we exclaim "How picturesque!" Travelling in Italy we see a piny mountain, a little dilapidated village on its declivity, the ruined temple of Jupiter or Apollo on its summit; a peasant with a bunch of roses hanging from his hat, and singing to his guitar, or a cotadina in her white veil and scarlet petticoat, and we exclaim "How picturesque!" but how different! Again—a tidy drill or a hay-cart, with a team of fine horses, is a very useful, valuable, civilized machine; but a grape-waggon reeling under its load of purple clusters, and drawn by a pair of oxen in their clumsy, ill-contrived harness, and bowing their patient heads to the earth, is much more picturesque. A spinning wheel is very convenient it must be allowed, but the distaff and spindle are much more picturesque. A snug English villa with its shaven lawn, its neat shrubbery, and its park, is a delightful thing—an Italian villa is probably far less *comfortable*, but with its vineyards, its gardens, its fountains, and statutes, is far more picturesque. A laundry-maid at her wash-tub, immersed in soap-suds, is a vulgar idea, though our [Pg 154] clothes may be the better for it. I shall never forget the group of women I saw at Terracina washing their linen in a bubbling brook as clear as crystal, which rushed from the mountains to the sea—there were twenty of them at least grouped with the most graceful effect, some standing up to the mid-leg in the stream, others spreading the linen on the sunny bank, some, flinging back their long hair, stood shading their brows with their hands and gazing on us as we passed: it was a *scene* for a poet, or a painter, or a melo-drama. An English garden, adorned at every turn with statues of the heathen deities (although they were all but personifications of the various attributes of nature,) would be ridiculous. Setting aside the injury they must sustain from our damp, variable climate, they would be *out of keeping* with all around; here it is altogether different; the very air of Italy is embued with the spirit of ancient mythology; and though "the fair humanities of old religion," the Nymphs, the Fauns, the

Dryads be banished from their haunts and live no longer in the faith of reason, yet still, whithersoever we turn, some statue, some temple in ruins, some fragment of an altar, some inscription half effaced, some name half-barbarized, recalls to the fancy those forms of light, of beauty, of majesty, which poetry created to people scenes for which mere humanity was not in itself half pure enough, fair enough, bright enough.

What can be more grand than a noble forest of English oak? or more beautiful than a grove of beeches and elms, clothed in their rich autumnal tints? or more delicious than the apple orchard in full bloom? but it is true, notwithstanding, that the olive, and cypress, and cedar, the orange and the citron, the fig and the pomegranate, the myrtle and the vine, convey a different and more luxuriant feeling to the mind; and are associated with ideas which give to the landscape they adorn a character more delightfully, more *poetically* picturesque.

When at Lord Grosvenor's or Lord Stafford's I have been seated opposite to some beautiful Italian landscape, a Claude or a Poussin, with a hill crowned with olives, a ruined temple, a group of peasants seated on a fallen column, or dancing to the pipe and the guitar, and over all the crimson glow of evening, or the violet tints of morning, I have exclaimed with others, "How lovely! how picturesque, how very poetical!" No one thought of saying "How *natural*!" because it is a style of nature with which we are totally unacquainted; and if some amateurs of real taste and feeling prefer a rural cattle scene of Paul Potter or Cuyp, to all the grand or lovely creations of Salvator, or Claude, or Poussin, it is perhaps, because the former are associated in their minds with reality and familiar nature, while the latter appear in comparison mere inventions of the painter's fertile fancy, mere visionary representations of what may or might exist but which do not come home to the memory or the mind with the force of truth or delighted [Pg 155] recollection. So when I have been travelling in Italy how often I have exclaimed, "How like a picture!" and I remember once, while contemplating a most glorious sunset from the banks of the Arno, I caught myself saying, "This is truly one of Claude's sunsets!" Now should I live to see again one of my favourite Grosvenor Claudes I shall probably exclaim, "How natural! how like what I have seen so often on the Arno, or from the Monte Pincio!"

And, in conclusion, let it be remembered by those who are inclined to smile (as I have often done) when travellers fresh from Italy *rave* almost in blank verse, and think it all as unmeaning as

> "Lutes, laurels, seas of milk, and ships of amber!"

let them recollect that it is not alone the *visible* picturesque of Italy which thus intoxicates; it is not only her fervid skies, her sunsets, which envelope one-half of heaven from the horizon to the zenith, in living blaze; nor her soaring pine-clad mountains; nor her azure seas; nor her fields, "ploughed by the sunbeams;" nor her gorgeous cities, spread out with all their domes and towers, unobscured by cloud or vapours;—but it is something more than these, something beyond, and over all—

> ——The gleam,
> The light that never was on sea or land
> The consecration, and the poet's dream!

Genoa, 30.—We arrived here late, and I should not write now, weary, weak, sick, and down-spirited as I am, did I not know how the impressions of one day efface those of the former; and as I cannot sleep, it is better to scribble than to think.

As to describing all I have seen, thought, and felt in three days, that were indeed impossible: I think I have exhausted all my prose eloquence, and all allowable raptures; so that unless I ramble into absolute poetry, I dare not say a word of the scenery around Sarzana and Lerici. After spending one evening at Sarzana, in lingering through green lanes and watching the millions of fire-flies, sparkling in the dark shade of the trees, and lost again in the brilliant moonlight—we left it the next morning about sunrise, to embark in a felucca at Lerici, as the road between Spezia and Sestri is not yet completed. The groves and vineyards on each side of the road were filled with nightingales, singing in concert loud enough to overpower the sound of our carriage-wheels, and the whole scene, as the sun rose over it, and the purple shadows drew off and disclosed it gradually to the eye, was so enchanting—that positively I will say nothing about it.

Lerici is a small fishing town on the Gulf of Spezia. Here I met with an adventure which with a little exaggeration and embellishment, [Pg 156] such as no real story-teller ever spares, would make an admirable morceau for a quarto tourist; but, in simple truth, was briefly thus.

While some of our party were at breakfast, and the servants and sailors were embarking the carriages and baggage, I sat down to sketch the old grey fort on the cliff above the town; but every time I looked up, the scene was so inexpressibly gay and lovely, it was with difficulty and reluctance I could turn my eyes down to my paper again; and soon I gave up the attempt, and threw away both paper and pencil. It struck me that the view *from* the castle itself must be a thousand times finer than the view of the castle from below, and without loss of time I proceeded to explore the path leading to it. With some fatigue and difficulty, and after losing myself once or twice, I reached the top of the rock, and there a wicket opened into a walled passage cut into steps to ease the ascent. I knocked at the wicket with three strokes, that being the orthodox style of demanding entrance into the court of an enchanted castle, using my parasol instead of a dagger, [Z] and no one appearing, I entered, and in a few moments reached a small paved terrace in front of the fortress, defended towards the sea by a low parapet wall. The massy portal was closed, and instead of a bugle horn hanging at the gate I found only the handle and fragments of an old birch-broom, which base utensil I presently applied to the purpose of a horn, viz. sounding an alarm, and knocked and knocked—but no hoary-headed seneschal nor armed warder appeared at my summons. After a moment's hesitation, I gave the door a push with all my strength: it yielded, creaking on its hinges, and I stepped over the raised threshold. I found myself in a low dark vaulted hall which appeared at first to have no communication with any other chamber: but on advancing cautiously to the end I found a low door in the side, which had once been defended by a strong iron grating of which some part remained: it led to a flight of stone stairs, which I began to ascend slowly, stopping every moment to listen; but all was still as the grave. On each side of this winding staircase I peeped into several chambers, all solitary and ruinous: more and more surprised, I continued to ascend till I put my head unexpectedly through a trap-door, and found myself on the roof on the tower: it was spacious, defended by battlements, and contained the only signs of warlike preparation I had met with; *videlicet*, two cannons, or culverins, as they are called, and a pyramidal heap of balls, rusted by the sea air.

I sat down on one of the cannon, and leaning on the battlements, surveyed the scene around, below me, with a feeling of rapture, not a little enhanced by the novelty and romance of my situation. I was alone—I had no reason to think there was a single human being [Pg 157] within hearing. I was at such a vast height above the town and the shore, that not a sound reached me, except an indistinct murmur now and then, borne upwards by the breeze, and the scream of the sea-fowl as they wheeled round and round my head. I looked down giddily upon the blue sea, all glowing and trembling in the sunshine: and the scenery around me was such, as the dullest eye—the coldest, the most *unimaginative* soul, could not have contemplated without emotion. I sat, I know not how long, abandoned to reveries, sweet and bitter, till I was startled by footsteps close to me, and turning round, I beheld a figure so strange and fantastic, and considering the time, place, and circumstance, so incomprehensible and extraordinary, that I was dumb with surprise. It was a little spare old man, with a face and form which resembled the anatomy of a baboon, dressed in an ample nightgown of flowered silk, which hung upon him as if it had been made for a giant, and trailed on the ground, a yard and a half behind him. He had no stockings, but on his feet a pair of red slippers, turned up in front like those the Turks wear. His beard was grizzled, and on his head he wore one of the long many-coloured woollen caps usually worn in this country, with two tassels depending from it, which nearly reached his knees. I had full time to examine the appearance and costume of this strange apparition as he stood before me, bowing profoundly, and looking as if fright and wonder had deprived him of speech. As soon as I had recovered from my first amazement, I replied to every low bow, by as low a courtesy, and waited till it should please him to begin the parley.

At length he ventured to ask, in bad provincial Italian, what I did there?

I replied that I was only admiring the fine prospect.

He begged to know, "*come diavolo*," I had got there?

I assured him I had not got there by any *diabolical* aid, but had merely walked through the door.

Santi Apostoli! did not my excellency know, that, according to the laws and regulations of war, no one could enter the fort, without permission first obtained of the governor?

I apologized politely: "And where," said I, "is the governor?"

Il Governatore son io per servirla! he replied, with a low bow.

You! *O che bel ceffo!* thought I—"and what, Signor Governor, is the use of your fort?"

"To defend the bay and town of Lerici from enemies and pirates."

"But," said I, "I see no soldier; where is the garrison to defend the fort?"

The little old man stepped back two steps—"*Eccomi!*" he replied, spreading his hand on his breast, and bowing with dignity.

It was impossible to make any reply: I therefore wished the governor and garrison good morning; and disappearing through my [Pg 158] trap-door, I soon made my way down to the shore, where I arrived out of breath, and just in time to step into our felucca.

If there be a time when we most wish for those of whom we always think, when we most love those who are always dearest, it must be on such a delicious night as that we passed at Sarzana, or on such a morning as that we spent at Lerici; and if there be a time when we least love those we always love—least wish for them, least think of them, it must be in such a moment as the noontide of yesterday—when the dead calm overtook us, half way between Lerici and Sestri, and I sat in the stern of our felucca, looking with a sort of despairing languor over the smooth purple sea, which scarcely heaved round us, while the flapping sails drooped useless round the masts, and the rowers indolently leaning on their oars, sung in a low and plaintive chorus. I sat hour after hour, still and silent, sickening in the sunshine, dazzled by its reflection on the water, and overcome with deadly nausea: I believe nothing on earth could have roused me at that moment. But evening so impatiently invoked, came at last: the sun set, the last gleam of his "golden path of rays" faded from the waters, the sea assumed the hue of ink; the breeze sprung up, and our little vessel, with all its white sails spread, glanced like a white swan over the waves, leaving behind "a moon-illumined wake." Two hours after dark we reached Sestri, where we found miserable accommodations; and after foraging in vain for something to eat, after our day's fast, we crept to bed, all sick, sleepy, hungry, and tired.

We leave Genoa to-morrow: I can say but little of it, for I have been ill, as usual, almost ever since we arrived; and though my little Diary has become to me a species of hobby, I have lately found it fatiguing, even to write! and the pleasure and interest it used to afford me, diminish daily.

Genoa, though fallen, is still "Genoa the proud." She is like a noble matron, blooming in years, and dignified in decay; while her rival Venice always used to remind me of a beautiful courtezan repenting in sackcloth and ashes, and mingling the ragged remnants of her former splendour with the emblems of present misery, degradation, and mourning. Pursue the train of similitude, Florence may be likened to a blooming bride dressed out to meet her lover; Naples to Tasso's Armida, with all the allurements of the Syren, and all the terrors of the Sorceress; Rome sits crowned upon the grave of her power, widowed indeed, and desolate, but still, like the queenly Constance, she maintains the majesty of Sorrow—

"This is my throne, let kings come bow to it!"

[Pg 159]

The coup-d'œil of Genoa, splendid as it is, is not equal to that of Naples, even setting poetical associations aside: it is built like a crescent round the harbour, rising abruptly from the margin of the water, which makes the view from the sea so beautiful: to the north the hills enclose it round like an amphitheatre. The adjacent country is covered with villas, gardens, vineyards, woods, and olive-groves forming a scene most enchanting to the eye and mind, though of a character very different from the savage luxuriance of the south of Italy.

The view of the city from any of the heights around, more particularly from that part of the shore called the Ponente, where we were to-day, is grand beyond description; on every side the church of Carignano is a beautiful and striking object.

There is but one street, properly so called, in Genoa—the Strada Nuova; the others are little paved alleys, most of them impassable to carriages, both from their narrowness and the irregularity of the ground on which the city is built.

The Strada Nuova is formed of a double line of magnificent palaces, among which the Doria Palace is conspicuous. The architecture is in general fine; and when not good is at least pleasing; the fronts of the houses are in general gaily painted and stuccoed. The best apartments are usually at the top; and the roofs often laid out in terraces, or paved with marble and adorned with flowers and shrubs.

I have seen few good pictures here: the best collections are those in the Brignolet and Durazzo palaces. In the latter are some striking pictures by Spagnoletto (or Ribera, as he is called here). In the Brignolet, the Roman Daughter, by Guido, struck me most. I was also pleased by some fine pictures of the Genoese painter Piola, who is little known beyond Genoa.

The church of the Carignano, which is a miniature model of St. Peter's, contains Paget's admirable statue of St. Sebastian, which Napoleon intended to have conveyed to Paris.

Beauty is no rarity at Genoa: I think I never saw so many fine women in one place, though I have seen finer faces at Rome and Naples than any I see here. The mezzaro, a veil or shawl thrown over the head and round the shoulders, is universal, and is certainly the most natural and becoming dress which can be worn by our sex:

the materials differ in fineness, from the most exquisite lace and the most expensive embroidery, to a piece of chintz or linen, but the effect is the same. This costume, which prevails more or less through all Italy, but here is general, gives something of beauty to the plainest face, and something of elegance to the most vulgar figure; it can make [Pg 160] deformity itself look passable: and when worn by a really graceful and beautiful female, the effect is peculiarly picturesque and bewitching.

It was a Festa to-day; and we drove slowly along the Ponente after dinner. Nothing could be more gay than the streets and public walks, crowded with holiday people: the women were in proportion as six to one; and looked like groups dressed to figure in a melodrame or ballet.

When once we have left Genoa behind us, and have taken our last look of the blue Mediterranean, I shall indeed feel that we have quitted Italy. Piedmont is not Italy. Cities which are only famous for their sieges and fortifications, plains only celebrated as fields of battle and scenes of blood, have neither charms nor interest for me.

On Monday we set off for Turin: how I dread travelling! and the motion of the carriage, which has now become *so* painful! Yet a little, a very little longer, and it will all be over.

FAREWELL TO ITALY.

Mira il ciel com'e bello, e mira il sole,
Ch'a se par che n'inviti, e ne console.

Farewell to the Land of the South!
Farewell to the lovely clime
Where the sunny valleys smile in light,
And the piny mountains climb!

Farewell to her bright blue seas!
Farewell to her fervid skies!
O many and deep are the thoughts which crowd
On the sinking heart, while it sighs,

"Farewell to the Land of the South!"

As the look of a face beloved,
Was that bright land to me!
It enchanted my sense, it sunk on my heart
Like music's witchery!
In every kindling pulse
I felt the genial air,
For life is *life* in that sunny clime,
—'Tis *death* of life elsewhere:
Farewell to the Land of the South!

The poet's splendid dreams,
Have hallowed each grove and hill,
And the beautiful forms of ancient Faith
Are lingering round us still.
And the spirits of other days,
Invoked by fancy's spell,
Are rolled before the kindling thought,
While we breathe our last farewell
To the glorious Land of the South!
[Pg 161]

A long—a last adieu,
Romantic Italy!
Thou land of beauty, and love, and song
As once of the brave and free!
Alas! for thy golden fields!
Alas! for thy classic shore!
Alas! for thy orange and myrtle bowers!
I shall never behold them more—
Farewell to the Land of the South!

Turin, May 10th.—We arrived here yesterday, after a journey to me most trying and painful: I thought at Novi and afterwards at Asti, that I should have been obliged to give up and confess my inability to proceed; but we know not what we can bear till we prove ourselves; I can live and suffer still.

I agree with — — who has just left me, that nothing can be more animating and improving than the conversation of intelligent and clever men, and that lady-society is in general very *fade* and tiresome: and yet I truly believe that no woman can devote herself exclusively to the society of men without losing some of the best and sweetest characteristics of her sex. The conversation of men of the world and men of gallantry, gives insensibly a taint to the mind; the unceasing language of adulation and admiration intoxicates the head and perverts the heart; the habit of *tête-à-têtes*, the habit of being always either the sole or the principal object of attention, of mingling in no conversation which is not personal, narrows the disposition, weakens the mind, and renders it incapable of rising to general views or principles; while it so excites the senses and the imagination, that every thing else becomes in comparison stale, flat, and unprofitable. The life of a coquette is very like that of a drunkard or an opium eater, and its end is the same—the utter extinction of intellect, of cheerfulness, of generous feeling, and of self-respect.

St. Michel, Monday.—I know not why I open my book, or why I should keep accounts of times and places. I saw nothing of Turin but what I beheld from my window: and as soon as I could travel we set off, crossed Mount Cenis in a storm, slept at Lans-le-bourg, and reached this place yesterday, where I am again ill, and worse—worse than ever.

Is it not strange that while life is thus rapidly wasting, I should still be so strong to suffer? the pang, the agony is not less acute at this moment, than when, fifteen months ago, the poignard was driven to my heart. The cup, though I have nearly drained it to the last, is not less bitter now than when first presented to my lips. But this is not well; [Pg 162] why indeed should I repine? mine was but a common fate—like a true woman, I did but stake my all of happiness upon one cast—and lost!

Lyons, 19th.—Good God! for what purpose do we feel! why within our limited sphere of action, our short and imperfect existence have we such boundless capacity for enjoying and suffering? no doubt for some good purpose. But I cannot think as I used to think:

my ideas are perplexed: it is all pain of heart and confusion of mind; a sense of bitterness, and wrong, and sorrow, which I cannot express, nor yet quite *suppress*. If the cloud would but clear away that I might feel and see to do what is right! but all is dark, and heavy, and vacant; my mind is dull, and my eyes are dim, and I am scarce conscious of any thing around me.

A few days passed here in quiet, and kind Dr. P** have revived me a little.

All the way from Turin I have slept almost constantly, if that can be called *sleep*, which was rather the stupor of exhaustion, and left me still sensible of what was passing round me. I heard voices, though I knew not what they said; and I felt myself moved from place to place though I neither knew nor cared whither.

All that I have seen and heard, all that I have felt and suffered, since I left Italy, recalls to my mind that delightful country. I should regret what I have left behind, had I not outlived all regrets—but one—for there, though

> I vainly sought from outward forms to win
> The passion and the life whose fountains are within;

all feeling was not yet worn out of my heart: I was not then blinded nor stupified by sorrow and weakness as I have been since.

There are some places we remember with pleasure, because we have been happy there; others, because endeared to us as the residence of friends. We love our country because it is *our country*; our home because it is *home*: London or Paris we may prefer, as comprehending in themselves, all the intellectual pleasures, and luxuries of life: but, dear Italy!—we love it, simply for its own sake: not as in general we are attached to places and things, but as we love a friend, and the face of a friend; there it was "*luxury to be*,"—there I would willingly have died, if so it might have pleased God.

Till this evening we have not seen a gleam of sunshine, nor a glimpse of the blue sky, since we crossed Mount Cenis. We entered Lyons during a small drizzling rain. The dirty streets, the black gloomy-looking house, the smoking manufactories, and busy looks of the [Pg 163] people, made me think of Florence and Genoa, and their "fair white walls" and princely domes; and when in the evening I heard the whining organ which some wretched Savoyard was grinding near us, I remembered even with emotion the delightful voices I heard singing "*Di piacer mi balza il cor*" under my balcony at Turin—my last recollection of Italy: and to-night, when they opened the window to give me air, I felt, on recovering, the cold chill of the night breeze; and as I shivered, and shrunk away from it, I remembered the delicious and genial softness of our Italian evenings—

22.—No letters from England.

Now that it is past, I may confess, that till now, a faint—a very faint hope did cling to my heart. I thought it might have been just possible; but it is over now—*all* is over!

We leave Lyons on Tuesday, and travel by short easy stages; and they think I may still reach Paris. I will hold up—if possible.

Yet if they would but lay me down on the road-side, and leave me to die in quietness! to rest is all I ask.

24.—St. Albin. We arrived here yesterday—

The few sentences which follow are not legible.

Four days after the date of the last paragraph, the writer died at Autun in her 26th year, and was buried in the garden of the Capuchin Monastery, near that city.—Editor.

THE END.

[Pg 164]

FOOTNOTES:

[A] First published in 1826.

[B] It must not be forgotten that this was written ten years ago: the aspect of Paris is much changed since then.

[C] By Christian Friederich Tieck.

[D]

"Rousseau, Voltaire, our Gibbon, and De Staël,
Leman! those names are worthy of thy shore."
Lord Byron.

[E] The sentence which follows is so blotted as to be illegible.—Ed.

[F] This was indeed ignorance! (1834.)

[G] Hail, O Maria, full of grace! the Lord is with thee! blessed art thou among women, and blessed is the fruit of thy womb, even Jesus. Holy Virgin Mary, mother of God! pray for us sinners—both now and in the hour of death! Amen.—Ed.

[H] The family of the Cenci was a branch of the house of Colonna, now extinct in the direct male line. The last Prince Colonna, left two daughters, co-heiresses, of whom one married the Prince Sciarra, and the other the Prince Barberini. In this manner the portrait of Beatrice Cenci cane into the Barberini family. The authenticity of this interesting picture has been disputed: but last night after hearing the point extremely well contested by two intelligent men, I remained convinced of its authenticity.

[I] TRANSLATION, EXTEMPORE.

Love, by my fair one's side is ever seen,
He hovers round her steps, where'er she strays,
Breathes in her voice, and in her silence speaks,
Around her lives, and lends her all his arms.

Love is in every glance—Love taught her song;
And if she weep, or scorn contract her brow,
Still Love departs not from her, but is seen
Even in her lovely anger and her tears.

When, in the mazy dance she glides along
Still Love is near to poize each graceful step:
So breathes the zephyr o'er the yielding flower.

Love in her brow is throned, plays in her hair,
Darts from her eye and glows upon her lip.
But, oh! he never yet approached her heart.

[J] Poor Schadow died yesterday. He caught cold the other evening at the Duke of Bracciano's uncomfortable, ostentatious palace, where we heard him complaining of the cold of the Mosaic floors: three days afterwards he was no more. He is universally regretted.—*Author's note.*

[K] A chasm occurs here of about twenty pages, which in the original MS. are torn out. Nearly the whole of what was written at Naples has suffered mutilation, or has been purposely effaced; so that in many parts only a detached sentence, or a few words, are legible in the course of several pages.—Editor.

[L] Was the letter addressed 'Alla Sua Excellenza *Seromfridevi,*' which caused so much perplexity at the Post Office and British Museum, and exercised the acumen of a minister of state, from Salvador to his illustrious correspondent?

[M] Quid times? &c.

[N] Wordsworth.

[O] Beyond Fondi I remarked among the wild myrtle-covered hills, a wreath of white smoke rise as if from under ground, and I asked the postilion what it meant? He replied with an expressive gesture, "Signora,—i briganti!" I thought this was a mere trick to alarm us; but it was truth: within twenty hours after we had passed the spot, a carriage was attacked; and a desperate struggle took place between the banditti and the sentinels, who are placed at regular distances along the road, and within hearing of each other. Several men were killed, but the robbers at length were obliged to fly.

[P] It is understood that this beautiful group has since been executed in marble for Sir George Beaumont.—Editor.

[Q] Written on an old pedestal in the gardens of the Villa Pamfili, yesterday (March 29th).

[R] See the admirable and eloquent "Essays on Petrarch, by Ugo Foscolo," which have appeared since this Diary was written—Editor.

[S] Corilla (whose real name was Maddaleno Morelli) often accompanied herself on the violin; not holding it against her shoulder, but resting it in her lap. She was reckoned a fine performer on this instrument; and for her distinguished talents was crowned in the Capitol in 1779.—Ed.

[T]

Othello—Thou mak'st me call what I intend to do
A murder,—which I thought a sacrifice.—

[U] Sestini died of a brain fever at Paris in November, 1822.—Ed.

[V] The allusion is to La Francia. When Raffaelle sent his famous St. Cecilia to Bologna, it was intrusted to the care of La Francia, who was his particular friend, to be unpacked and hung up. La Francia was old, and had for many years held a high rank in his profession; no sooner had he cast his eyes on the St. Cecilia, than struck with despair at seeing his highest efforts so immeasurably outdone, he was seized with a deep melancholy, and died shortly after.—Ed.

[W] Forsyth complains of some celebrated Madonnas being *unimpassioned*: with submission to Forsyth's taste and acumen—*ought* they to be *impassioned*?

[X] Dr. Holland once told me, that when travelling in Iceland, he had heard one of Mozart's melodies played and sung by an Icelandic girl, and that some months afterwards he heard the very same air sung to the guitar by a Greek lady at Salonica. Yet the son of that immortal genius, who has dispensed delight from one extremity of Europe to the other, and from his urn still rules the entranced senses of millions—Charles Mozart, is a poor music master at Milan! this should not be.

[Y] What Beccaria said in his day is most true of ours, "on paie les musiciens pour émouvoir, on paie les danseurs de corde pour étonner, et la plus grande partie des musiciens veulent faire les danseurs de corde."

[Z]

"With dagger's hilt upon the gate,
Who knocks so loud and knocks so late?"—Scott.

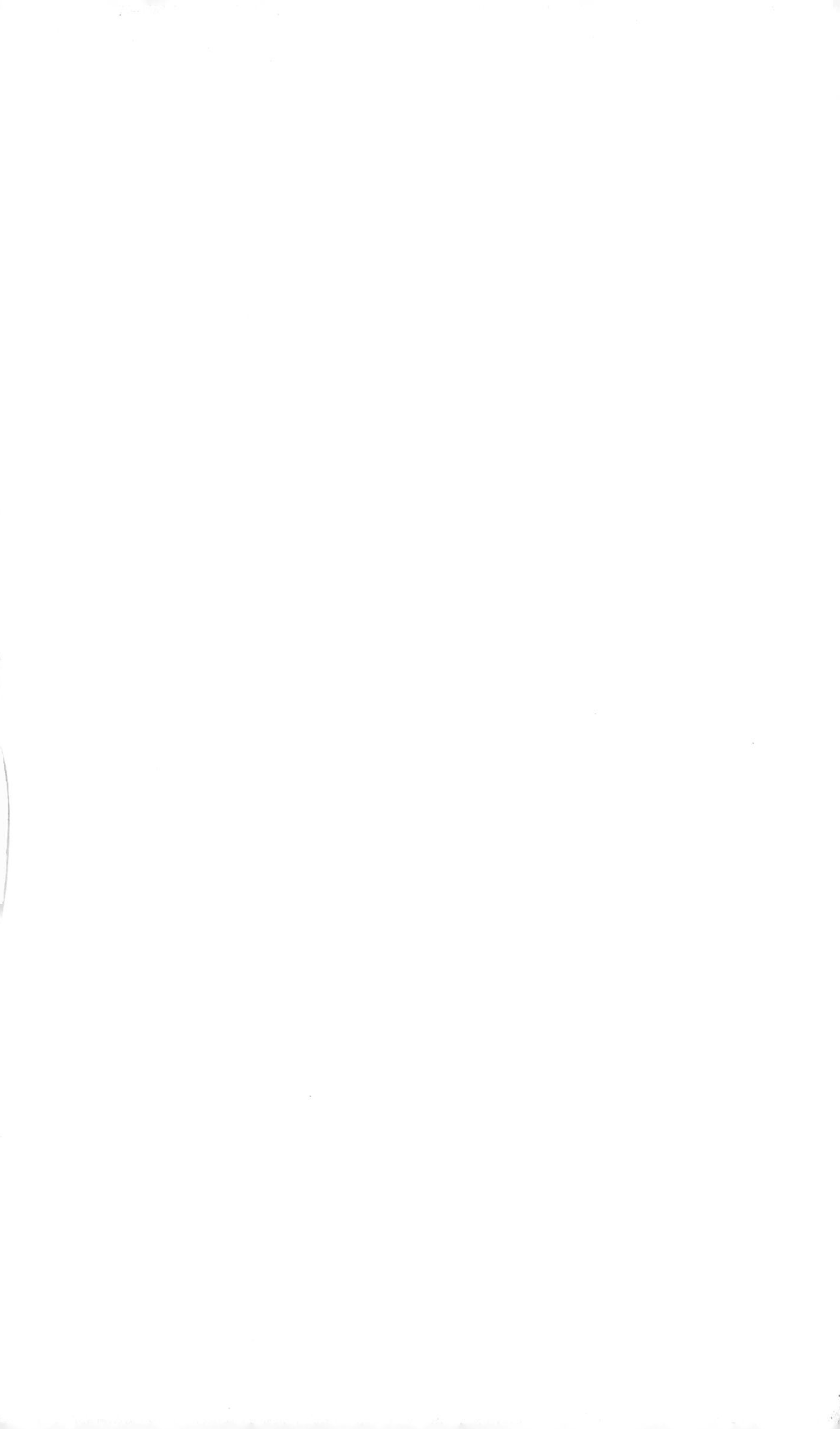